CONTEMPORARY SOUTH AFRICAN DEBATES

CONTEMPORARY SOUTH AFRICAN DEBATES

Other titles available in this series:

From apartheid to nation-building
by Hermann Giliomee and Lawrence Schlemmer
ISBN 0 19 570550 5

Critical choices for South Africa: An agenda for the 1990s
edited by Robert Schrire
ISBN 0 19 570574 2

No place to rest: Forced removals and the law in South Africa
edited by Catherine O'Regan and Christina Murray
ISBN 0 19 570580 7

Towards justice?

Crime and state control in South Africa

Edited by
Desirée Hansson and Dirk van Zyl Smit

CONTEMPORARY SOUTH AFRICAN DEBATES

1990
Oxford University Press
Cape Town

Oxford University Press
Walton Street, Oxford OX2 6DP, United Kingdom

Oxford New York Toronto
Delhi Bombay Calcutta Madras Karachi
Petaling Jaya Singapore Hong Kong Tokyo
Nairobi Dar es Salaam Cape Town
Melbourne Auckiand

and associated companies in
Berlin Ibadan

ISBN 0 19 570579 3

Cover: Pen and ink wash by Paul Sibisi entitled *Unrest II*.

Published by Oxford University Press Southern Africa
Harrington House, Barrack Street, Cape Town, 8001, South Africa

DTP conversion by Bellset in 10 on 11,5 pt Garamond
Printed and bound by Clyson Press, Maitland, Cape

Contents

Preface

Some of the contributions in this book were commissioned, while the theses argued in several others were first presented at a conference organized by the Institute of Criminology at the University of Cape Town in May 1989. All of the contributions have been substantially updated to reflect, as far as possible, the dramatic changes that have taken place in South Africa during the past year.

As editors we have sought to impose a measure of uniformity of style without departing from the authors' original ideas. Thus, the ideas expressed in this book remain those of the authors. Like many commentators on South Africa, we abhor ethnic classifications which carry connotations of racial discrimination. In South Africa, however, it is impossible to avoid such classifications when describing official practices, one of the central themes of this book. Accordingly, we have used, without quotation marks, the official terms white, coloured, and Asian/Indian. Further, we have used the term African for people whom the state classifies as black, and have reserved the term black to refer to all those people who are not classified as white.

Our sincere thanks goes to all our friends and colleagues who have contributed to the production of this volume. In particular, we wish to thank Beattie Hofmeyr for organizing the 1989 Criminology Conference, the Canadian Embassy for their financial support, and Janet McCurdie for assisting us in meeting our final deadline.

We hope that this book will encourage those who are working to develop a criminology for a democratic South Africa.

Desirée Hansson and Dirk van Zyl Smit
Cape Town
February 1990

Contributors

DENNIS DAVIS is Professor of Law at the University of Cape Town and National Director of the Society for the Abolition of the Death Penalty in South Africa.

DERRICK FINE is a member of the Legal Education Action Project (LEAP) at the Institute of Criminology at the University of Cape Town.

DESIRÉE HANSSON is Chairperson of the Social Justice Resource Project and a lecturer at the Institute of Criminology at the University of Cape Town. She is also a registered clinical psychologist working in the area of violence against women.

DIRK VAN ZYL SMIT is Dean of the Faculty of Law and Professor of Law at the University of Cape Town. He was Director of the Institute of Criminology at the University of Cape Town from 1982 to 1989.

DON FOSTER is Professor of Psychology at the University of Cape Town.

DULLAH OMAR is an advocate of the Supreme Court of South Africa, a member of the Cape Town Bar, and the National Vice-President of the National Association of Democratic Lawyers (NADEL).

ELRENA VAN DER SPUY is a lecturer in Sociology at the University of Stellenbosch.

JULIA SLOTH-NIELSEN is a lecturer in Law at the University of Cape Town.

NICHOLAS HAYSOM is an attorney and a senior research officer at the Centre for Applied Legal Studies (CALS) at the University of the Witwatersrand.

NICO STEYTLER is Professor of Law at the University of the Western Cape.

WILFRIED SCHÄRF is the Director of the Institute of Criminology and a senior lecturer in Criminology at the University of Cape Town.

INTRODUCTION

Contextualizing criminology in contemporary South Africa

Dirk van Zyl Smit

Introduction

In South Africa, as elsewhere, criticism of the methods used by the state to control conduct defined as criminal is hardly new or unusual. Indeed, the history of the evolutionary development of the system of criminal justice in South Africa is inextricably linked to the history of the critical ideas developed both by criminal justice practitioners and academic criminologists. Nevertheless, the ideas expressed in this volume differ from much of the preceding thought in this field. The authors represented here are working within a radical intellectual framework which differs from its predecessors both in its analysis of the dynamics of South African society which underlie the functioning of the criminal justice system, and in its prescriptions of how theory should be converted into practice.

Such a typification would be misleading, however, if it were to imply that the work presented in this volume exists in isolation from other intellectual frameworks which have been applied to the study of criminal justice in South Africa. First, the intellectual frameworks are not *pure* or *ideal* types. The notion that South African criminology has undergone clear shifts of paradigm has rightly been criticized as exaggerated (Unterhalter, 1985). Secondly, when discussing criminological thought, in South Africa in particular, one is often dealing with a form of practical reasoning in which theoretical approaches are used in a somewhat *eclectic* and *pragmatic* manner in order to justify or make sense of current practices.

With all these caveats, therefore, what are the intellectual conditions which have underpinned the South African criminal justice system? Three such traditions or approaches can be identified: legal reformist criminology, Afrikaner nationalist criminology, and critical criminology. Each can be linked to specific developments in the administration of criminal justice, although these links are mediated both by interaction between the traditions and by the broader political processes in society.

Legal reformist criminology

In South Africa, legal reformist criminology was firmly rooted in the reorganization of the South African state which took place shortly after Union in 1910. Its earliest and perhaps most articulate practitioner was Jacob de Villiers Roos, the first Secretary of Justice and Director of Prisons of the Union (Chisholm, 1987). Roos, who was a lawyer by training and who had extremely strong links with the new élite who came into power in 1910, was primarily responsible for the consolidation of the South African prison system and for the creation of the first welfare organizations for ex-prisoners. (Toussaint van Hove, 1962; and Erasmus, 1985). Roos saw himself as a reformer and a modernizer. He applied not only the principles of enlightened, legal neo-classicism to dispense finally with *barbaric* punishments, such as the treadmill and the stocks, but also the most up-to-date techniques of the empiricist criminology of the time to measure the amount of crime found among different race groups. From this basis Roos initiated reforms which were *economical*, as they were designed to inculcate the discipline of work in those who were processed through the criminal justice system. An important aspect of Roos's criminology, as it was presented in the detailed Annual Reports of the Director of Prisons and in Roos's many public speeches, was its appeal to a consensus view of society. In this society, the Afrikaners and the English could work together and through (capitalist) enterprise build a new nation within the broader imperial framework. This consensus, with its neo-classical emphasis on formal equality before the law, was thought of as including primarily the *European races* (British and Boer) who had recently been at war in southern Africa. Whites who committed crimes were considered to be a serious problem as they were seen to be 'indicative of the moral disease in the body politic of Southern Africa' (Chisholm, 1987: 55). Black crime, on the other hand, was portrayed as being more widespread. In the newspaper editorials black crime was portrayed as part of the 'white man's burden in South Africa' (*South Africa*, 18 March 1911 in Chisholm, 1987: 55). The solution propagated was essentially paternalistic. Blacks should be treated fairly, but should be accustomed by punishment to hard work when they transgressed. They should gradually be brought to understand the *justice* of the criminal courts and the *punishments* meted out by them.

Roos's legacy continued long after his departure as Director of Prisons in 1918. The Lansdown Commission, which reported in 1947 on Penal and Prison Reform, not only quoted Roos at great length[1], but adopted the same mixture of legal reformism based on a consensus view of society, together with an attitude of benign paternalism toward those whom it described as *non-Europeans*. For example, the Commission explained:

> If ultimately [the educated native] can find no suitable outlet for his activities, he frequently suffers from a bitterness of mind and a frustration which engender in him feelings of racial animosity (The Lansdown Commission, 1947: 13–14).

On the other hand, all was not gentle liberalism. The Commission did not favour the abolition of corporal punishment, even for adults 'in the present state of the country' (The Lansdown Commission, 1947: 71). Perhaps the tone of the Commission's paternalism is best captured in its concluding comment on the problem of crime amongst *urban Natives* or Africans:

> Means must be found to ensure that the Natives in town become decent members of society, and obey European standards of morality in order to lessen crime. (The Lansdown Commission, 1947: 6).

Legal reformist criminology had, and has, both conservative and liberal-humanitarian elements. Prominent among earlier liberals was the famous novelist Alan Paton, who from 1935 to 1948 served as head of the Diepkloof Reformatory for African *juvenile delinquents*. In this capacity he introduced numerous innovations which were described by Paton himself and by sympathetic outsiders as important experiments in using 'freedom as a reformatory instrument' (Paton, 1986: 17). Thus Paton described how dormitories were unlocked and Diepkloof was changed, internally at least, into an *open institution*. He also noted how the simple decision to allow a ration of tobacco to boys over the age of sixteen and a ration of sweets to all boys under the age of sixteen led to a drastic reduction in the number of beatings for *disciplinary offences*.[2]

There were indeed significant changes in the regime at Diepkloof,

---

1. See, The Lansdown Commission (1947: 92–3).
2. Corporal punishment was retained at Diepkloof for other offences (Paton, 1986: 101).

which followed the model of the English Borstal system. A close analysis of the Diepkloof regime suggests, however, that the changes were not as profound as Paton himself claimed (Chisholm, 1989). Certainly, Paton did not seek through his work in the reformatory to challenge the broader status quo in which the successful products of the reformatory would take their lowly places as law-abiding members of society.[3]

Afrikaner nationalist criminology[4]

The ideology of a broad *South Africanism* with its support for imperial institutions and capitalist enterprise was the ideological home of legal reformism. From the twenties onward, however, this South Africanism was increasingly challenged by an emerging Afrikaner nationalism which made much of the social and economic impoverishment of the Afrikaner people. An important base for this newly assertive nationalism was the campaign to alleviate the *poor white* problem which arose during the economic depression of the late twenties and early thirties. Part and parcel of the campaign was the popularization of social theories which attributed crime to social rather than to individual pathologies (Groenewald, 1984). To some extent, therefore, the criminology which was affiliated to Afrikaner nationalism and which emerged in the thirties drew on a model of social relations which recognized that there were deeper, economically determined divisions in society. At the same time, criminology was used as a vehicle to express nationalist sentiments of the most xenophobic kind. The first South African criminology text introduced its section on crime problems of the Union by highlighting the role of *volksvreemde geldsoekers,* literally seekers after money, that is, speculators who were foreign to the nation (Willemse & Rademeyer, 1933). This single concept combined the two major themes of the tradition, namely its emphasis on national units as bulwarks against crime and deviance, and its distrust of imperial capital.

Unlike the legal reformists, Afrikaner nationalist criminologists were intellectuals and *not* practitioners. The leading figures of this school, Professors G. Cronjé and W. A. Willemse, were social scientists who had been trained in Europe and who had been strongly influenced both by the economic determinism of the Dutch criminologist Wilhelm Bonger, and by the doctrine of fascism. Their project was to develop a coherent intellectual base for policies which would promote the interests of the

3. Much the same approach was adopted by other *reformist* heads of institutions for juveniles in the thirties and forties (Chisholm, 1989).
4. For a more detailed account of this tradition, see Van Zyl Smit (1989).

Afrikaner nation. Among these interests was the combating of crime and deviance, particularly among those Afrikaners who had been impoverished during the depression. The solution suggested for the crime problem, as for other social and economic ills, was the policy of *apartheid* which was designed to protect poor, Afrikaner whites from *unfair* economic competition and from crime-related contact with *lesser races.* Thinking about crime thus became inextricably linked to thinking about apartheid. Racial segregation was propagated in criminology texts and overtly racist forms of discourse became part of the explanations of why particular groups, such as the mixed race coloureds, were particularly prone to commit crime. These explanations, in turn, were used to underline the necessity of protecting whites from the contamination which would result from integration.

Initially, Afrikaner nationalist intellectuals did not have direct access to the top echelons of government, although there was much sympathy for their ideas among, for example, the rank and file of the police.[5] However, the accession to power of the Nationalist government in 1948 coincided with the establishment of criminology as a separate university discipline in Pretoria. In the fifties, Cronjé, with the assistance of his two most successful graduate students, H. J. Venter and P. J. van der Walt, made conscious efforts to bring the influence of their brand of criminology to bear upon the upper echelons of the police force and the prisons service. In this they were successful. Qualifications from their departments[6] became the passport to promotion within the police force and the department of prisons, and the terminology of apartheid found its way into the *academic* writings of a new generation of practitioners. Thus, for example, a student of Venter's could explain the legislative formalization of the long-standing practice of segregation in prison as the implementation of South Africa's apartheid policy (Steyn, 1962: 48).

Interactions

The academic criminology of Afrikaner nationalism did not represent as clear a break with what went before as might be thought at first glance. Firstly, in the first three decades of this century the racist discourse which formed part of academic criminology was widely used, not only among white South Africans of all political persuasions, but

---

5. See the contribution by Van der Spuy in Chapter 4 of this volume.
6. Venter and Van der Walt became the first professors of criminology in South Africa at the University of Pretoria and the University of South Africa (UNISA) respectively.

also in intellectual circles throughout the world (Dubow, 1987). Secondly, the anti-capitalist elements of Afrikaner nationalist criminology were soon de-emphasized. *Communism* became a bogey to be set alongside *liberalism* and the dangers of *integration* and *racial mixing*. In this demonology the various ideologies were not always clearly distinguished. For example, P. J. van der Walt was highly critical of the views of 'liberalists' because they blamed discriminatory legislation for the high rate of incarceration of Africans and thus,

> … lost sight of the fact that the natives, because of the nature of their lower economic, social, constitutional and intellectual development, clash more easily and more quickly with the judicial system[7] (Van der Walt, 1964: 128).

The examples of the work of *liberalists* that Van der Walt quoted included the writings of R. F. H. Hoernle, a leading liberal in the thirties and forties, and H. J. Simons, who was later to become one of South Africa's foremost Marxist scholars[8].

One may speculate that attacks on capitalism subsided as new intellectuals themselves became part of the ruling Afrikaner nationalist élite. A further factor which discouraged the emergence of competing approaches to criminology was that legal reformists concentrated their energies on challenging lawyers, who in general retained their commitment to formal legal equality, while academic criminologists concentrated on the institutions of the police and prisons. Of course, some changes were felt: Paton at Diepkloof, for example, was replaced by someone more in tune with the philosophy of apartheid and with the limited role that was to be assigned to Africans under *Bantu education* (Chisholm, 1989).

By the late seventies the scene was set for a revival of legal reformism. The zeal of the early apartheid ideologists had been tempered and this was reflected in the academic criminology of the period, which abandoned most of its racist explanations of crime causation.[9] Instead, the dominant text books of the period reflect the recycling of *middle-range* American criminological theory, made applicable to South Africa only in the most general terms. The initiative in the early seventies was taken by Mr. Justice J. H. Steyn. Using his chairmanship of the National Institute for Crime Prevention and the Rehabilitation of Offenders (NICRO) as a base, Steyn soon became involved in a wide range of reforms designed to reassert liberal and humanitarian values in the

---

7. Author's translation of Afrikaans original.
8. He is also one of the political exiles who is to return to South Africa shortly.
9. But not all. See, for example, Venter (1972) and even Stevens (1983).

sphere of criminal justice. NICRO, which had its roots in Roos's reforms of more than half a century earlier, was revitalized. A journal was started[10] and the first judicial commission of inquiry into the penal system since the Lansdown Commission in 1947 was convened under the chairmanship of Mr. Justice G. Viljoen.

The Viljoen Commission in 1976 confirmed the revival of legal reformism. Although it included at least one Afrikaner nationalist criminologist[11] among its members, there was a curious disjunction between its criminological review of the causes of crime, which hardly addressed the reality of crime in South Africa at all and spoke generally of, for example, the dangers of permissiveness, and its analyses of the criminal justice system, which proposed detailed reforms to sentencing and parole practices. In its broad assumptions about social consensus and even in its toleration of corporal punishment, because it was alleged that Africans supported the use of such punishments (The Viljoen Commission, 1976: 130), it differed not at all from the Lansdown Commission of almost thirty years earlier.

The development of a criminology for a democratic South Africa

Mr. Justice Steyn's other major initiative was the founding of the Institute of Criminology at the University of Cape Town in 1977. This event was preceded by a large international conference in Cape Town in 1975, to which criminologists from all over the world were invited to lend their intellectual weight to the new enterprise (*Acta Juridica*, 1975). The new Institute, complete with a Board of Patrons which was to include representatives of the judiciary, the prosecuting authorities, the police, the prisons service, and various welfare organizations, was clearly designed to propose reforms which could operate within the established framework of the criminal justice and penal systems.

Almost from the start, members of the Institute staff found that they could not work within this framework. The space for intellectual manoeuvre was simply too small. They were confronted by a stark choice: Either they had to deny their conclusions in order to work within the system, or publish and take the consequences. The very first study

---

10. *Crime Punishment and Correction* which appeared from 1972 to 1976, after which it was replaced by the *South African Journal of Criminal Law and Criminology* between 1977 and 1987, which was in turn succeeded by the *South African Journal of Criminal Justice* from 1988 to date.
11. Professor P. J. van der Walt of UNISA.

published by the Institute, on tattooing in prison (Slabbert & Van Rooyen, 1978), brought down the wrath of the prisons service. The first director, Professor J. H. van Rooyen, resisted the pressure applied by the prisons service and has been *persona non grata* ever since. Subsequent studies, such as McLachlan's work on children in custody in 1984 and 1986, and the research of Foster, Davis, and Sandler on the psychological effects of detention in 1987, to name just two, have continued to evoke the displeasure of the authorities. In all these cases the authors have chosen courageously to defend their conclusions.

The type of criminology which has emerged from the Institute has *not* been only a product of determined academics doing research which has led them to empirically-based conclusions that have contradicted the notion of a consensus so central to legal reformism, it has also been a product both of a change in the broader South African context and of international developments in criminological theory. The late sixties and early seventies saw major and exciting advances in criminological theory in the Western world. The study of crime and deviance became central to social theory in a way that it had not been since the thirties. Criminologists began to ask different and more fundamental questions, such as *What is crime?* and *How does the criminal justice system deal with offenders?*, rather than concentrating exclusively on the *causes* of criminal behaviour. These questions soon led to a wider enquiry about the distribution of power and wealth in society and about the nature and function of the state. The foundations were thus laid for a radical critique of institutions of social control as an inherent part of criminology. From the mid-seventies onwards, a new generation of South African criminologists was influenced by fresh ideas from abroad.

The founding of the Institute of Criminology at the University of Cape Town, and the introduction of criminology at the University of the Witwatersrand, coincided, perhaps fortuitously, with the Soweto uprising of 1976 and with the beginning of a fundamental shift in the power relations of South African society. These changes undoubtedly provided the context for the emergence, at these more *open* universities, of a critical criminology which focused on the social conflict so manifest in South African society.

Even in its relatively closed world, academic Afrikaner nationalist criminology has been affected by the dramatic demise of the apartheid ideology, if not of its practice. Its response has, however, not been to rethink its theoretical base in order to come to grips with the realities of South African society. The quest for a coherent social theory to explain crime has simply been abandoned. The resultant *atheoretical* criminology has both a benign and a sinister form. At best it has concerned itself with the practicalities of assisting the victims of *traditional* crime (Cilliers, 1986). If it has any theory at all, it is that of the consensual theory of society which underpins the legal reformist approach and which it has finally, if belatedly, adopted.

At worst, mainstream South African criminology of the eighties has focused on techniques for dealing with *terrorists* (Venter, 1981). It is seen as an important ally

> ... in the national interest — especially in the light of the increasing animosity towards South Africa and the infiltration of undesirable elements (Visse, 1982: 3).

In this guise, criminology has not only eschewed any critical understanding of the excesses of the agents of social control, but has involved itself actively in devising tactics for ensuring the survival of the current South African state. The eighties saw increasing co-operation between the security forces and criminologists. This movement found expression in the National Symposium on Crimes of Violence in South Africa in 1980, where much attention was paid to 'spiritual preparedness', and even to how the population could be controlled and persuaded to support 'the suspension of certain specified rights' (Schutte, 1982: 245). At the Symposium the definition of crime was stretched extraordinarily widely to accord with the pretensions of the ruling élite. Thus *ideological violence* in South Africa was described as

> ... a method applied by a group or groups to eliminate the existing order in the country by means of non-parliamentary conduct (Du Preez, 1982: 210).

The fact that the majority of the population is not represented in Parliament at all was not mentioned.

Academic criminology in this tradition was given institutional recognition in 1986 with the formation of the Criminological Society of Southern Africa (CRIMSA), which draws its members from academics, the police, the prisons service, and security officers. Particular attention has been paid to *military criminology* from a position perhaps best illustrated by this exhortation made by Stevens and published in the first issue of *Acta Criminologica*, the journal of CRIMSA:

> In a time such as the present when a total onslaught is being made on the RSA, indiscipline, bad behaviour and crime cannot be afforded! Everything must be thrown into the battle to prevent and combat crime in the defence force ... (Stevens, 1988: 22).[12]

It is clear that a radical or critical criminology should not have any

---

12. Author's translation from the Afrikaans original.

truck with a criminology which sees its function as providing techniques for bolstering the power of the South African state. But how does it, and how should it, react to the crises of the past decade? There seem to be three possible reactions, of which two have already been mentioned.

First, is to continue to expose what is happening, to highlight the differences between the *law in books* and the *law in action*, and to point out abuses in the exercise of state power. This must continue to be a vital part of any critical South African criminology. The gibe that a piece of research is mere descriptive journalism has no place in a society in which the press is subject to restrictions and where the normal checks and balances of the democratic process are absent.

Secondly, criminology must not cease to be a *serious intellectual* enterprise. It must continue to attempt to explain what is defined as crime and the responses of the state to *crime* in terms of a broader sociological understanding of South African society. Most importantly, it must not posit consensus where none exists. A shared commitment to social justice must be cherished, but it should not blind us to the class and status differences in our society. Part of the success of Afrikaner nationalist criminology in the thirties and forties can be attributed to the fact that, in spite of the *blinkers* of its racism, it recognized that there *were* real divisions in society between the *haves* and the *have nots*, and that these distinctions should figure in explanations of the causes of crime.

The third reaction is that of *practical intervention*. Here one is confronted by a paradox. Internationally, critical criminology of the sixties and seventies emerged as a reaction against a criminology which was only concerned with practice, that is, the practice of studying criminals in order to control them more effectively. The result was that the first generation of critical criminologists concentrated their energies on developing explanations of crime in terms of broad social forces. They did *not* consider the *real suffering* of the broader mass of people, both at the hands of the state and as a result of conventional crimes. In recent years a group which styles itself *left realist* has emerged. These realists have launched scathing attacks on much of the earlier critical criminology, which they have condemned as mere *left idealism* (Young, 1986).

In South Africa we cannot allow ourselves the luxury of an *abstract* debate which could lead to quite unnecessary polarization between *theorists* and *practitioners* who share the same ideals. Nor have we. The Legal Education Action Project (LEAP) of the Institute of Criminology at the University of Cape Town and the Centre for Applied Legal Studies (CALS) at the University of the Witwatersrand in Johannesburg are

practical responses to current conditions. They aim to help disadvant-
aged individuals and communities by fulfilling a legal or para-legal
function and by educating lay people in their legal rights. However,
these approaches do not neglect the other two necessary types of
responses mentioned above. Thus, they play their part in exposing
abuses and are also contributing material which will allow the further
development of South African criminological theory. We have much to
offer our critical colleagues abroad, who only now are beginning to
consider ways in which their work can be made more relevant to the
population as a whole.

South African criminology in relation to previous dilemmas

It remains to consider how this book relates to the intellectual context
of South African criminology and to ask how it contributes to the
aspirations implicit in the three reactions to the dilemmas which have
been outlined. While there can be no doubt that the contributors share
the broad aspirations of critical criminology, it is significant that they
have adopted modes of analysis which are also intellectually indebted
to the two other frameworks which have been outlined, namely legal
reformist criminology and academic Afrikaner nationalist criminology.

The openness to other influences is well illustrated by Omar's contribution on state lawlessness in Chapter 1. At one level this chapter can
be read as a powerful exposé of the materialist motives for much of the
state lawlessness that has been perpetrated in this century. At another
level, Omar is at pains to point out how this lawlessness has been
perpetrated in contravention of the rule of law. By invoking this standard he opens the way for dialogue with the liberal tradition within legal
reformism, which has used analytical concepts such as the rule of law
as the basis for its critique of the criminal justice system. In essence,
Omar's contribution is a challenge to transcend the limits of legalism,
without abandoning the values inherent in doctrines such as the rule of
law. In this way Omar is opening a dialogue, which is also being
furthered by others such as Albie Sachs (1989). Such thinkers recognize
the importance of inviolable guarantees of classical due process rights
as *part* of any future bill of rights, but they emphasize that South African
circumstances demand that, at the same time, appropriate recognition
be given to *social and economic rights*.

Academic Afrikaner nationalist criminology features less prominently
as a source of ideas, but the critique by Van der Spuy, in Chapter 4, of

a recent history of the South African Police can be read as an account of what has become of the Afrikaner nationalist tradition. Van der Spuy is devastatingly critical of what she describes as an *apologist* and *ethnocentric* history of the police. Yet, at the same time, she notes how the historian in this tradition is able to analyse sensitively the impact of conflict in white society on the development of policing prior to and during the Second World War. In this respect the police historian shares the valuable insight of the earlier Afrikaner nationalist criminologists, who rejected the assumption that consensus existed in South Africa where, in fact, conflict reigned. The failure to see as clearly the causes of similar conflicts involving blacks, both then and subsequently, amounts to a tragic failure of the sociological imagination. Ethnic blinkers would, however, have to be removed before a fuller account of the dynamics of the history of South African policing could be given. Implicit in Van der Spuy's critique is the theoretical framework within which a more complete account would have to be informed.

The chapter by Hansson on state strategy generally in the last decade, Chapter 2, offers a fascinating codicil to the conclusion reached earlier in this introduction, namely, that mainstream academic criminology has become implicated in the strategies of the state in general, and of the military in particular, for the maintenance of order at all costs. The evidence presented goes beyond this conclusion, for it suggests that the work of military theorists became dominant in police practice in the eighties, to the extent that even those criminologists who supported the status quo were largely ignored. This might be a further indication of the theoretical paucity of mainstream South African criminology.

This chapter by Hansson can also be read simply for the full picture it provides of an aspect of the activities of the South African state which would otherwise remain concealed. It is complemented by the information contained in Haysom's account in Chapter 3 of vigilantes in the townships and of the support which the state has provided there, and also by Steytler's study in Chapter 5 of the role that death squads are alleged to have played in the policing of the *unrest*. A particular contribution that Steytler makes is to analyse the phenomenon he describes in terms of the occupational subculture of the police. In so doing he contributes not only to a theoretical understanding, but also indicates how a *cop culture* is maintained and, therefore, what steps will have to be taken if the fundamental attitudes of the police are to be changed.

The importance of contextualizing specific legal practices is the theme of a number of the chapters. Thus Sloth-Nielsen in Chapter 9 explains why the South African state has retained corporal punishment in the face of widespread international rejection. She emphasizes that a gradual abolition is not a natural or inevitable historical process. A move towards abolition should be seen as part of a broader campaign of recognition of the essential humanity of all the subjects of the state. Such a shift would require fundamental changes in South African society. Similarly, Davis in Chapter 6 places the doctrine of common purpose in its social context. He shows that the developments to which the doctrine has been subject are a product of its application in murder trials that have resulted from killings in township conflicts. The politicization of the concept has led to its general re-evaluation and to re-examination of the fundamental legal tenet that criminal liability should be based on individual culpability. It has also led to a wider re-examination of the death penalty in South Africa, both by extra-parliamentary forces and, latterly, by the government. Here too the relationship between change in the application of the law and shifts in political power in the state are revealed.

The contributions on expert testimony by Foster in Chapter 7, and by Hansson and Fine in Chapter 8 directly combine the legal and the practical. In his analysis of several cases in which expert witnesses have been involved, Foster deals not only with the well-known problem of the lack of fit between legal and psychological concepts, but also suggests that, in their desire to assist individual accused persons facing the sentence of death, both lawyers and psychologists have underplayed the structural and political context of collective violence. An analysis of collective violence that does not decontextualize such activity by denying its political nature would, in Foster's view, be a more acceptable ground for extenuation. Such an analysis would also make a greater contribution to criminological theory and would allow for the further consideration of how both specific policing practices and the wider political processes would have to be structured if such collective violence is to be avoided. Hansson and Fine's contribution on expert testimony on community attitudes to sentencing in Chapter 8 can be read as an informative case study of the attitudes of a single community confronted by a particularly traumatic political killing. This study complements Foster's analysis, because it deals with a single case of experts being used in a different sphere, yet at the same time it raises many of the same issues about the role of expert witnesses. Hansson and Fine's further account of how the court refused to hear the expert testimony which had been carefully collected, because it regarded the testimony as *irrelevant*, raises, in a different form, the difficult question of how courts are supposed to divine the opinion of those people on whose behalf they have been called to act. While it is easy enough to be sceptical about whether individual white judges know or appreciate the sentiments of African communities, the broader questions are whether a court composed entirely of professional judges can *ever* perform this function and of what alternative arrangements would be more just.

The two concluding chapters, Chapter 10 by Fine and Hansson, and Chapter 11 by Schärf, both deal with community responses to problems of crime. Police abuse of power and street gangs are found in most societies, but South African conditions greatly aggravate these forms of crime. Both chapters are valuable criminological accounts of these phenomena. However, their primary contribution is to describe what *can be done*, under current circumstances, to limit these crimes. Fine and Hansson pay close attention to the role of lawyers and are able to indicate both technical pitfalls which face legal practitioners and the difficulties and challenges of working closely with communities in a manner which is sufficiently flexible to encourage them to determine their *own* responses to state abuses of power. Schärf focuses more directly on communities' particular responses to street gangs. However, he also raises questions about the limits of such responses when they are not supported by the state. In the democratic South Africa of the future there will be a need to build links with the police and other agents of formal control. It is necessary, therefore, to consider the forms of state control of crime which will be compatible with such a democratic ideal.

Taken together, all the contributors to this volume have responded to the challenges of state control in contemporary South Africa. In the process they have described abuses, considered theoretical issues, and, at the same time, proposed practical courses of action. It is the fervent hope of the editors that in these various ways this volume will make its contribution *towards justice* in South Africa.

Bibliography

Books and articles

Acta Juridica (1975). (Annual Law Journal of the Faculty of Law). Cape Town: University of Cape Town.

Chisholm, L. (1987). 'Crime, Class and Nationalism: The Criminology of Jacob de Villiers Roos 1869–1918'. *Social Dynamics* 13: 46–59.

Chisholm, L. (1989). Reformatories and Industrial Schools in South Africa: A Study in Class, Colour and Gender, 1882–1932. Unpublished Ph.D. Dissertation. Johannesburg: University of the Witwatersrand.

Cilliers, C. H. (1986). *Viktimologie.* Pretoria: HAUM.

Davis, D. & Slabbert, M. (1985). *Crime and Power in South Africa.* Cape Town: David Philip.

Dubow, S. (1987). 'Race, Civilization and Culture: The Elaboration of Segregationist Discourse in the Inter-War Years'. In *The Politics of Race, Class and Nationalism in Twentieth Century South Africa.* (Eds.) Marks, S. & Trapido, S. Essex: Longman.

Du Preez, J. A. (1982). 'Ideological Crimes of Violence in South Africa'. In *Crimes of Violence in South Africa.* (Ed.) Van der Westhuizen, J. Pretoria: University of South Africa.

Erasmus, W. P. (1985). Die Vestiging en Ontwikkeling van die Kriminologie in Suid Afrika met Spesiale Verwysing na die Penitensiêre Inligting tussen 1910–1961. Unpublished Ph.D. Dissertation. Pretoria: University of South Africa.

Foster, D., Davis, D. & Sandler, D. (1987). *Detention and Torture in South Africa: Psychological, Legal and Historical Studies.* Cape Town: David Philip.

Groenewald, C. J. (1984). Die Institutionalisering van die Sosiologie in Suid-Afrika. Unpublished Ph.D. Dissertation. Stellenbosch: University of Stellenbosch.

McLachlan, F. (1984). *Children in Prison.* Cape Town: Institute of Criminology, University of Cape Town.

McLachlan, F. (1986). *Children: Their Courts and Institutions in South Africa.* Cape Town: Institute of Criminology, University of Cape Town.

Paton, A. (1986). *Diepkloof — Reflections of Diepkloof Reformatory.* Cape Town: David Philip.

Sachs, A. (1989). A Bill of Rights for South Africa. Unpublished paper. New York: Columbia University.

Schutte, S. H. (1982). 'Urban Terrorism and the Role of Community in Combating it'. In *Crimes of Violence in South Africa.* (Ed.) Van der Westhuizen, J. Pretoria: University of South Africa.

Slabbert, M. & Van Rooyen J. H. (1978). *Some Implications of Tattooing in and outside Prison.* Cape Town: Juta.

Stevens R. (1983). Introduction to Criminology. Johannesburg: MacMillan.

Stevens, R. (1988). 'Misdaad in die Weermag'. *Acta Criminologica*

1: 17–27.

Steyn, J. C. (1962). Die Nuwe Wet op Gevangenisse. Unpublished MA Dissertation. Pretoria: University of Pretoria.

The Lansdown Commission (1947). *Report of the Lansdown Commission on Penal and Prison Reform.* Pretoria: Government Printer.

The Viljoen Commission (1976). *Report of the Viljoen Commission of Inquiry into the Penal System of the Republic of South Africa.* Pretoria: Government Printer.

Toussaint van Hove, T. (1962). Rehabilitation of Adult White Offenders: An Analysis of Extra Institutional Specialized Services of the Republic of South Africa. Unpublished D.Phil. Dissertation. Stellenbosch: University of Stellenbosch.

Unterhalter, D. (1985). 'Review of "Crime and Power in South Africa"'. *South African Journal on Human Rights* 1: 284–7.

Van der Walt, P. J. (1964). *'n Sosiologiese Klassifikasie van Misdade.* Pretoria: Nasou.

Van Zyl Smit, D. (1989). 'Adopting and Adapting Criminological Ideas: Criminology and Afrikaner Nationalism in South Africa'. *Contemporary Crises* 13: 227–51.

Venter, H. J. (1972). *Kriminologie: 'n Handleiding vir Studente in die Kriminologie.* Pretoria: Published Privately.

Venter, H. J. (1981). *Terrorisme.* Pretoria: HAUM.

Visse, J. (1982). 'In the National Interest'. In *Crimes of Violence in South Africa.* (Ed.) Van der Westhuizen, J. Pretoria: University of South Africa.

Willemse, W. A. & Rademeyer, C. I. (1933). *Kriminologie.* Pretoria: Afrikaanse Pers.

Young, J. (1986). 'The Failure of Criminology: The Need for a Radical Realism'. In *Confronting Crime.* (Eds.) Matthews, R. & Young, J. London: Sage.

CHAPTER ONE

An overview of state lawlessness in South Africa

Dullah Omar

Introduction

Contemporary South Africa is sometimes described as being a *society in transition*. The brutal slaying of South African democrat Dr. David Webster on May Day of 1989, however, hardly characterizes a society in transition, but more realistically a *society in crisis*. Although South Africa is pregnant with change, it refuses to change. The crisis is occasioned by the fact that the dominant section of the ruling bloc is determined to prevent a transition of our society from one based on apartheid, racial oppression, and economic exploitation, to a society of free citizens who have an equal say in the running of the country and an equal share in its wealth. In essence, the history of South Africa since 1910 represents a shameful chapter in world history. Whilst a few have amassed fortunes under the protective political umbrella of apartheid, the lot of the vast majority of the population has deteriorated. For the Nationalist regime, however, this is not seen to be the cause of the present crisis. The state's concern is that since 1912 the disenfranchised oppressed have resisted apartheid. Their struggles have, despite all difficulties, increased in momentum and in the last decade the state has lost its hegemony to the mass liberation movement against apartheid. As this movement has won legitimacy at one level after another, so the state has resorted increasingly to violence in order to retain its power. This is the root cause of the phenomenon known as *state lawlessness*. In this chapter, the concept is clarified and an overview of state lawlessness in South Africa is provided.

The concept of state lawlessness

Geof Budlender has explained that state conduct may be lawless even if it is *legal*:

> … if the exercise of state power [is] unconstrained by any limits or by any control by an independent system of judicial power. Laws [which] place such unrestrained powers in the hands of State Officials [make] the exercise of state power effectively lawless, that is, there is no independent judicial control over the exercise of power. One of the critical elements of the rule of law is that the law should be reasonably certain and predictable. The subject should know what conduct is commanded and what conduct is prohibited, and what criterion will be followed in applying the power of the state. Arbitrary power may be legal but it is fundamentally lawless (Budlender, 1988: 2).

In so far as black South Africans and all democrats are concerned, apart from conquest, the greatest historical act of lawlessness has been the Act of Union introduced by British Parliament. The Act of Union placed the stamp of approval on conquest and land dispossession. It was the instrument for the imperialist exploitation of the subcontinent, and laid the basis for white domination over blacks. Importantly, it also laid the foundation for state lawlessness in South Africa. Lest it be thought that these words are unduly harsh, consider what Cecil John Rhodes, one of the architects of the future Union, had to say in the Cape Parliament:

> I will lay down my own policy on this Native question. Either you have to receive them on an equal footing as citizens or to call them a subject race. I have made up my mind that there must be class legislation, that there must be Pass Laws and Peace Preservation Acts, and that we have to treat Natives where they are in a state of barbarism, in a different way to ourselves. We are to be the lords over them. These are my politics and these are the politics of South Africa. The Native is to be treated as a child and denied the franchise; he is to be denied liquor also. We must adopt a system of despotism such as works so well in India, in our relations with the barbarians of South Africa. We have given them no share in the government — and I think quite rightly too (Rhodes, 1887 cited in Mnguni, 1988: 135–6).

In 1911, two significant acts were passed. The Mines and Works Act 12 of 1911 reserved skilled jobs on the mines for whites. The Native Labour Regulation Act 15 of 1911 placed African labour under the Department of Native Affairs[1] and provided for a Director of Native Labour, who was to be in charge of Native commissioners, inspectors, and pass officers.

---

1. Set up in terms of Section 147 of the South Africa Act of 1909.

In 1913, the infamous Land Act, the long title of which describes it as an 'Act to make further provision as to the purchase and leasing of land by Natives' was introduced (The Land Act 27 of 1913). It is interesting to note that if South Africa's statutes are judged solely by their titles, the conclusion would be that there has not been a single piece of discriminatory legislation, nor any statute which has deprived people of their rights. In effect, however, the innocuous sounding land laws, of which the Land Act 27 of 1913 was a key element, the franchise laws, and the labour laws reduced blacks to a state of helplessness, rightlessness, and poverty.[2] Pass laws and the migratory labour system drove blacks from their homes to the mines and farms where their labour was required, and then drove them back to the Native Reserves when their labour was no longer required, or when they were able to labour no more. Rhodes explained the purpose of his law relating to land as follows:

> Every Black man cannot have three acres and a cow. We have to face the question and it must be brought home to them that in the future nine-tenths of them will have to spend their lives in daily labour, in physical work, manual labour. They never go out to work. It is our duty as a government to remove these poor children from this life of sloth and laziness and to give them some gentle stimulus to come forth and find out the dignity of labour (Rhodes, 1884 cited in Mnguni, 1988: 136).

The success of the diamond and gold mines was made possible by the systematic dispossession, disenfranchisement, impoverishment, and proletarianization of the black population. It is ironic that the British accomplished these goals using the very people it had defeated in the Afrikaner *vryheidsoorlog*[3]. The economic aims of British imperialism could not be achieved, however, without control over the subcontinent as a whole. An apartheid state, the Union of South Africa, was thus imposed on the indigenous inhabitants of this land and the dual political system of a parliamentary democracy for whites and a dictatorship for blacks was born. It is thus hardly surprising that J. H. Hofmeyr wrote,

> … the great majority of wage earners in South Africa are Natives, Asiatic or Coloured. They are the proletarians upon whose shoulders is borne the South African White aristocracy of labour (Hofmeyer, cited in Mnguni, 1988: 150).

---

2. Other examples include the Bantu (Abolition of Passes and Co-ordination of Documents) Act 67 of 1952, which did not abolish passes but extended pass laws to women, and the Extension of University Education Act 45 of 1959, which ushered apartheid into universities.
3. Literally, the War of Freedom, more commonly the Anglo-Boer War of 1899 to 1902 or, from the British side, the South African War.

State lawlessness, therefore, is not of recent origin. Blacks have been the victims of state lawlessness ever since Union and before.

The rule of law

The rule of law has been used as a yardstick to measure whether state action or conduct is lawless. The rule of law is,

> … a constitutional doctrine governing the state–subject relation, [which] consists of the following distinct but inter-related principles:
>
> (1) The acts of the Government towards the subject, particularly those affecting his rights to freedom of the person, speech and association, and the right of choosing representatives to make the laws, shall be in accordance with previously established general rules having a reasonable specific reference.
> (2) The rights enumerated in paragraph 1, being essential to the operation of law as an order designed to regulate human affairs according to reason, shall be maintained as part of the legal system but subject to;
> (a) well recognized limits upon their exercise;
> (b) limitations consequential upon the need to reconcile them with one another; and
> (c) qualification of such rights in times of exceptional crisis.
> (3) The interpretation and application of the general rules referred to in paragraph 1, and adjudication upon the necessary limitations referred to in paragraph 2, shall be under the control or supervision of an independent judicial body with effective remedial powers and acting according to fair trial procedures (or the requirements of procedural due process) (Mathews, 1971: 31).

Professor Mathews explains that the first of these principles expresses the notion of legality and demarcates its most appropriate area of operation. The second provides for the protection of certain basic principles and qualifications thereto, and the third principle relates to the institutional form in which the ideals of the rule of law can and must be clothed, if they are to be realized. An independent judiciary is perhaps the most important institutional requirement of the rule of law. In criminal law the *principle of legality* is the basis of the rule of law, whereas in criminal procedure it is *due process*. The latter includes the right to a fair trial before an impartial court, which recognizes the right to legal defence and which adheres to certain basic rules of evidence, notably the presumption of innocence and the privilege against self incrimination.

Although a full critique of the rule of law is not within the scope of this chapter, it is important to highlight a central limitation of liberal notions of the concept. Traditional liberal definitions of the rule of law neglect social and economic considerations. In South Africa this has serious implications, for it merely:

> ... lay[s] down certain "guides to conduct" in the field of procedure. A person should not be deprived of his life, liberty or property without access to a proper court of law; he should not be treated differently from other citizens by the law, and if he has a substantive right, he should have legal machinery available to assert that right (Dugard, 1978: 45).

Today, the affirmation of both the substantive as well as the procedural rights of the individual and the protection of human rights have assumed importance. The 1948 Universal Declaration of Human Rights is perhaps the best known document embodying these concerns. In 1959 the International Commission of Jurists adopted the Delhi Declaration, in which it was recognized that it was necessary to establish the social, economic, educational, and cultural conditions under which a person's legitimate aspirations and dignity can be realized (Dugard, 1978). The socio-economic situation in South Africa is characterized by glaring disparities between the rich and the poor, the powerful and the powerless, and by giant monopoly conglomerates who own about 80 per cent of the country's means of production. In this context, any legal or constitutional provision designed to protect existing property rights and wealth accumulation will, in essence, serve only to preserve the status quo. The narrow meaning ascribed to liberal notions of the rule of law does *not* challenge class exploitation, a root cause of poverty in South Africa. Thus for the working people, freedom from exploitation and the redistribution of wealth are priorities which must find their place in a future constitution.

Law and state lawlessness in South Africa

Background

Thus far the roots of state lawlessness in South Africa, rather than its history, have been outlined. The focus now shifts to the extent to which South Africa has departed from the principles of the rule of law, the extent of state lawlessness. This involves dictatorship, the arbitrary exercise of power, oppressive and repressive conduct, as well as different forms of violence used to elicit compliance or to overcome resistance. The point to stress at this juncture is that all of these forms of state lawlessness occur within, and serve to legitimate, the law and the legal system in South Africa. The courts will only intervene where the person or authority exercising arbitrary power acts *outside* the scope of that person's or authority's power, or in the event of procedural irregularities.

The law is concerned with the regulation and control of the exercise of power. Historically, in South Africa, the law has been an important instrument used by the highly interventionist state to create and maintain conditions favourable for the supply of cheap labour and for monopoly capitalist exploitation. It has served to legalize the conquest and the subjugation of the black working class, as well as the monopolization of political power by the white minority. The law has authorized lawless, dictatorial, and arbitrary powers which have frequently led to gross violations of human rights and the rule of law. Furthermore, in South Africa the law has never been independent, for the constitution has made it a servant of the state. It may at times have been independent of the government of the day, but it has always been the handmaiden of the state, whose victims have been black people in general, and the proletarianized and landless black masses in particular. This is stated with all due respect to those few courageous members of the bench who have tried to stem the tide of arbitrary powers. In South Africa, therefore, it may be said that state lawlessness *is* the law.

The context: Reform, repression, and resistance

Phillips and Swilling (1988) have described the eighties as a period of reform, repression, and resistance. They explain that for a state to be legitimate, the right of its apparatuses to regulate society as a whole needs to be broadly accepted at the level of civil society. It is here that hegemony is won through active or passive consent. During the eighties in particular, the South African state lost both legitimacy and hegemony. Caught in a stranglehold of international sanctions, conscious of its loss of legitimacy and of the rise of a powerful resistance movement, the state responded with a total strategy to destroy extra-parliamentary opposition.

Since this counter-revolutionary strategy is detailed in the next chapter, a brief summary will suffice at this point. Between 1979 and 1982 the *total strategy* planners, having just introduced reform on the labour front, believed that some reform was possible without disturbing existing hierarchies of power and the capitalist economic system itself. Reform was planned in the four major areas of labour, urbanization, regional development, and the constitution. In essence, the policy was one of co-option or incorporation. In general, a massive propaganda campaign ensured that the majority of whites supported the state's new strategy. Whites came to see these changes as a bold move away from grand apartheid. Sustained black resistance, however, blew the fuses of total strategy. The government's urban policy failed and the local government system was soon in ruins. Tricameralism itself was a hopeless failure and although Botha was forced to retreat on the issue of black citizenship, at the time this book goes to press, there is still no recognition of a single South African citizenship for all. In the face of continued and increasing black resistance, the state has been forced to adopt more sophisticated counter-revolutionary strategies such as *low intensity conflict* and *winning hearts and minds*. In more and more areas of life in South Africa security has become the prime consideration. This has meant increasing state lawlessness in the form of repression.

State lawlessness, state violence, and state-inspired violence have also been *unlawful*, in the legal sense of the word. For example, people have been assaulted, tortured, and a variety of actions have been taken by the security forces in townships, in schools, and at gatherings, and cross-border raids have been conducted. Many of these *illegal* forms of state lawlessness are discussed in the chapters that follow. Right-wing violence and intimidation of all kinds produced by the apartheid system, its ideology, its traditions, teachings, and propaganda should *not* be excluded from this category. Further repressive measures employed by the state have included media restrictions; mass detentions without trial; the use of vigilantes and death squads; eviction, forced removals, and relocations; the occupation of townships by the defence force; the restriction and banning of organizations; the use of criminal charges, in particular treason; the imposition of the death penalty in offences deemed to be politically-motivated; and the continued imprisonment of political prisoners.[4] Furthermore, the infamous National Management System (NMS) was used to rip black communities apart, to extract the leadership from their hearts, and to reconstruct them according to the state's blueprint.

State lawlessness with regard to Section 29 and Section 31: Detainees

One area of state lawlessness which has not yet been mentioned relates to evidence and the admissibility of statements under the Criminal

---

4. The passing of the Labour Relations Amendment Act 83 of 1988 is also significant, although it is not, strictly speaking, an example of state lawlessness.

   The continued imprisonment of political prisoners, and, indeed, the criteria used to categorize prisoners as *political* or *criminal* offenders has proved to be one of the stumbling blocks to negotiations between the government and the ANC.

Procedure Act 51 of 1977, for certain categories of detainees. In South Africa, existing legal provisions make a mockery of rules of fair play and procedural justice. Confessions and admissions have generally been admissible as evidence only if they were made *freely, voluntarily,* and *without undue influence.* Two new sections, Sections 217(1) and 219A, of the Criminal Procedure Act 51 of 1977, however, have removed the onus on the state to prove, beyond reasonable doubt, that admissions and confessions have been made freely and voluntarily. When such statements are made to a magistrate, they are presumed to have been made freely and voluntarily. The accused now bears the onus of proving otherwise on a balance of probabilities.

This shifting of the onus onto the accused has resulted in very few statements being rendered inadmissible. Section 29 of the Internal Security Act 74 of 1982 provides that a person may be arrested and detained, usually in solitary confinement, for an indefinite period, for the purpose of interrogation. A person may be so detained until, *inter alia,* the Commissioner orders their release, when satisfied that the said person has replied satisfactorily to all questions under interrogation, or that no useful purpose will be served by their further detention under this Section. Thus, such a detainee is *compelled by law* to answer questions. The fact that indefinite detention is known to have serious psychological effects and is likely to break the resistance of most detainees supports the argument that all statements made by detainees, held under Section 29, should be rendered inadmissible (Foster et al., 1987).

Consider what is likely to happen to detainees arrested and held under Section 29. They are held in solitary confinement and are denied access to anyone except the police, interrogators, a magistrate, and an inspector of detainees. Their families are not told where they are being held. They are kept in a small cell for twenty-three hours per day, with only the barest of necessities, and are totally at the mercy of their interrogators, who warn the detainees that they will be held until they have answered the interrogator's questions satisfactorily. Not surprisingly, their resistance breaks, they answer the questions, and make statements to the police. After the police have obtained the information they desire or confirmation of their own version of events, the detainees are taken to a magistrate. In most circumstances, the police allege that it was the detainees who had requested to see the magistrate, or that they had chosen from various alternatives put to them to go to a magistrate. Detainees who are later charged invariably state that they were told, or asked, by their interrogators to make a statement to a magistrate or to face further detention. Whatever the position, the detainees usually find themselves in the presence of a magistrate. They are asked a number of preliminary questions. While replying to these questions and making their statement to the magistrate, the detainees are conscious that both they and their statement will be returned to the Security Police, who are waiting outside the magistrate's office. After the detainees are charged, their statements to the magistrate are handed to the court as a confession. How the courts can accept such a statement as having been made freely and voluntarily, is beyond comprehension!

The late Professor Barend van Niekerk was the last person who exhorted judges to oppose the Terrorism Act 83 of 1967. As a result he was charged and convicted of the offence of attempting to defeat or obstruct the course of justice.[5]

Often a number of persons are detained under Section 29 and their statements are extracted. The police then sift through these statements, charge some of the detainees and use others as state witnesses under Section 31 of the Internal Security Act 74 of 1982. Section 31(1) permits the Attorney General of each province to issue a warrant for the detention of a witness if, in the Attorney General's opinion, there is any danger that such a witness may abscond or be tampered with or intimidated, or if the Attorney General deems such detention to be necessary in the interests of justice. Again the police decide who is entitled to see detainees held under Section 31. When such detainees are brought to court and compelled to take the witness stand, they have no choice *in law*. Furthermore, Section 204 of the Criminal Procedure Act 51 of 1977 states that Section 31 detainees are compelled to give evidence, even if such evidence is self incriminatory. It seems trite to state that the detainee held under Section 31 has no choice.

In conclusion, the process and consequences of detention under Sections 29 and 31 are grossly and totally contrary to the rules of fair play and justice, for detainees held under these provisions are at the mercy of the Security Police. This can only be a form of state lawlessness and it makes a mockery of the system of justice in South Africa.

Conclusion

It is hoped that this overview of state lawlessness will not discourage lawyers from seeking constructive ways of re-introducing justice to such an unjust system. There is an important role to be played by lawyers

---

5. The Terrorism Act was the forerunner of the current Internal Security Act 74 of 1982. For a moving account of Professor Van Niekerk's clash with the authorities see Kahn (1981).

who see the need to curb the exercise of arbitrary powers and dictatorial rule. Although we may differ in our interpretations of the rule of law and its limitations, fighting to prevent the exercise of arbitrary powers, and working toward human rights and fairness inside and outside the courtroom is a basis for unified effort. It is also a challenge we dare not refuse.

Bibliography

Books and articles

Budlender, G. (1988). Law and Lawlessness in South Africa. Unpublished paper. Cape Town.

Dugard, J. (1978). *Human Rights and the South Africa Legal Order*. Princeton: Princeton University Press.

Foster, D., Davis, D. & Sandler, D. (1987). *Detention and Torture in South Africa: Psychological, Legal and Historical Studies*. Cape Town: David Philip.

Kahn, E. (1981). 'In Memoriam: Barend van Niekerk'. *South African Law Journal* 8: 402–11.

Mathews, A. S. (1971). *Law Order and Liberty in South Africa*. Cape Town: Juta.

Mnguni (Jaffe, H.) (1988). *Three Hundred Years*. Cumberwood: APUDSA.

Phillips, M. & Swilling, M. (1988). The Politics of State Power in the 1980s. Unpublished paper. Johannesburg: Centre for Policy Studies, University of the Witwatersrand.

Acts and declarations

The Bantu (Abolition of Passes and Co-ordination of Documents) Act 67 of 1952.

The Criminal Procedure Act 51 of 1977.

The Extension of University Education Act 45 of 1959.

The Internal Security Act 74 of 1982.

The International Commission of Jurists. The Delhi Declaration of 1959.

The Labour Relations Amendment Act 83 of 1988.

The Land Act 27 of 1913.

The Mines and Works Act 12 of 1911.

The Native Labour Regulations Act 15 of 1911.

The South Africa Act of 1909.

The Terrorism Act 83 of 1967.

The Universal Declaration of Human Rights of 1948.

CHAPTER TWO

Changes in counter-revolutionary state strategy in the decade 1979 to 1989[1]

Desirée Hansson

Introduction

'FW's reign marks the end of the "total strategy" era' (*The Star*, 29 November 1989). A decade of rule under the Botha government is now over and South Africa and the world presently await the impact of the new De Klerk administration. Much has already been written on the state's counter-revolutionary strategy during the post-Soweto period. Nevertheless, it is important at this significant political juncture to bring together the central ideas and to reflect upon *total strategy*. This chapter thus provides an overview of the development of state strategy as revealed in the discourse of strategic thinkers and state policy planners in state structures, in legislative changes, and in practice.

In dealing with political resistance in South Africa, the state has functioned neither as omnipotent initiator, nor as fearful reactionary. It is essential, therefore, that analyses of state strategy neither exaggerate nor underestimate the power of the state. Furthermore, it is important that state strategy is not oversimplified, for:

> ... current state strategies cannot be reduced to a single "masterplan", but are constantly being shaped by the struggles of the oppressed classes and their organisations, and by struggles between different institutions within the South African state (Boraine, 1989: 47).

1. Acknowledgement is made to all those who assisted me with this chapter. Special thanks to Margie Crawford, Robin Petersen, and Wilfried Schärf. The central thesis of this chapter was first presented in Hansson (1987).

Total strategy has not been uniform either in policy or practice. In 1986, there was a major shift of emphasis in the overall approach to countering revolution in South Africa. The state's initial reliance on overt repression and token political reforms was replaced by a focus on *winning the hearts and minds* (WHAM) and social reform. The overall aim of this chapter, then, is to provide a macro context for understanding subsequent discussions of state control in this book.

National security ideology

National security ideology was developed in the United States soon after the Second World War and has since been adopted widely in the West (Merrifield, 1987). In South Africa, this ideology provided a legitimation for the state's counter-revolutionary total strategy of the early eighties. The central premise of national security ideology is the notion of an international communist onslaught against capitalism, a '[c]ommunist-inspired subversion from outside' (Seegers, 1988: 22). The communist states, the Soviet Union and it's allies, are cast as the antagonists in world conflict, whereas capitalist states, the United States of America and it's allies, are seen as acting in defence. In the words of Caspar Weinberger, the then United States Secretary of Defence:

> [O]ne out of every four countries around the globe is at war. In virtually every case, behind the mask is the Soviet Union and those who do its bidding (Weinberger, cited in Martin, 1986: 9).

The communist strategy of *total onslaught* is said to involve the use of non-military tactics to exploit grievances in all spheres of social life. A total strategy is thus required to ward off this total onslaught (Malan, cited in Giliomee, 1987). 'The ascension to power in South Africa remains Moscow's principal long-term objective' (The United States Department of Defence, cited in *The Argus*, 7 September 1988). Since the mass liberation movement in South Africa is seen to be aligned with the South African Communist Party (SACP) and the African National Congress (ANC), it is viewed as part of the international communist onslaught (Vlok, cited in Schneider, 1987).

Total strategy, 1979 to mid-1986

Background

For South Africa, the eighties heralded the rise to power of Mr. P. W. Botha and the state's adoption of total strategy to counter revolution.[2] P. W. Botha, in his capacity as Minister of Defence, introduced this approach in his 1977 White Paper on Defence:

> Total strategy co-ordinates all aspects of national life — the military, economic, political, sociological, technological, ideological, psychological and cultural — in an integrated defence of the nation (Botha, 1977: 2).

When total strategy was first implemented, however, repression was its cornerstone, the justification being that political reform was only possible once a state of *law and order* had been re-established (Huntington, 1986; and Vlok, cited in Schneider, 1987). Repression by the security forces was intense, widespread, and violent (Frederikse, 1986). For example, between July 1985 and March 1986, 18 569 people were detained without trial under the security emergency regulations[3] (*Hansard*, 1985: col. 1352) and there is evidence that detainees were severely tortured (Foster et al., 1987). Furthermore, the South African Police (SAP) killed 1 113 township residents in *unrest related incidents* between July 1985 and July 1986 (*Hansard* 1986: col. 255617). During this phase of total strategy, political reforms were limited and comprised carefully engineered and related changes to policies regarding urbanization, labour, regional development, and the constitution[4] (Swilling, 1988). All of these reforms involved processes of *deracialization* and *reracialization*, namely, the substitution of overtly racist and, therefore, politically controversial policies and structures, with more covert mechanisms to ensure white domination[5] (Morris & Padayachee, 1988).

Reforms in urbanization policy

Grand apartheid, based on the system of bantustans, influx control, and pass laws, was designed to restrict and control the movement and settlement of the African labour force in urban and white areas.[6] On the whole, however, the bantustans have lacked political legitimacy among the African population and proved to be economically non-viable. Influx controls were gradually, but increasingly, ignored, and settled

2. Derived from the ideas of a Second World War, French general, Beaufre (Swilling, cited in *Engineering Week*, 28 April 1989). For details see Chapter 3.
3. Under Regulation 3(1).
4. The urban and labour reforms were part of the state's monetarist policy, discussed in Morris & Padayachee (1988).
5. See Burdzik & Van Wyk (1987) for a full account of apartheid legislation.
6. Coloureds and Asians were not subject to influx controls. Instead, their settlement was regulated within South Africa by group areas legislation (The Group Areas Act 36 of 1966).

'regional proletariats' formed on the peripheries of many white metropolitan areas[7] (Cobbett et al., 1989: 23). In the late seventies, the trade unions started campaigning for higher wages for migrant workers. In turn, organized industry and commerce put pressure on the state to relax influx controls, in order to encourage the development of a stable urban African labour force (Morris & Padayachee, 1988).

By 1980 the state could no longer ignore the fact that apartheid had not only failed to control African urbanization, but was serving to fuel resistance to the Botha government, both nationally and internationally.

A new urbanization policy, based on the recommendation of the Rieckert Commission (1979), was thus introduced. Those Africans having residence rights under Section 10 of the Black Urban Areas Consolidation Act 25 of 1945 were granted permanent urban residence,[8] and the rights to trade, to purchase property, to sell labour without a contract, and to constitute labour unions. Those with temporary employment contracts, domiciled in the bantustans, were denied these rights and were subjected to stricter influx controls[9] (Hindson, 1987).

These reforms in urbanization policy were based on the state's principle tactic of *divide and rule*. One of the central objectives was to decrease unity among the African majority by creating a small, relatively privileged class of urban Africans, whilst relegating the remainder of the African population to the bantustans. It was also hoped that the exclusion of rural Africans would ease the unemployment problem and the housing shortage in urban areas, both of which had become politically contentious issues (Morris & Padayachee, 1988). Overall, it was a way of maintaining white dominance, particularly in urbanized South Africa, whilst appearing to begin a process of redistribution.

Reforms in regional development policy

In 1982 a new regional development policy was adopted, which took cognizance of the fact that the forty-four planning regions, established in 1975, had proved to be economically counter-productive. This was largely due to the fact that these regions had been defined according to the artificially imposed boundaries required by apartheid's bantustans

---

7. For example, Durban and Pretoria.
8. Although this right was still subject to the availability of, what the state defined as, suitable accommodation and employment.
9. It became the task of the Development Boards and the Tribal Labour Bureaux to regulate the movement of Africans from rural to urban areas within the bantustans. Stricter fines were also introduced for employers and employees who contravened these provisions (Hindson, 1987).

and group areas. In contrast, the new plan was based on a 'soft borders approach' (Buthelezi, cited in Cobbett et al., 1989: 27). Nine development regions[10] corresponding with existing sources of capital and labour were to replace the existing planning regions:

> These form functional economic, social and political administrative units. They cut across and include Bantustan borders. Administratively all departments and state structures are being defined by these borders[11] (Crawford, 1989: 5).

In March 1983 the Science Committee of the President's Council reported its findings, which showed *inter alia* that the state family planning programme had only succeeded in reducing fertility rates among an urbanized élite. In essence, it was argued that *population* planning rather than *family* planning is necessary if South Africa is to keep its population growth rate in line with its resources.[12] The Committee proposed that the way to achieve this goal is to improve the standard of living and quality of life for all (Science Committee of the President's Council, 1983). On this basis, the Department of Constitutional Development and Planning formulated a new regional development plan, known as the Population Development Programme (PDP).[13] Figure 2.1 details the central aims, objectives, and tactics of the PDP. A national and a regional community development strategy were devised to implement the PDP, and state structures were introduced to facilitate the execution of these strategies. Figure 2.2 shows the relationships between development, welfare, and PDP structures.

---

10. In the long term, the plan was for these development regions to replace the bantustans and the provinces (Cobbett et al., 1989).
11. For example, the boundaries of Regional Welfare Boards, Joint Management Centres (JMCs), Regional Development Associations, and Regional Services Councils.
12. It has been estimated that available resources, particularly water, can support a maximum of 80 million people. With a fertility rate of 2,1 for all racial groups, this limit will be reached in 2020 (Lund, 1985).
13. The PDP is now located in the General Affairs Department of National Health and Population Planning, but is implemented by each of the racially segregated own affairs departments, i.e. the Departments of Health Services and Welfare for Whites, Health Services and Welfare for Coloureds, Health Services and Welfare for Asians, and Development and Planning for Africans. It is interesting to note that programmes like the PDP have been a part of the strategy of low intensity conflict in the Phillipines, which is experiencing political conflict similar to that in South Africa (Crawford, 1989).

FIGURE 2.1: THE AIMS, OBJECTIVES, AND TACTICS OF THE POPULATION DEVELOPMENT PROGRAMME (PDP)*

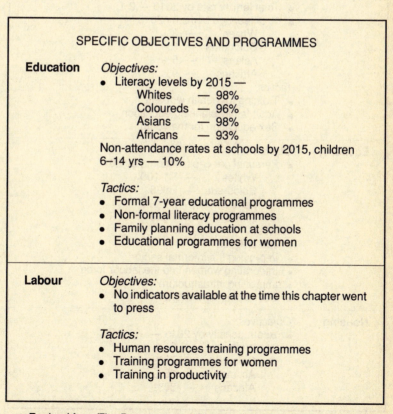

CENTRAL AIMS

- Ensuring a balance between natural resources, socio-economic potential & population size
- Enhancing the quality of life
- Accelerating development
- Integrating family planning with development programmes
- Involving communities in the PDP

SPECIFIC OBJECTIVES AND PROGRAMMES

Education   *Objectives:*
- Literacy levels by 2015 —
    Whites   — 98%
    Coloureds   — 96%
    Asians   — 98%
    Africans   — 93%
  Non-attendance rates at schools by 2015, children 6–14 yrs — 10%

Tactics:
- Formal 7-year educational programmes
- Non-formal literacy programmes
- Family planning education at schools
- Educational programmes for women

Labour   *Objectives:*
- No indicators available at the time this chapter went to press

Tactics:
- Human resources training programmes
- Training programmes for women
- Training in productivity

* *Revised from The Department of Constitutional Development and Planning, 1989.*

Health	*Objectives:*
	• Infant mortality rate by 2015 — 8 deaths per 1 000 per year
	• Life expectancy by 2015 —
	Whites — 74 years
	Coloureds — 74 years
	Asians — 74 years
	Africans — 69 years
	Tactics:
	• The provision of basic services such as sanitation, water & garbage removal
	• Educational programmes
Population	*Objectives:*
	• Total fertility rate by 2010 — 2,1
	• % of teenage births by 2015 —
	Whites — 3%
	Coloureds — 6%
	Asians — 5%
	Africans — 9%
	Tactics:
	• Training for health workers
	• Adult family planning education
	• Sex education for the youth
Economy	*Objectives:*
	• Personal per capita income by 2015** —
	Whites — R1 100
	Coloureds — R998
	Asians — R1 070
	Africans — R846
	Tactics:
	• Job creation
	• Improving the informal sector
	• Integrating women into the labour force
	• Improving infrastructure
	• Developing agriculture
Housing	*Objectives:*
	• Room density by 2015 —
	Whites — 65%
	Coloureds — 72%
	Asians — 65%
	Africans — 80%

** *January 1989 monetary values.*

Housing	*Tactics:*
	• Lowering building standards
	• Self-building schemes
	• Home-ownership schemes
	• The provision of basic services

The national community development strategy was the state's first co-ordinated community development programme. Previously, the Department of Community Development had focused on forced removals (Lund, 1985). The PDP, together with the community development strategy and the Black Communities Development Act 4 of 1984, were indications of a formal institutionalization of the notion of *community development* in South Africa (Groenewald, 1984). The following comment made by the Chief of Social Planning in the Department of Constitutional Development and Planning in 1984 conveys the essence of the state's conception of community development:

> [T]he onus rests on the individual and his community to undertake constructive efforts to improve its socio-economic position[14] (Chief of Social Planning in the Department of Constitutional Development and Planning, cited in Crawford, 1989: 4).

Community development is clearly in accordance with the government's policy of *own affairs*, for it emphasizes self-help and the responsibility of racially segregated local communities for improving their quality of life. The central contradiction of this approach is that:

> ... [p]eople whose lives are a struggle to meet basic needs are hardly well-placed to "improve their own quality of life" by somehow "improving their socio-economic position" by "constructive effort" (Lund 1985: 17).

Furthermore, one of the premises of community development is that communities must identify their own needs, yet problems arise when local needs do not correspond with the aims of the PDP. This has frequently been the case when African communities have prioritized their need for national political rights.

Since the role played by the PDP in counter-revolutionary strategy only became apparent in 1987, this is discussed in detail later in this

---

14. This approach stands in contrast to the socialist basic needs approach, which acknowledges structural constraints imposed on communities by the broader economic and political system and so stresses the central state's duty to redistribute resources (Breytenbach, 1984).

FIGURE 2.2: THE STRUCTURES OF AND INTER-RELATIONS BETWEEN THE POPULATION DEVELOPMENT PROGRAMME, DEVELOPMENT AND WELFARE BODIES*

POPULATION DEVELOPMENT PROGRAMME STRUCTURES

THE DEPARTMENT OF NATIONAL HEALTH & POPULATION DEVELOPMENT

Functions:
- The home department of the PDP
- Oversees the planning and implementation of the PDP

Members:
- Chaired by the Director General
- Liaison Officers are employed to implement the PDP in communities

DEVELOPMENT STRUCTURES

THE NATIONAL REGIONAL DEVELOPMENT ADVISORY BOARD

Functions:
Reports to the Cabinet & to the Demographic Planning Committee of the President's Council

Members:
- The 11 Director Generals of the Inter-Departmental Committees
- The 9 Chairpersons of the Regional Development Advisory Committees
- Representatives from the South African Welfare Council

WELFARE STRUCTURES

THE SOUTH AFRICAN WELFARE COUNCIL

---

9 REGIONAL DEVELOPMENT ADVISORY COMMITTEES

Functions:
- Oversee developments in each of the 9 development regions
- Advise the National Regional Development Advisory Board

Members:
- A Chief Community Liaison Officer for each region
- Representatives from the Regional Development Associations
- Representatives from the Regional Welfare Boards

36 REGIONAL WELFARE BOARDS

One for each racial group in each of the 9 development regions

---

INTER-DEPARTMENTAL COMMITTEES

Functions:
- Decides PDP policy
- Allocates budgets

Members:
The 11 Director Generals of —
- National Health and Population Development
- Constitutional Development and Planning
- Co-operation and Development
- Community Development
- National Education
- Education and Training
- Internal Affairs
- Manpower
- Industry, Commerce, and Tourism
- Agriculture
- Environmental Affairs

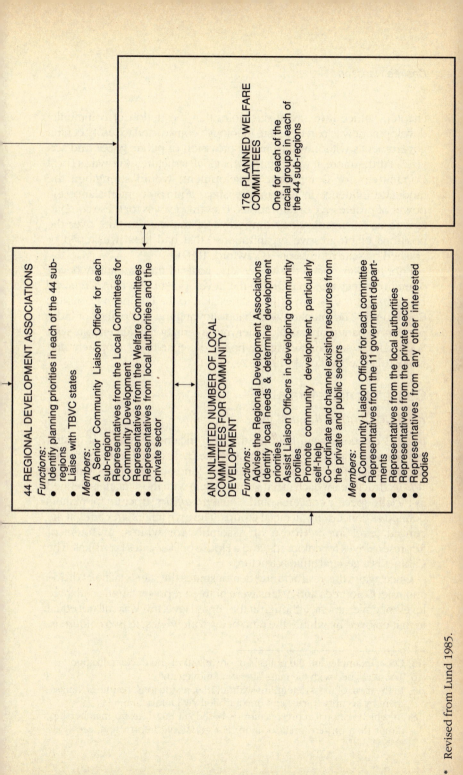

176 PLANNED WELFARE COMMITTEES

One for each of the racial groups in each of the 44 sub-regions

44 REGIONAL DEVELOPMENT ASSOCIATIONS

Functions:
- Identify planning priorities in each of the 44 sub-regions
- Liaise with TBVC states

Members:
- A Senior Community Liaison Officer for each sub-region
- Representatives from the Local Committees for Community Development
- Representatives from the Welfare Committees
- Representatives from local authorities and the private sector

AN UNLIMITED NUMBER OF LOCAL COMMITTEES FOR COMMUNITY DEVELOPMENT

Functions:
- Advise the Regional Development Associations
- Identify local needs & determine development priorities
- Assist Liaison Officers in developing community profiles
- Promote community development, particularly self-help
- Co-ordinate and channel existing resources from the private and public sectors

Members:
- A Community Liaison Officer for each committee
- Representatives from the 11 government departments
- Representatives from the local authorities
- Representatives from the private sector
- Representatives from any other interested bodies

* Revised from Lund 1985.

chapter. Suffice it to say at this point that the notion of community development was part of a state ideology[15] constructed to justify central government's withdrawal from the provision of public goods and services. Furthermore, it was intended that PDP structures, known as Local Committees for Community Development, would strengthen the moderate influence in African townships and so counterbalance the power of progressive organizations. The strategy was for these committees to assist organizations supportive of the state to take over the positions of progressive organizations[16] that had been weakened or crushed by state repression[17] (Crawford, 1989).

Prior to 1985, one of the longer-term goals of the community development strategy was to promote the development of a *consociational confederation*[18] of South African states akin to the European Economic Community. The intention was that, following the acceptance of independence, bantustans would enter into international agreements with South Africa, so maintaining the policy of separate development and white rule (Cobbett et al., 1989).

Constitutional reforms

Restructuring at the first tier

In 1983 elections were held for the new tricameral system of central government with its three racially separate parliaments and sets of state departments. This system involves two kinds of structures, an *own affairs* structure for each racial group to deal with those matters defined as racially specific concerns, and a *general affairs* structure for matters defined as concerning all racial groups. The own affairs structures at the central level are a House of Assembly for whites, a House of Representatives for coloureds, and a House of Delegates for Asians. The Cabinet is a general affairs structure.

Once again, this restructuring demonstrates the state's tactic of divide and rule. Coloureds and Asians were granted representation at all three levels of government, although at the central level this was still not equal to that enjoyed by whites, the ratio being four whites, to two coloureds,

---

15. Other examples are the policies of privatization and decentralization.
16. Those aligned with the mass liberation movement.
17. In the form of mass detentions without trial, restrictions, bannings, harassment by security forces, and uncontrolled vigilante action.
18. In which national representation is based on racial group membership, rather than on territorial location. For additional information, see Bolle (1984).

to one Asian. At this stage, Africans were represented on Black Local Authorities (BLAs) only, the lowest level of government. This apparent democratization tactic aims:

> ... at integrating a small part of the "moderate" opposition into the government-controlled political process, and isolating other opposition forces (Hippler, 1987: 35).

Restructuring at the second tier

The restructuring of second-tier government remained at the stage of planning during the 1984–5 period. It was only in 1986 that changes were implemented, beginning with the replacement of the Provincial Councils with nine general affairs structures, known as Executive Committees, one for each of the new development regions. Each Executive Committee is responsible for local authorities, regional development, transport, and for controlling the movement of labour in its particular region. During the early eighties, however, a supportive planning network had already been developed. This infrastructure comprised the Regional Development Advisory Committees, the planning branch of the Department of Constitutional Development and Planning and the Development Boards, and for those regions that included independent bantustans, Regional Liaison Committees (Cobbett et al., 1989).

Restructuring at the third tier

During 1984 and 1985 the third tier of government was reconstituted as a consociational structure, intended as the foundation for the Tricameral Parliamentary system (Morris & Padayachee, 1988). Each racial group was represented at the local level by a self-financing local authority to deal with own affairs. At the metropolitan level, self-financing, multiracial Regional Services Councils (RSCs) were set up to handle general affairs. African permanent residents were granted the right to elect representatives to the BLAs, but were excluded, at least initially, from representation on the RSCs.

This system keeps the decision-making power in white hands, for each local area is allowed one RSC representative for every 10 per cent of the RSC services it uses. RSCs are financed from new taxes on turnover, wages, and salaries.[19] Like the community development strategies, this devolution of responsibility to local authorities was

---

19. The Regional Establishment Levy and the Regional Services Levy, respectively.

intended to allow the central government to shed the responsibility of providing public goods and services. It was also designed to deflect political resistance based on social grievances away from the first to the third tier of government, thus fragmenting the national liberation struggle. Furthermore, it was a means of getting black residents to pay for urban upgrading via the covert route of forcing businesses to raise consumer prices,[20] rather than by using the politically contentious method of local authority increases in rent and service charges.

Public reaction to state strategy

In effect, these political reforms did not challenge the fundamentals of apartheid.[21] It is hardly surprising, therefore, that instead of quelling extra-parliamentary opposition, these token reforms actually fuelled mass-based resistance. Squatters, faced with the option of returning to the more serious poverty of the bantustans and denied urban rights, refused to move. Forced removals, such as the Crossroads debacle, caused public outcry and a loss of support for the state. The African unions rejected the new labour policy which excluded migrant workers. There were mass boycotts of the elections for the Tricameral Parliament and nation-wide resistance was expressed against the BLAs.[22] By April 1985 only three of the original thirty-four BLAs were still functioning[23] (*The Rand Daily Mail*, 16 March 1985), and as early as mid-1983, the majority of the bantustans had rejected the proposed consociational confederation in favour of a non-racial constitutional plan (South African Institute of Race Relations (SAIRR), 1983).

The state response

By this stage, 'the scope for concessionary economic reforms' was being curtailed by a deepening economic recession (Cobbett et al., 1989: 19). The state had experienced a marked loss of ideological and economic support on the international front as a result of its extensive use of violent repression. Faced with hegemonic and economic crises, the government not only had to counter revolution, but had to begin re-establishing its legitimacy. Further concessionary reforms were thus made.

---

20. Due to the new RSC taxes on businesses.
21. Unequal political representation across racial groups, the system of bantustans and group areas, as well as influx control.
22. Mainly due to rent and service charge increases introduced to finance the BLAs.
23. It was intended that 104 BLAs would be operating by the end of 1984.

In 1986 the pass laws were repealed, prohibitions on mixed marriages and the ban on multiracial political parties were lifted. Africans were granted representation on the multiracial RSCs.[24] The state gave assurances that the system of tricameral government was a short-term reform and that the full franchise for blacks was being investigated (Merrifield, 1987). The National Forum was renamed the National Statutory Council.[25] This body was originally set up in 1983 to investigate African urbanization. It now took on the new role of negotiating ways of including Africans at higher levels of formal political decision-making. P. W. Botha endorsed the possibility that African permanent residents could be represented at central government level by a black assembly (Merrifield, 1987). It was envisaged that the resulting *quadcameral* parliament would be co-ordinated by a council of state, a general affairs structure comprising representatives from each of the Houses of Parliament, as well as from the bantustans.

By 1985, the strategy of splitting African *insiders* from *outsiders* had still not succeeded (Cobbett et al., 1989). Further legislation and a policy of orderly urbanization were thus introduced. This policy was based on the premise that African urbanization is both inevitable and desirable, but that it must nevertheless be regulated.[26] Costly, direct restrictions on the physical presence of Africans in urban areas and in white South Africa were replaced with more economical, indirect controls. Fines for employing illegal workers were increased. New legislation was passed, including the Abolition of Influx Control Act 68 of 1986, and amendments were made to the Slums Act 46 of 1979 and the Prevention of Illegal Squatting Act 52 of 1951. The provision of housing in African townships was privatized. African urban residents were to be limited by available accommodation and employment. In this way apartheid's separate development was being replaced by *intra-urban social engineering* (Morris & Padayachee, 1988). The intention was to create class divisions in the urban African population, namely, a class of privileged home-owners in formal townships within metropolitan areas; a class of lower-income, site-and-service residents on the peripheries of the townships and the metropoles;[27] and a very low income class of residents in

---

24. Third-tier structures, one level above that of the BLAs.
25. In 1987 it was renamed the National Council.
26. Orderly urbanization was informed by the PDP's recommendation that increased urbanization can decrease the population growth rate.
27. For example, in July 1986 the BLA forced 200 people in the Western Cape to move from Langa township to Khayelitsha.

regulated squatter areas, on the furthermost metropole peripheries[28] (Cobbett et al., 1989).

Orderly urbanization was linked to a change in focus from financial to industrial capital and to the promotion of productivity in the manu-facturing sector (Morris & Padayachee, 1988). To this end orderly urbanization included a policy of industrial deconcentration designed to limit development in highly urbanized areas, while encouraging growth in industrial development points, areas selected for their growth potential. Economic incentives and disincentives[29] were designed to coax industry to development points and it was envisaged that these would provide employment for Africans who were forced to settle on the peripheries. A process of deregulation was introduced as a way of boosting employment in the informal sector. In particular, minimum wage levels and health and safety regulations were abolished.

Public reaction to additional state reforms

These additional reforms also proved ineffectual in countering popular resistance. The majority, denied access to national representation, had been mobilized around social grievances at a grassroots level. Shared everyday problems such as high rentals, poor housing, low wages, and inadequate education served to unify and extend extra-parliamentary opposition. It was inferior military strength and the lack of formal political power, however, which prevented the extra-parliamentary opposition from achieving a revolution (Bundy, 1988).

By mid-1985 it was clear that the total strategy approach of overt, widespread repression and token political reforms had failed. The state, constrained by a policy of non-concession to radical demands (Hunt-ington, 1986), was now threatened by a growing mass-based resistance and increasing economic pressure. To retain control, it once again resorted to 'rule by the big stick' (De Villiers, 1988: 6) and a partial State of Emergency was declared on 12 June 1985.[30] Since many of Botha's supporters were moderates (Webster, 1987), this regression to the use of widespread violence lost the Botha government further support, both nationally and internationally. A rapid change in state strategy thus became essential.

---

28. This is the first time that the Nationalist government was to allow squatting.
29. Especially the new RSC taxes.
30. Four consecutive national States of Emergency have since been declared: on 12 June 1986, 12 June 1987, 11 June 1988, and 9 June 1989. The fourth was still in operation at the time this book went to press.

Total strategy, mid-1986 to 1989

Low intensity conflict and revolutionary onslaught

From mid-1986 the notion of total onslaught was gradually replaced with that of revolutionary onslaught, an ideology in which South Africa's problems are attributed to its Third World status, rather than to an externally-inspired communist onslaught (Seegers, 1988). Accordingly, state spokesmen began to speak of a change in counter-revolutionary state strategy. The key elements of this new approach are highlighted in the following statements by the then State President P. W. Botha in 1986, and the Minister of Law and Order, Mr. Adriaan Vlok in 1987:

> I believe you can't control violence only with violence and force — you also need socio-economic and other measures to stop the onslaught against South Africa (Botha, cited in Merrifield, 1987: 1).

> We have made studies of similar situations in the rest of the world,[31] which show that if you are to win a revolutionary war there are three important aspects which must be borne in mind. You have to address the security situation, secondly, you have to address grievances and bring good government to ordinary people and, thirdly, you have to address the situation. This is exactly what the government is doing at the moment (Vlok, cited in Merrifield, 1987: 9).

This approach is based on the principles of low intensity conflict,[32] 'a post-Vietnam counterinsurgency doctrine' (Waghestein, cited in Martin, 1986: 9) developed by the United States to prevent a repetition of the type of defeat they had experienced in the Vietnamese war. In the early eighties, the strategy of low intensity conflict emerged internationally as a key counter-revolutionary strategy and has been described thus:

> Counterinsurgency, [is] the keystone of low-intensity conflict ... Military force is an important element — and an instrument — of this strategy, but it is not equivalent to the strategy. The basic goal is to separate anti-government guerrilla forces from the population. The separation can be either civilian or military (resettlement programs or aerial bomb attacks against civilians); the instruments are selected according to effectiveness: anything from large scale massacres to "social reforms" ... [low intensity conflict] recognizes that the roots of insurgences generally are intolerable social, economic, and political conditions ... Some counterinsurgency

---

31. For example, Malaya, Algeria, Chile, and El Salvador (Merrifield, 1987).
32. Alternatively termed low intensity warfare.

planners even like to talk about "addressing the causes" of insurgences. But fundamental change is the goal of the insurgents. [low intensity conflict] aims at a status quo reformed only to the extent needed to continue in place (Hippler, 1987: 34).

At this time, the potential advantages of low intensity conflict (for the South African government) were substantial. It is 'a fight without appearing to fight' (Hippler, 1987: 37), so military objectives can be achieved more covertly without losing popular support. Of equal importance, in times of economic recession, is the fact that low intensity conflict lowers the economic cost of war and allows military expenses to be defrayed across other budgets.

In South Africa, the adoption of a strategy of low intensity conflict constituted a significant change in counter-revolutionary approach from that employed during the previous phase of total strategy. Although it was still to involve a reliance on the use of repression to re-establish and maintain a base level of control by the state, the type of repression that was to be employed was to be less overt and was to be focused more selectively on the leaders of the resistance movement and guerrilla insurgents. Most importantly, reform, although it was to remain limited and highly selective in nature, was to be extended beyond the political, to the social sphere. In essence:

> ... the security action took out the leaders of the UDF[33] while the welfare action cut the ground from under their feet (Wandrag, Chief of Riot Police, cited in *The Star*, 29 November 1989).

The central goal of this low intensity conflict phase of total strategy was to reduce extra-parliamentary opposition to a minimum, using the least overt and state-aligned force possible, while maintaining and strengthening public support for the government, or winning the hearts and minds (WHAM) of the people.[34] Special attention was to be paid to those who would not be dissuaded from active opposition, particularly the leadership. It was accepted that this group had to be separated from its mass base and that violence was justified to achieve this goal. Furthermore, it was essential that *law and order* was re-established and maintained by the security forces, before reforms were initiated. The rationale was that reforms conceded during periods of civil conflict increase the strength of the resistance, by according the opposition victory (Grassroots, August 1988).

---

33. United Democratic Front.
34. WHAM is one aspect of the broader strategy of low intensity conflict.

Restructuring state power relations

For this change in state strategy to succeed, however, a number of serious problems in government had to be overcome. The civil bureaucracy had long been dogged by corruption, inefficiency, and a lack of co-ordination. Security intelligence was impeded by rivalry among the state security bodies and by a lack of up-to-date information about activities at the local level. The core problem seemed to be a gap between planning and execution. This context was ripe for the acceptance of a military solution that stressed co-ordination and efficiency (Seegers, 1988). The office of Executive State President, instituted in the new constitution of 1983, was a ready basis for a more executive style of government. It was hardly surprising then that power relations within the state were restructured toward an executive dominated by the military. The National Security Management System (NSMS), subsequently renamed the National Management System (NMS), was the symbol of this process (Morris & Padayachee, 1988), and it enabled the military to *clean up* government (Seegers, 1988). One of the aims of the NMS was to improve efficiency by training civilian bureaucrats in a military style.

Since its introduction in 1979, the NSMS had supplied the State Security Council (SSC)[35] and the Cabinet with information concerning security. It was not until 1986, however, that the NSMS's capacity for monitoring political resistance at a grassroots level and on a daily basis, and its potential for co-ordinating the executive functions of civil government and the military, were exploited.

Figure 2.3 is a schematic representation of the structure of the NMS. In late 1986, the operational headquarters of the then NSMS, the National Joint Management Centre, was set up. This centre was chaired by the Deputy Minister of Law and Order, whose position was created for this specific purpose. Figure 2.3 shows that the structure of the NMS facilitated the participation of all government institutions at every level. In particular, the split into security and welfare subsystems reflects the dual focus of the strategy of low intensity conflict. The way in which the NMS was employed to facilitate the implementation of this strategy will be detailed in the text that follows. Suffice it to say at this point that the NMS's matrix system of management, which linked the efforts of functionally separate departments from the local to the national level, enabled a greater co-ordination of counter-revolutionary interventions.

---

35. Introduced in 1972 in an attempt to co-ordinate intelligence (Seegers, 1988).

FIGURE 2.3: THE STRUCTURE OF THE NATIONAL MANAGEMENT SYSTEM (NMS)*

STATE PRESIDENT

STATE SECURITY COUNCIL (SSC)
- The State President — Chair
- Ministers of 6 departments:
  - Foreign Affairs
  - Defence
  - Law and Order
  - Justice
  - Finance
  - Constitutional Development & Planning
- Chiefs of:
  - SADF (Army, Airforce & Navy)
  - Intelligence
  - Police

CABINET

3 CABINET COMMITTEES

Constitutional Committee	Economic Committee	Social Committee

WELFARE SECRETARIAT

JOINT WORKING COMMITTEE
- The Deputy Minister of Law and Order — Chair
- Heads of State Departments

SSC SECRETARIAT
Representatives from:
- National Intelligence Service
- SADF
- SAP
- Department of Foreign Affairs

Administrative Branch	National Intelligence Service	Strategic Communications Branch	Strategy Branch

13 INTER-DEPARTMENTAL COMMITTEES

Manpower	Security Forces	Civil Defence	Transport	Security	National Supplies & Resources	Government Funding	National Economy	Telecommunications & Electrical Power Supply	Service & Technology	Community Services	Culture	Political Affairs

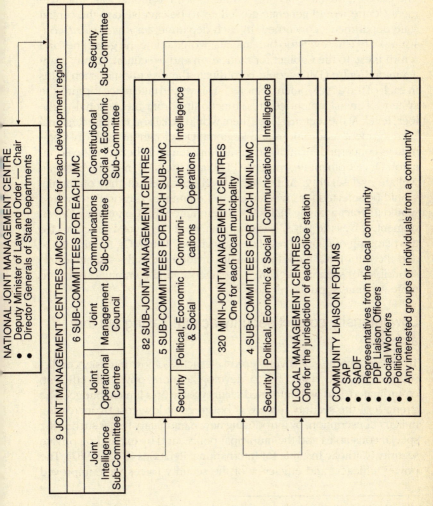

NATIONAL JOINT MANAGEMENT CENTRE
- Deputy Minister of Law and Order — Chair
- Director Generals of State Departments

9 JOINT MANAGEMENT CENTRES (JMCs) — One for each development region

6 SUB-COMMITTEES FOR EACH JMC

| Joint Intelligence Sub-Committee | Joint Operational Centre | Joint Management Council | Communications Sub-Committee | Constitutional Social & Economic Sub-Committee | Security Sub-Committee |

82 SUB-JOINT MANAGEMENT CENTRES

5 SUB-COMMITTEES FOR EACH SUB-JMC

| Security | Political, Economic & Social | Communications | Joint Operations | Intelligence |

320 MINI-JOINT MANAGEMENT CENTRES
One for each local municipality

4 SUB-COMMITTEES FOR EACH MINI-JMC

| Security | Political, Economic & Social | Communications | Intelligence |

LOCAL MANAGEMENT CENTRES
One for the jurisdiction of each police station

COMMUNITY LIAISON FORUMS
- SAP
- SADF
- Representatives from the local community
- PDP Liaison Officers
- Social Workers
- Politicians
- Any interested groups or individuals from a community

* Revised from Swilling & Phillips, 1988; and *The Pretoria News*, 29 November 1989.

Figure 2.4 shows the NMS, developmental, and other government structures in parallel.

The planning function of the NMS was designed to operate as follows: The Cabinet, the State Security Council, or the National Joint Management Centre would generate guidelines to be circulated to the central state departments concerned. In each department a *nodal point*, consisting of five to seven top bureaucrats, would refine the guidelines and return these to the Cabinet for ratification and execution. A Joint Management Centre (JMC) would co-ordinate the execution of such plans in each of the development regions.[36] This would take place through the system of management centres, functioning from the regional to the local level. At the regional level, there would be liaison with the Regional Development Associations and Regional Development Advisory Committees concerned.[37] This indicates an important link between the Population Development Programme (PDP) and the NMS, namely, between welfare and security. At the local level, members of the community would be selected for involvement in Community Liaison Forums and would interact with the PDP's Local Committees for Community Development. It was the JMCs, however, that were the pivotal structures for the planning of counter-revolutionary tactics. The JMCs, the sub-JMCs, and the mini-JMCs were functionally divided into sub-committees responsible for security, welfare,[38] intelligence, and communications, or, more accurately, public relations.[39]

Low intensity conflict security action: Taking out the activists

To implement the selectively repressive tactics of low intensity conflict successfully, the state had to develop a more powerful, efficient, co-ordinated, and well-informed security force on a limited budget. The strength of the security force was bolstered at low cost by increasing military conscription, by introducing new paramilitary forces such as the special constables and the municipal police, and by expanding private security (Catholic Institute for International Relations (CIIR), 1987). The power, efficacy, and efficiency of the security forces were improved

---

36. These also overlap with the command areas of the South African Defence Force (SADF).
37. See Figure 2.2.
38. Including constitutional, economic, and social matters.
39. Also known by their Afrikaans acronyms VEIKOM, SEMKOM, GIK, and KOMKOM, respectively.

FIGURE 2.4: GOVERNMENT, DEVELOPMENT, AND NATIONAL MANAGEMENT SYSTEM (NMS) STRUCTURES IN PARALLEL*

NATIONAL MANAGEMENT SYSTEM	GOVERNMENT BODIES	DEVELOPMENT BODIES

State President

Cabinet

NATIONAL LEVEL

State Security Council

3 Cabinet Committees

Economic Committee	Constitutional Committee	Social Committee

National Joint Management Centre

Tricameral Parliament

House of Assembly	House of Delegates	House of Representatives

National Regional Development Advisory Council

REGIONAL LEVEL

Joint Management Centres

Provincial Administrations

Regional Development Advisory Committees

SUB-REGIONAL LEVEL

Sub-Joint Management Centres

Mini-Joint Management Centres

Regional Services Councils

Regional Development Associations

LOCAL LEVEL

Local Management Centres

Local Authorities

Local Committees for Community Development

Community Liaison Forums

* Revised from Lund, 1985.

through the operation of the NMS. Military control of the NMS ensured the priority of security imperatives. The NMS structure, which allowed the civil bureaucracy of government to be bypassed, enabled very rapid responses by the security forces.

As was mentioned above, one of the central functions of the NMS was intelligence gathering. A JMC's intelligence sub-committee would collect and provide the security sub-committee with information on the plans, activities, and problems of activists and progressive organizations[40] in it's area. The security sub-committee would then use this information to design counter-revolutionary interventions and, in particular, to select targets. These interventions included a range of tactics, such as, assassination, detention without trial, torture, banning, restriction, direct attacks on guerrilla forces outside the South African borders, and assistance to anti-communist groups outside South Africa,[41] as well as to anti-revolutionaries within the country,[42] particularly vigilante groups[43] (Theological Exchange Programme (TEP), 1987).

Simultaneously, the state launched a WHAM campaign to repair the tarnished public image of the security forces. The JMC's communications sub-committees were central to this campaign. Through liaison with the intelligence and security sub-committees, communications sub-committees instituted *disinformation* campaigns to besmirch the national liberation movement and to disrupt their activities. Television played an important role in building a positive image of the security forces and in discrediting the national liberation movement. Another public relations tactic was the involvement of security forces in civic action programmes. For instance, South African Defence Force (SADF) personnel and equipment were used to construct sports fields and national servicemen were employed in educational and medical facilities in African townships. Furthermore, whenever possible, paramilitary units rather than the security forces were used to conduct overtly repressive operations.

Low intensity conflict welfare action: Cutting the ground from under the feet of the revolutionaries

Besides the fundamental difference in the repressive aspects of the first and second phases of total strategy, in practice the latter emphasized

---

40. Those aligned with the national liberation movement.
41. Like UNITA and RENAMO.
42. Like the Witdoeke, Inkatha, and Ama-Afrika.
43. Vigilantism is discussed in detail in Chapter 3.

social rather than political reform. The strategy had changed from a focus on negotiating political representation to negotiating development (Seegers, 1988). From this perspective, welfare became an important site for counter-revolutionary intervention. Until the state adopted the policy of orderly urbanization, the exclusion of Africans from state-provided collective consumption[44] had been justified on the grounds that Africans were not South African citizens. Once the urban African proletariat was officially recognized and communities began to organize around social grievances, their demands for public goods and services could no longer be ignored. The central aim of the welfare action of low intensity conflict, therefore, was to ameliorate those social problems around which the extra-parliamentary opposition was being mobilized. Major General Charles Lloyd, the then Secretary of the State Security Council, explained the rationale for welfare action as follows:

> We must, of course, give the enemy as little opportunity as possible to exploit the situation psychologically, and therefore that is why the very first principle of counter-revolutionary war is good government ... So therefore you must work on things like soccer fields and transport and housing (Lloyd, Secretary of the State Security Council cited in *The Weekly Mail*, 23 June 1989).

Given the economic recession and the enormous backlog in public facilities and services in black areas, the state was forced to prioritize it's upgrading initiatives. The NMS and the PDP functioned to select townships and to plan, facilitate, and co-ordinate upgrading programmes (Crawford, 1989). *Oilspots*, highly politicized black townships in which the material conditions were particularly bad, were identified as priority targets for upgrading. Thirty-four areas, including Mamelodi in the Transvaal, New Brighton in the Eastern Cape, and Bonteheuwel, Manenberg, and Crossroads in the Western Cape, were specified as priorities for substantial upgrading. In addition, about 200 other areas were noted for lower-level upgrading (Boraine, 1988). The state acknowledged that oilspots were chosen for strategic reasons, rather than on the basis of human need (Lloyd, cited in Seegers, 1988).

PDP personnel, in liaison with the Regional Development Advisory Committees, the Regional Development Associations, and the Local Committees for Community Development, worked closely with state

---

44. Such as social welfare, subsidized education, housing, and unemployment insurance.
45. PDP personnel were already functioning as advisers, planners, and co-ordinators in the various departments of Social Welfare and Community Development (Crawford, 1989).

officials from key government departments[45] in the JMC's welfare sub-committees. In this way the civil administration of those functions identified as being crucial to countering revolution[46] were co-ordinated (Lund, 1985; and McKendrick, 1988). The JMC's intelligence sub-committees supplied the welfare sub-committees with up-to-date information about the most volatile social grievances and the attitudes of black communities to state welfare interventions (Hansson, 1987; and Swilling, cited in *Engineering Week*, 28 April 1989). This information was combined with community profiles drawn up by community liaison officers from the PDP,[47] and proved essential to the planning and execution of effective and strategic welfare actions in black communities (Crawford, 1989). Initially, the public were not aware of the clear links between the PDP and the NMS, namely, between welfare and security. The PDP was thus able to take on a central role in upgrading, as public suspicion and rejection of the NMS grew.

Welfare actions were also used to win the hearts and minds. It was the goal of the JMC's communications sub-committees to build government support by ensuring that the state was accredited publicly for upgrading projects.

The restructuring of welfare[48]

Since welfare had become a key political arena, it was restructured to afford the central state greater control. As was explained above in connection with the community development strategy, the conception of state-provided social welfare had already been replaced with the notion that development was to be the responsibility of communities themselves. The Black Communities Development Act 4 of 1984 had already laid the foundation for community development through the BLAs. The Community Welfare Act 104 of 1987 also embodied this new notion of community development for the coloured population.[49] Furthermore, community development involved an expansion of the sphere encompassed by welfare to include all conditions necessary for the physical, emotional, social, and environmental health of individuals, families, and groups (April in Anonymous, 1987).

---

46. Such as roads, education, welfare, health, and manpower.
47. Profiles of housing, health, education, welfare, sport, recreation, leadership, community relations, and basic safety.
48. For more detailed discussions of the restructuring of welfare, see Jinabhai (1986) and Lund (1988).
49. Since welfare is an own affair, each of the Houses may introduce different welfare legislation at different times.

In the context of this process of restructuring, the state had to deal with the contradiction between its policy of decentralizing power, which was promoted in the service of political reform, and its social reform goal of increasing centralized control over welfare. In reconciling this contradiction, the state sought to ensure that changes made in the sphere of welfare effectively increased central control, whilst appearing to decentralize power. To illustrate: In keeping with the goal of decentralization, local authorities were given responsibility for a wider range of more important issues than their predecessors, the city councils. Local authorities had to provide housing, set and collect rents and rates, and control local health services and schools, duties which the government itself labelled 'community sensitive' (*Grassroots*, August 1988). In effect, however, the central state maintained ultimate control over local welfare by appointing staff, deciding policy, and setting budgets at the local level. Clearly, this tactic served another important strategic function. It blurred the lines of accountability, so deflecting the focus of the opposition away from the central state. This made the raising of political consciousness increasingly difficult and aimed to 'depoliticise the role of the central state and decentralise conflict' (Glaser, 1987: 385).

The old policy of funding welfare agencies and individual social workers' posts, which had made it difficult for the state to keep abreast of and to control welfare activities, especially at the grassroots level, was replaced. The new policy required the submission of detailed funding proposals to the central state and stipulated that subsidies were to be allocated on the basis of welfare programmes.

Regional Welfare Boards, new structures staffed by ministerial appointment, were set up to 'coordinate and control the actions of welfare organisations in "periods of crisis"' (Anonymous, 1987: 5).[50] More specifically, these boards were designed to collect information about all existing and planned welfare programmes in their designated areas. All bodies involved in welfare activities had to register with the boards in order to raise funds. In this way welfare endeavours which were not supportive of the state could be curtailed by refusing to register the organizations concerned.

Since state-provided social welfare for Africans had been extremely limited, African social welfare had to be reformed. In 1986, the Abolition of the Development Boards Act 75 of 1986 was passed and Development Boards were replaced with provincial authorities. Provincial Departments of Community Services and Community Development were

---

50. See Figure 2.3.

set up to deal with welfare-type services[51] and community development for Africans (Crawford, 1989).

Public responses and problems

The greatest impediments to the success of welfare action under low intensity conflict have been insufficient finance and a lack of legitimacy in black communities. Swilling notes that:

> … [t]he highly publicised upgrade programme is having a major effect in no more than three or four townships around the country. Even if the state and the economy were able to meet the demands which have accumulated over the last 40 years however, there is no evidence that a new materially comfortable population will forget that it lacks political representation. The converse may in fact be true (Swilling, cited in *Engineering Week*, 28 April 1989).

Although at first the NMS seemed to be an awesome counter-revolutionary mechanism in the hands of the military, in practice a number of problems were encountered. It's secretive nature created a great deal of public suspicion and widespread rejection. The NMS was criticized for being a 'silent coup' for the military, which 'prized power from elected bodies and entrusted it to a secret operation run by the military' (*The Weekly Mail*, 3 October 1987), and a 'shadow government' that shirked public accountability (*The Weekly Mail*, 23 June 1989).

Furthermore, a substantial section of the civil bureaucracy came to resent the dominance of the military in the NMS. Discontent was expressed over the fact that civilian government had been subordinated to the military and associated with state repression. Some bureaucrats maintained that the security policy providing information on a *need to know* basis only impeded the co-ordination of state interventions (Seegers, 1988). The NMS functioned with varying degrees of success across geographic areas. More specifically, in areas that faced low levels of political resistance, there was little incentive to be involved in the NMS and, as resentment grew on the part of civil servants toward the military, participation in the NMS by lower-level government officials became inconsistent.

Substantial sections of the African population rejected the PDP as a state-imposed form of token consultation and a covert means of trying to strengthen and legitimate the system of local authorities. The legitimacy of the PDP was eroded further as its role in the military-aligned NMS

---

51. Such as pensions, grants, and statutory work under the Child Care Act 74 of 1983.

was exposed. Even the Local Committees for Community Development did not enjoy significant community support. In particular, investigations into the spheres of basic safety, leadership, and community relations, conducted under the auspices of the Local Committees, came to be viewed as subtle forms of political surveillance.

In summary then, although security action weakened the extra-parliamentary opposition and welfare action *won the hearts and minds* of a small number of blacks, this low intensity conflict phase of total strategy succeeded in *managing* rather than *destroying* political opposition[52] (*New Nation*, December 1989). During the post-1986 period, the mass liberation movement was rebuilt, international pressure did not abate, and despite somewhat drastic economic measures, the South African economy did not recover. Succinctly put:

> This year has witnessed the defeat of the cosy theory that the South African Government could prevent a revolution by giving blacks electricity and flushing loos (*The Sunday Tribune*, 3 December 1989).

Conclusion: The De Klerk era

The recently inaugurated President, F. W. de Klerk, seems to be putting a rapid and somewhat dramatic end to the strategies of the Botha government. In the first month of the new presidency newspaper headlines proclaimed: 'FW pulls down the house that PW built' (*The Weekly Mail*, 1 December 1989), and 'Wham goes a pet Nat[53] theory' (*The Sunday Tribune*, 3 December 1989). Although it would be premature at this early stage to attempt a description of the De Klerk approach, it is nevertheless useful to conclude this chapter by noting aspects of what will develop into the state's new counter-revolutionary strategy.

Already, F. W. de Klerk appears to have acknowledged the failure of P. W. Botha's strategy and to have realized the fundamental importance of political reform in South Africa:

> You cannot simply have a counter-insurgency approach, because it may be that the enemy is the majority of the population (De Klerk, cited in *The Weekly Mail*, 1 December 1989).

> Winning the hearts and minds is fine, but it is only a way of calming a situation and not an end in itself ... [T]he only way to prevent a revolution is a negotiated political settlement that can win majority credibility among

---

52. Furthermore, WHAM has not only failed to re-establish hegemony in South Africa, but also in Namibia (*Sunday Times*, 3 December 1989).
53. Abbreviation for Nationalist.

all population groups (De Klerk, cited in *The Sunday Tribune*, 3 December 1989).

More specifically, De Klerk has stated that he aims to remove civilian government from military dominance (De Klerk, cited in *The Weekly Mail*, 1 December 1989). The first step in this direction has been the abolition of the stronghold of the military, the NMS. National security will no longer be handled by the SSC, but by a new, yet ordinary, Cabinet Security Committee[54] (*The Pretoria News*, 29 November 1989). The National Joint Management Centre is to be replaced by a number of Senior Officials' Task Groups[55] and at the regional and local levels, JMCs will be replaced with co-ordinating centres. Figure 2.5 shows the structure of the old NMS in parallel with that of the new system. As yet, it is too early to ascertain whether this new structure will turn out to be the NMS by yet another name, for after all the NMS was originally called the National *Security* Management System. It has also been speculated that the role of military intelligence is to be downgraded in favour of the National Intelligence Service (Cilliers, cited in *The Weekly Mail*, 1 December 1989). The proposed cuts in the defence budget and the transfer of expenditure to policing are said to signify a reduction in the role that will be played by the military in countering revolution and a corresponding increase in the role that will be played by the police force, namely, a move from a 'boys on the border' approach to that of 'bobbies on the beat' (*The Sunday Times*, 3 December 1989).

On the liberal front, talk of a constitutional settlement based on geographic federalism intensified during 1989. This has been proposed as a political solution that is superior to both apartheid and to majority rule in a unitary state. Liberals, especially those in big business, fear that the latter system will cause the collapse of industrial capitalism in South Africa. Specific fears of a socialist system include the nationalization of property, confiscatory taxation, an increase in the minimum wage level, administrative chaos resulting from too rapid an advancement of blacks in the civil service, and, of course, violence against whites. These groups prefer geographic federalism, for its powerful regional authorities would serve to fragment the national majority and the power of any single group would be limited by the system's checks and balances. The State President has not yet taken a public stand on this matter. The proposal has not been well received by the Mass Democratic Movement

---

54. Comprising the President, the Ministers of Justice, Defence, Law and Order, and Foreign Affairs (*The Pretoria News*, 29 November 1989).
55. Accordingly the portfolio of Deputy Minister of Law and Order has also been abolished.

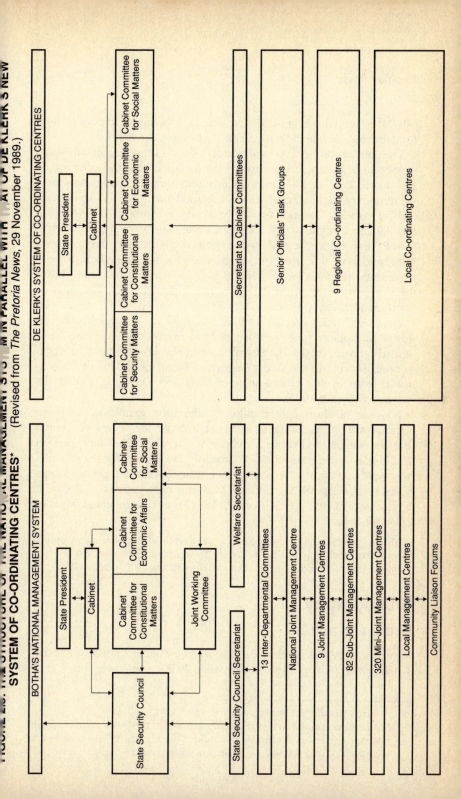

FIGURE 2.3. THE STRUCTURE OF THE NATIONAL MANAGEMENT SYSTEM IN PARALLEL WITH THAT OF DE KLERK'S NEW SYSTEM OF CO-ORDINATING CENTRES*
(Revised from *The Pretoria News*, 29 November 1989.)

BOTHA'S NATIONAL MANAGEMENT SYSTEM

- State President
- Cabinet
- Cabinet Committee for Constitutional Matters
- Cabinet Committee for Economic Affairs
- Cabinet Committee for Social Matters
- Joint Working Committee
- State Security Council
- State Security Council Secretariat
- Welfare Secretariat
- 13 Inter-Departmental Committees
- National Joint Management Centre
- 9 Joint Management Centres
- 82 Sub-Joint Management Centres
- 320 Mini-Joint Management Centres
- Local Management Centres
- Community Liaison Forums

DE KLERK'S SYSTEM OF CO-ORDINATING CENTRES

- State President
- Cabinet
- Cabinet Committee for Security Matters
- Cabinet Committee for Constitutional Matters
- Cabinet Committee for Economic Matters
- Cabinet Committee for Social Matters
- Secretariat to Cabinet Committees
- Senior Officials' Task Groups
- 9 Regional Co-ordinating Centres
- Local Co-ordinating Centres

(MDM) in which it is generally perceived as being an impediment to fundamental change in South Africa (Cobbett et al., 1989).

The date 2 February 1990 will no doubt be recognized as an important milestone in South African history. In his speech at the opening of parliament, F. W. de Klerk announced a number of dramatic and somewhat unexpected reforms. These included the intention to release Nelson Mandela unconditionally[56] and the unbanning of the ANC, the Pan African Congress (PAC), and the South African Communist Party (SACP). Exiled members of these organizations are now free to return home and those who are imprisoned merely for being members of these organizations are to be released. Restrictions were lifted from thirty-three organizations of the MDM including the UDF, the Congress of South African Trade Unions (COSATU), the National Education Crisis Committee (NECC), and the South African Student Congress (SANSCO). Restrictions placed on 374 ex-detainees were removed. The State President also promised that the State of Emergency would be lifted as soon as possible and that the Media Emergency Regulations[57] and the Education Emergency Regulations are to be abolished (De Klerk, cited in *The Argus*, 2 February 1990).

It would be short-sighted indeed to deny the significance of these reforms. A word of caution is, however, in order, for it is not yet certain that 'the season of violence is over' in South Africa (De Klerk, cited in *The Argus*, 2 February 1990). Whatever De Klerk's strategy, it will necessarily be constrained by 'its own historical starting point' (Morris & Padayachee, 1988: 11), and it is from this perspective that it should be assessed. Maybe then it is best, at least for the moment, to adopt the following stance:

> This is clearly a move away from a previous style of government into something different and we will have to wait and see whether it is an improvement (Van der Merwe, cited in *The Citizen*, 29 November 1989).

Bibliography

Books and articles

Anonymous (1987). *Behind the New Welfare Policy: A Guide for Social Workers*. Pamphlet published anonymously in Cape Town.

---

56. Nelson Mandela was subsequently released on 11 February 1990.
57. With the exception of a regulation which prevents the publication of visual material related to the unrest situation. This regulation has now been incorporated into the Security Emergency Regulations.

Bolle, L. J. (1984). *South Africa and the Constitutional Option: A Consociational Analysis.* Cape Town: Juta.

Boraine, A. (1988). Wham, Sham or Scam? — Security Management, Upgrading and Resistance in a South African Township. Unpublished paper. Cape Town: Centre for African Studies, University of Cape Town.

Boraine, A. (1989). 'Security Management in the Black Townships'. *Transformation* 8: 47–63.

Botha, P. W. (1977). *White Paper on Defence.* Pretoria: Government Printer.

Breytenbach, W. J. (1984). 'The New South African Constitution and its Implications for Development'. *Development Southern Africa* 1: 65–81

Bundy, C. (1988). Around which Corner? Revolutionary Theory and Contemporary South Africa. Unpublished paper. Cape Town: Centre for African Studies, University of Cape Town.

Burdzik, J. & Van Wyk, D. (1987). 'Apartheid Legislation 1976–1986. *Acta Juridica*: 119–64.

Catholic Institute for International Relations (CIIR) (1987). *Now Everyone is Afraid: The Changing Face of Policing in South Africa.* Cape Town: CIIR.

Cobbett, W., Glaser, D., Hindson, D. C. & Swilling, M. (1989). 'A Critical Analysis of South African State Reform Strategies in the 1980s'. In *State, Resistance and Change in South Africa.* (Eds.) Frankel, P., Pines, N. & Swilling, M. Johannesburg: Southern Books.

Crawford, M. (1989). Social Welfare and Community Development Structures: Their Relationships with the National Security Management System. Unpublished paper. Cape Town: Institute of Criminology, University of Cape Town.

De Villiers, M. (1988). 'Rule by the Big Stick: State of Emergency Repression in the Eastern Cape'. *Reality* 2: 3–6.

Foster, D., Davis, D. & Sandler, D. (1987). *Detention and Torture in South Africa: Psychological, Legal and Historical Studies.* Cape Town: David Philip.

Frederikse, J. (1986). *South Africa: A Different Kind of War.* Johannesburg: Ravan.

Giliomee, H. (1987). 'In Gesprek met Genl. Magnus Malan'. *Die Suid*

Afrikaan 8: 12–13.

Glaser, D. (1987). 'Ruling Groups and Reform in the Mid-1980s'. *South Africa Review Four*. Johannesburg: Ravan.

Groenewald, C. J .(1984). 'Evaluasie in Gemeenskapsontwikkeling'. *South African Journal of Sociology* 15: 129–37.

Hansson, D. S. (1987). Warfare through Welfare: The New State Strategy of Low Intensity Warfare and some of its Implications for Progressive Social Services in South Africa. In *Mental Health, Struggle and Transformation*. (Eds.) Eagle, G. Hayes, G. & Bhana, A. Durban: Organization for Appropriate Social Services in South Africa (OASSSA).

Hindson, D. C. (1987). 'Orderly Urbanisation and Influx Control: From Territorial Control to Regional Spatial Reordering in South Africa'. In *Regional Restructuring under Apartheid: Urban and Regional Policies in South Africa*. (Eds.) Tomlinson, R. & Addleson, M. Johannesburg: Ravan.

Hippler, J. (1987). 'Low-Intensity Warfare: Key Strategy for the Third World Theater'. *Middle East Report* Jan/Feb: 32–8.

Hansard (House of Assembly Debates) April 1985. Pretoria: Government Printer.

Hansard (House of Assembly Debates) September 1986. Pretoria: Government Printer.

Huntington, S. P. (1986). 'Whatever has Gone Wrong with Reform'. *Die Suid Afrikaan* 8: 19–22.

Jinabhai, C. C. (1986). The Apartheid Welfare System: From State Security to Social Security. Unpublished paper. Amsterdam: Institute for Social Studies, University of Amsterdam.

Lund, F. J. (1985). A Description and Preliminary Assessment of South Africa's National Community Development Strategy. Unpublished paper. Durban: Centre for Applied Social Sciences, University of Natal.

Lund, F. J. (1988). 'State Restructuring of Welfare'. *Transformation* 6: 22–37.

Martin, P. (1986). 'No more Vietnams: Old Slogans, New Visions'. *NACLA Report on the Americas* July/August: 3–25.

McKendrick, B. (1988). *Introduction to Social Work in South Africa*. Pinetown: Owen Burgess.

Merrifield, A. (1987). Recent Changes in State Strategy: JMCs, National Security and Low Intensity Warfare. Unpublished paper. Cape Town: Department of Political Science, University of Cape Town.

Morris, M. & Padayachee, V. (1988). 'State Reform Policy in South Africa'. *Transformation* 7: 1–26.

Schneider, M. (1987). 'Adriaan Vlok'. *Leadership* 6: 28–32.

Science Committee of the President's Council (1983). *Report on Demographic Trends*. Pretoria: Government Printer.

Seegers, A. (1988). The National Security Management System: A Description and Theoretical Enquiry. Unpublished paper. Cape Town: Department of Political Science, University of Cape Town.

South African Institute for Race Relations (SAIRR) (1983). *Survey of Race Relations*. Johannesburg: SAIRR.

Swilling, M. (1988). Reform, Security and White Power: Rethinking State Strategies in the 1980s. Unpublished paper. Cape Town: Centre for African Studies, University of Cape Town.

Theological Exchange Programme (TEP) (1987). *Low Intensity Conflict: South Africa under Threat*. (Pamphlet). Cape Town: TEP.

The Riekert Commission (1979). *Report of the Commission of Enquiry into Legislation affecting the Utilisation of Manpower*. Pretoria: Government Printer.

Webster, D. (1987). 'Repression and the State of Emergency'. *South Africa Review* 4: 141–72.

Newspaper articles

Engineering Week (28 April 1989).

Grassroots (August 1988).

New Nation (3 December 1989).

The Argus (7 September, 1988).

The Argus (2 February 1990).

The Citizen (29 November 1989).

The Pretoria News (29 November 1989).

The Rand Daily Mail (16 March 1985).

The Star (29 November 1989).

The Sunday Times (1 December 1989).

The Sunday Tribune (3 December 1989).

The Weekly Mail (3 October 1987).

The Weekly Mail (23 June 1989).

The Weekly Mail (1 December 1989).

Acts

The Abolition of Influx Control Act 68 of 1986.

The Abolition of the Development Boards Act 75 of 1986.

The Black Communities Development Act 4 of 1984.

The Black Urban Areas Consolidation Act 25 of 1945.

The Child Care Act 74 of 1983.

The Community Welfare Act 104 of 1987.

The Group Areas Act 36 of 1966.

The Population Registration Act 30 of 1950.

The Prevention of Illegal Squatting Act 52 of 1951.

The Slums Act 46 of 1979.

CHAPTER THREE

Vigilantism and the policing of African townships: Manufacturing violent stability

Nicholas Haysom

Introduction

Trade unionists in the Pietermaritzburg area refer to the nearby Edendale Valley as the *valley of widows*. It has more widows, they claim, than any other valley in South Africa. Since vigilante violence erupted in that region, over 1 500 people have died, thousands have been subjected to violence against their person and property, and an estimated 30 000 people have become *internal refugees* (Congress of South African Trade Unions (COSATU), 1989). In April 1989, the monthly fatality rate in Pietermaritzburg dropped to thirty-four. This was considered to be a distinct improvement on the death rates of the preceding eleven months, even though this represents more than one violent death per day (*The Star*, 23 May 1989). To place these figures in context, consider the fact that in 1988 more than twice as many persons died as a result of vigilante and counter-vigilante violence in the Greater Pietermaritzburg area than died in Beirut during the same period, that is, 682 compared with 312 (Centre for Adult Education, 1989). While South African television viewers were regularly exposed to the Beirut conflict, they saw little, if any, of the human tragedy occurring in the Edendale Valley (Tomaselli, 1988). Township residents in South Africa are now far more likely to die in vigilante violence than as a result of confrontations with the South African Police (SAP). By October 1988, over 90 per cent of *unrest-related* deaths were caused by vigilante and counter-vigilante violence (*The Star*, 10 November 1988).

For Edendale residents, the vigilante phenomenon has become the most terrifying manifestation of a conflict-ridden society. How is it that such extreme violence can be tolerated by the forces of *law and order?* How can it continue with such little official concern and such limited attention from the local and international media? The purpose of this chapter is to answer these questions. To do so, it is necessary to trace not only the emergence of the vigilante phenomenon in South Africa, but the emergence of similar groups in other parts of the world. The roots of this phenomenon arise not in policing practices, but in the contemporary counter-insurgency doctrine of *low intensity conflict.*

In this chapter it is argued that the operation of vigilante groups in South Africa's black areas since 1985 is an expression of the militarization of South Africa. The prevalence and operation of these groups should be seen as the internal equivalent of the strategy of destabilizing neighbouring states. It is a low intensity civil war which appears to be conducted at arm's length from an aggressive state. In fact, however, the state benefits in a variety of ways from the conflict it licenses, indeed, more so than it would from more direct intervention.

Low intensity conflict[1]

Commentators have noted that there is a strong parallel to be drawn between vigilante violence in South Africa and that in El Salvador and the Philippines (Dionko, 1988). In these countries, violence by vigilante and civilian units has become a central component of the mode of repression adopted by the governing regimes (Caceres, 1988). The doctrine of low intensity conflict stresses *total war* and incorporates a tactic of *winning the hearts and minds* (WHAM). Low intensity conflict is a solution to the dilemma of destroying popular insurgency without appearing to be waging war directly on the populace. It is this strategic approach which has been adopted in the civil wars sanctioned by the United States in Central America, the vigilante movements in the Philippines, and in the destabilization of southern African states. One of the central tactics of low intensity conflict is the clandestine creation of surrogate armed forces which appear to emerge spontaneously from *the people*. It is then claimed that groups like the CONTRAS and UNITA in southern Africa and the Philippines vigilantes are an expression of popular support or popular rebellion, as the case may be.

The explicit adoption of low intensity conflict as a counter-revolution-

---

1. See Chapter 2 for a more detailed discussion of this strategy.

ary state strategy in South Africa appears to fall into two phases (Phillips & Swilling, 1988). The adoption and implementation of the military establishment's strategic blueprint coincided with the accession to power of Mr. P. W. Botha as State President and General Magnus Malan as Minister of Defence, and signified the entrenchment of military dominance. This blueprint has been a direct application of the military theories of Andre Beaufre, a French general in the Algerian civil war (*The Star*, 10 November 1989). Beaufre argued for a military approach that acknowledged the existence of a battlefield extended to include all aspects of civil society, particularly the social and ideological spheres. According to Beaufre, the proper concern of the military should be expanded to encompass the co-ordination of all aspects of civil society (Beaufre, 1963).

The dissolution of the boundaries between military and civil society, as Beaufre proposed, has now passed into the South African political lexicon as *total strategy* in response to *total war*. The clearest adoption of Beaufre's recommendations, and equally the clearest expression of the influence of the military establishment in South African politics, has been the elaborate security structure known as the National Management System (NMS), which is discussed at length in Chapter 2. It should be mentioned that as a young lieutenant, Magnus Malan, now Minister of Defence, served as a military observer in Algeria under the command of General Beaufre (Phillips & Swilling, 1988). It is thus hardly surprising that Beaufre's book, *Introduction to Strategy* (Beaufre, 1963) has long been prescribed reading at the South African Military Academy (Cawthra, 1988; and Ebersohn, cited in *The Star*, 10 November 1988)

In the mid-eighties, South African strategists appeared to favour the more practical theories of Colonel McCuen, who developed his ideas on counter-insurgency warfare in Vietnam (McCuen, 1966). McCuen's writing belongs to the genre of low intensity conflict theory, which has become dominant among counter-insurgency theories in the United States. In particular, low intensity conflict has supplanted the *Westmorland strategy* that was applied in Vietnam. General Westmorland's approach to counter-insurgency was for the military to make maximum use of technologically superior resources and fire-power to destroy a *Third World enemy*. The Westmorland school believed in *asphalting Vietnam* (Miles, 1986).

In her informed review of low intensity conflict in Central America, Miles reveals some of its distinctive features (Miles, 1986). She points out that low intensity conflict is no less violent than conventional warfare. The premise is simply that there should be no direct security force intervention, for if the security forces have to intervene in a conflict situation, they have already lost the strategic initiative. Military involvement can win *battles*, but it will lose *counter-insurgency wars*. Under low intensity conflict there are neither battlefields nor victories, for this is a war of destruction in which optimum circumstances for strategic responses are created. Victory is measured in terms of the 'avoidance of outcomes' and in 'attitudinal changes' in a target group (Miles, 1986: 19). This redefinition of victory means that even where there is no outright victory, enough physical and political damage is done to ensure that revolutionaries cannot win. The new generation of counter-insurgency experts recognize that the objective is *pacification* of the *population not the territory* (Miles, 1986). Low intensity conflict is thus a war of counter-organization. In the southern African scenario this is illustrated by the apparent unwillingness of those who back groups like UNITA in Mozambique to allow these groups to actually seize power.

In essence, low intensity conflict is total war at the grassroots level. Whether it is used *offensively*, as has been the case in Nicaragua and Angola, or *defensively*, as has been the case in El Salvador and the Philippines, the aim remains constant. Apparently popular groups, composed of grassroots civilians, are either created or existing groups are used to engage in *revolutionary* violence. The role of the military is confined to co-ordinating the distribution of economic aid to target social groups and to supplying logistic and informational support to surrogate, armed groups. *Foreign* forces, such as the United States in Central America and the South African Defense Force (SADF) in our townships, cannot *win over* the local population. According to Miles (1986), contemporary United States military strategists are less concerned with winning battles than with separating the enemy from its mass base and neutralizing its social structures (Miles, 1986; and Lloyd, cited in *The Weekly Mail*, 23 June 1989). Apart from the violence that it introduces, low intensity conflict is also a *dirty war*, for:

> ... '[i]t penetrates into homes, families, the entire fabric grass-roots social relations; there are no "civilians" in a low intensity conflict ... it is a science of warfare whose goal of controlling the qualitative aspect of human life merits the term "totalitarian"' (Miles, 1986: 45).

In 1986 General Meiring, the former general of the South West Africa Territorial Force, expressed his preference for McCuen's theories over the abstractions of Beaufre. He argued that the former approach was more practical in that it offered both *hard war tactics*, such as the creation of counter-revolutionary groups, and *soft war* or WHAM tactics, including the electrification of the townships (Meiring, in Phillips & Swilling, 1988). By late 1986, McCuen's ideas had been reduced to a

75-page précis entitled, 'The Art of Counter-Revolutionary Warfare', which was then to be distributed throughout the NMS (Phillips & Swilling, 1988).

It is apparent from McCuen's approach and the speeches of its South African proponents that a political solution for the South African government required the reconstruction of political forces from the bottom up, and *not* a commitment to political bargaining or top-down reform. The move from total strategy to active low intensity conflict was in effect a subtle move from controlling dissent to reorganizing politics. It should be emphasized that this shift occurred between 1985 and 1986, at the same time that vigilante groups were emerging (Phillips & Swilling, 1988).

Vigilantes

Patterns and activities

It is necessary to begin by describing the emergence and operation of vigilante groupings in South Africa. In this section the patterns and implications of vigilante activities will be discussed, rather than specific details of various vigilante groupings.[2]

The term vigilante is itself a source of confusion. In South Africa, the term connotes violent, organized, and conservative groupings operating within black communities. Although these groups receive no official recognition, they are politically directed in the sense that they act to neutralize individuals and groupings that are opposed to the apartheid state and its institutions. These features and the fact that vigilante groups are alleged to enjoy varying degrees of police support, are the only characteristics that link groups like the A-Team, Ama-Afrika, Phakatis, Mabangalala, Amadoda, the Witdoeke, Amosolomzi, Amabutho, Mbhokhoto, and the Green Berets.

Vigilantes are not an entirely new phenomenon in South Africa. Between June and October 1983, vigilantes supervised by the Ciskeian authorities terrorized the inhabitants of Mdantsane during the course of a bus boycott (Haysom, 1984; and Lakob, 1984). In 1985, however, there was a sudden proliferation of these groups and their more complex urban counterparts began to emerge. A survey in 1986 of fourteen

---

2. Full accounts of these groups can be found in Aitcheson (1988); Haysom (1986); Phillips & Swilling (1988); and The Catholic Institute for International Relations (CIIR) (1987).

communities[3] that had experienced vigilante violence revealed a distinct pattern in this new phenomenon, which has been confirmed in subsequent reports (Haysom, 1986; and The Catholic Institute for International Relations (CIIR), 1988). Community leaders from the Cape to the Transvaal have reported that nation-wide vigilante activity, in the form of violence against members of anti-apartheid organizations, commenced in 1985. The fact that vigilantes emerged as the political crisis in South Africa deepened indicates an intimate connection between these two phenomena. Furthermore, as the crisis of state control over black areas expanded geographically, so did the incidence of vigilante activity.

The composition of the vigilante leadership and the victim groups has been consistent across regions. In general, the leadership of vigilante groups have functionaries in the state authorities, for example, chiefs in the homeland governments and, in the urban areas, state officials like the police and community councillors, or members of the embryonic middle-class who have an interest in stability and a natural inclination to conservatism (Seekings, 1986: 27). The victim groups have been those perceived to be resisting apartheid institutions, whether they are students campaigning against *Bantu education*, community leaders creating alternative black municipal structures, or communities resisting the jurisdiction of homeland authorities.

Another central feature of vigilante violence is that the vigilantes appear to enjoy police support, operating brazenly as if their extra-legal violence has no legal consequence. It cannot be proven that all vigilante groups have received direct sanction or open support from the security forces, although this is alleged to have been the case in several areas (CIIR, 1988). Direct support, however, is not necessary for the generation of vigilante conflict. A mere reluctance to curb vigilante activity, or a failure to intervene in conflict in the townships, allows a *favoured* group a substantial advantage over an *unfavoured* group. The effect is much the same whether the police actively sanction and support vigilantes, or whether they merely appear incapable of, or reluctant to, curb vigilante activities. This is particularly the case where a vigilante group has access to firearms. It has been alleged that the police were passive while a vigilante gang killed Mayise, a community leader, in Leandra in

---

3. Crossroads, Ashton, and KTC in the Western Cape; Queenstown and Fort Beaufort in the Eastern Cape; Huhudi in the Northern Cape; Thaburg in the Orange Free State; Umlazi, Inanda, and Lamontville in Natal; Leandra, Moutse, and Ekangala in the Eastern Transvaal; and Soweto in the Transvaal.

the Transvaal; while Inkatha supporters marched into Lamontville in Natal; and while the Mbhokhoto leaders pursued an intensive regional campaign of intimidation in KwaNdebele. This is a stark contrast to the active role played by the police in dispersing gatherings of the United Democratic Front (UDF) and in policing members of anti-apartheid organizations and trade unions. When victim communities or organizations have attempted physical contest with vigilantes, police intervention has been supportive of the vigilantes.

Vigilantes' use of council facilities, notably in Thabong and Ashton, and of resources provided by homeland governments, in KwaNdebele and the Ciskei, reveals that support for vigilante activities may take a variety of forms. A copy of minutes of a meeting between a senior police officer and black traders in the Vaal Triangle area, suggests that the police could have *actively* prompted the formation of vigilante groups in some areas. At this meeting the police officer concerned offered to arm the traders and encouraged them to form an organization for self-protection (Haysom, 1986). Here it should be mentioned that it is nearly impossible for a black South African to acquire a firearm license without police approval. In Natal, many of the vigilante warlords carry firearms openly. There is evidence to suggest that the police have allowed warlords to carry firearms without permits (Haysom, 1986).

A distinctive feature of vigilantism is the extreme and brutal nature of their violence. Thus, vigilante violence is associated with the brutalization of the body of the victims, including dismemberment or decapitation. Vigilante violence is extreme and symbolic terror. Although the specific composition and operation of these groupings does vary from region to region, the following random, but representative, incidents illustrate the distinctive pattern of vigilantism which is described above.

Phakatis in Thabana

During April and May 1985, a vigilante grouping calling themselves the Phakatis emerged in Thabong township in the Orange Free State. This group made use of the municipal authority's facilities openly and embarked on a campaign of indiscriminate assaults on youths, whom they believed were involved in a school boycott. One night they apprehended a boy, David Mabenyane, on the streets, whipped him severely, and then delivered him to the local police station. The boy subsequently died (Haysom, 1986).

Amabutho in Umlazi

During August 1985, armed gangs of Amabutho vigilantes took to searching houses in Umlazi in Natal. They claimed to be looking for UDF *trouble-makers*. Mr. B, a UDF supporter, was at home one night when the Amabutho arrived at his house, surrounded it, and set it alight. His brother attempted to flee with his infant niece, but was shot in the head. His elder sister was also shot as she tried to escape the flames. Mr. B recognized one of three armed men as a member of the KwaZulu government (Haysom, 1986).

Mbhokoto in KwaNdebele

In 1985 the Chief of the KwaNdebele homeland, Simon Skosana, launched a vigilante organization called Mbhokoto. On 1 January 1986, a large group of Mbhokoto vigilantes abducted over 400 men from Moutse, a district that had resisted the jurisdiction of the KwaNdebele homeland authorities. The men were taken to a community hall in the capital of KwaNdebele, where they were ordered to strip and were severely beaten for several hours before being released. The Prime Minister of KwaNdebele at the time supervised the assaults. Although some of the victims identified their assailants to the police, none have as yet been apprehended (Haysom, 1986).

Ama-Afrika in KwaNobuhle

In KwaNobuhle, a township bordering on Uitenhage in the Eastern Cape, a vigilante group calling itself Ama-Afrika emerged in the latter part of 1986. On 4 January 1987, a group of the Ama-Afrika launched a twelve-hour attack in this township. They destroyed the houses of fourteen activists and killed two people. Most of these houses were the homes of members of UDF-affiliated organizations, such as the Uitenhage Youth Congress and UDF Area-Committees. A report on the incident commented:

> One of the most disturbing aspects of the day's events was that the KwaNobuhle Municipal Police and the South African Police apparently made little effort to curtail the violence and destruction. It appears to have been pre-arranged by the two parties with the understanding that the destructions and assaults would be perpetrated by the vigilantes with the police monitoring the events to ensure the safety and success of Ama-Afrika. They also used it as an opportunity to take more detainees (Human Rights Trust, 1988: 48).

Vigilantes in Leandra

The events in Leandra, a black township on the East Rand, illustrate many of the elements of vigilantism. In 1985 Leandra residents were involved in a grassroots campaign to improve their living conditions and to prevent the forced removal of the inhabitants of the township. To this end they had formed the Leandra Action Committee (LAC), a civic structure alternate to the officially-approved municipal council. By late 1985, the organizational strength of the LAC was such that the authorities were compelled to negotiate with one of its leaders, Chief Ampie Mayise, instead of the officially-recognized black councillors. Shortly thereafter, vigilantes began brazenly attacking members of the LAC. This culminated in a mob assault on Chief Mayise's house on 11 January 1986, during which Mayise was publicly hacked to death. A policeman, alerted to the attack by Mayise's call to the nearby police station for assistance, was ordered not to intervene. Shortly thereafter, youths in the township were forced to flee the area in fear of their lives and the house of one of the LAC leaders was attacked. The LAC subsequently disbanded (Haysom, 1986).

Witdoeke in Crossroads and KTC

In January 1986 vigilantes calling themselves Witdoeke emerged in the squatter camps of Crossroads and KTC in the Cape Peninsula. For several years these communities, comprising nearly 70 000 people, had been engaged in a struggle with the authorities over their right to live in these squatter settlements. Despite being detained without trial and threatened by the authorities, they had persisted in their campaign. In May and June 1986 the Witdoeke, with the police allegedly intervening only to assist them, tore through the camps, destroying and burning houses and driving out inhabitants. Squatter camp tenants allege that on 17 May police cleared the way for Witdoeke to penetrate the camp by dispersing those who attempted to resist. Police watched the assaults and the illegal destruction of property, and allegedly intervened whenever the Witdoeke were under attack. Similarly, the police were alleged to have broken the defence-line formed by residents during the attack on KTC on 9 June. The Witdoeke also took people prisoner and tortured them without police intervention (Lawyers Committee for Human Rights, 1987; CIIR, 1988; and Phillips & Swilling, 1988). In the two attacks, fifty-three people were killed and 7 000 homes were demolished (Lawyers Committee for Human Rights, 1987). The government has denied any responsibility for this tragedy. The vigilantes accomplished in a few weeks what the state had failed to achieve in ten years. The 70 000 refugees were compelled to seek refuge in other townships, including Khayelitsha, the government-designated option.

Why vigilantes?

A mere description of vigilante activities does not answer two other important questions: why did vigilantism emerge as a control tactic for the repression of popular organizations, and why did vigilantes emerge only in 1985?

To understand why vigilantes emerged in 1985, it is necessary to review briefly the intensity and scale of political crises during the period 1984 to 1986. In 1984 the UDF, along with other organizations, launched a nation-wide campaign of opposition to the exclusion of blacks from the new constitution. This opposition was also directed at what came to be known as the Koornhof Bills. The success of the campaign was evident in the very low percentage polls in the Asian and coloured parliamentary elections and in the elections for community councillors (South African Institute for Race Relations (SAIRR), 1984–5). The consequence of this success was a rapid politicization of black communities.

By this time, the economic climate in South Africa had begun to deteriorate. A recession was making itself felt and unemployment had reached extremely high levels. In the urban areas, short-sighted parsimony by the authorities responsible for black local government led to pressure on the community councils to become self-financing. In turn, the community councils sought to impose increases in rentals and service charges in order to meet their budgets. A number of civic associations began to orchestrate protest against these bodies, which they perceived to be corrupt and self-serving. Protests took the form of marches, attacks on councillors, and a rent boycott which involved up to 300 000 people and which cost the state over 188 million rand (*The Sunday Tribune*, 31 August 1986). During this period South Africa also experienced an increasing number of national and local wage disputes. School pupils commenced a nation-wide campaign against inadequate education. When they were confronted with an authoritarian response, a school boycott spread throughout the country, and by late 1984 even the bantustans had been affected. One of the largest stayaways in South African history took place when 800 000 trade union members joined with township residents and school children to protest against inferior education, poor township conditions, and police brutality (Haysom, 1985: 85).

This confluence of political and economic factors produced intense, widespread, and diverse protests in the townships in the Vaal Triangle area from September 1984, and, subsequently, in other townships throughout South Africa. Under this pressure the existing structures of local government collapsed in the majority of urban areas in the Transvaal and the Eastern Cape. By 1985 only five of the thirty-eight Black Local Authorities (BLAs) were operating effectively and community councillors and police officers who had not yet resigned were being housed *outside* townships for their own safety (SAIRR, 1984–5).

The first response to this civil rebellion was a policing policy of *maximum force*, which was later reinforced by emergency powers and additional military personnel. The police, however, were unable to control this rebellion which took a myriad of different forms. In one area they were called upon to deal with a strike, in another a consumer boycott or a stayaway, a demonstration, a march on municipal council offices, or a school boycott. The rebellion was the converse of total strategy, it was *total resistance.* In order to re-impose and bolster the power of government institutions, particularly the community councils, the police were supplemented by SADF units. Regular security force patrols seemed to confirm township residents' fears that they were under siege by an occupying army. The mushrooming rate of clashes between security forces and township residents came to a head in June 1985, when the government declared a State of Emergency. By the end of 1985 it was estimated that over 10 000 people had been detained under laws relating to the security of the state and homeland security legislation (Detainee's Parents Support Committee (DPSC), 1986). Over 1 000 people died in *unrest-related* events between 1984 and 1986 (*Hansard* (House of Assembly Debates), 25 April 1986: col. 11423–6).

The distinctive feature of the police policy of *maximum force* was the attempt to control and deter the rebellion by means of fire-power. The incidents that illustrate this policing practice are: the Langa massacre, in which nineteen mourners were shot dead at a funeral; the Mamelodi massacre, in which twelve unarmed protesters were shot dead; and the Trojan Horse incident, in which three people were shot dead by police who were hidden in a truck that was stoned. These incidents show that the police were willing to use lethal force indiscriminately to dissuade township residents from participating in protests.

It is in this context of a crisis in state control over black areas and the failure of the police to restore *order* that vigilantes emerged and attempted to alter the balance of power in the townships, albeit under the slogan of *law and order.* By mid-1985 it was clear that the strategy of policing by maximum force was failing. That grizzly index of *unrest*, the daily death rate, had not been reduced by the State of Emergency. In

August 1985 the rate had climbed to 5,3 deaths per day (Haysom et al., 1986: 110). Ironically, these policing practices had further politicized the black community and had created a degree of social cohesion among township residents. What the state needed was a strategy for *disorganizing*. In line with the doctrine of low intensity conflict, vigilantes emerged to fulfil this function. Vigilante groups were better suited to achieve disorganization because they were less constrained by the threat of adverse publicity and by legal considerations that hampered the South African Police (SAP) and the SADF. Vigilantes, on the other hand, could risk perpetrating the extreme terror and violence needed to combat popular organizations. The security forces could not publicly hack a popular leader to death and avoid prosecution or civil claims. However brutal these vigilante groups may have been, by purporting to act under the banner of *restoring law and order*, they could legitimate their actions, elicit at least some sympathy from the white public and, in some cases, play on a broader disgruntlement with the disruption caused by the unrest, particularly where vanguard youth groups had been undemocratic in imposing community boycotts.

Furthermore, the security forces could not coerce support for community councils nor could they administer townships. A Soweto councillor clearly expressed his frustration with conventional responses to township opposition. In a speech to a Sofasonke party rally, he stated that he had asked the government to allow councillors to avenge attacks on their homes, and to embark on full-scale vigilante activities aimed at rooting out trouble-makers in the townships. He added that, 'Hopes that security forces would bring peace were a pipe dream' (Seekings, 1986: 28). This statement implied a realization that councillors must appear to their own constituencies to have the power to use force.

Unlike the random and indiscriminate violence which takes place when the police confront popular organizations, vigilante terror can target the leaders of organizations more accurately. The terror comes from *within* the community, thus rupturing confidence and cohesion, and this makes it difficult for popular organizations to function openly. In 1985 vigilantes in magisterial districts not covered by the State of Emergency disrupted civic and youth organizations to a greater extent than did the detentions and actions of the security forces in townships under the emergency regulations.

Vigilantes have the added advantage of being economical. Lennox Sebe, Prime Minister of the Ciskei, rationalized the formation of the Green Berets by saying that the vigilantes were acting as low-cost police auxiliaries. In this sense the vigilante phenomenon represents a *Reaganomic* tendency in one of South Africa's growth industries, the privatization of repression. Its proponents argue that privatization has ideological benefits. Vigilante violence, reported locally and internationally as *black-on-black* violence, seems to justify police presence in the townships on the grounds that the residents have a racial propensity to internecine strife. More importantly, the destruction of organizational opposition to the state is accomplished without the intervention of the security forces, and without the same public outrage that would result from brutalities committed by the security forces. Although the persistent use of the label *black-on-black* violence by the Bureau for Information and the media has as much heuristic value as describing the Second World War as *white-on-white* violence, the label does obscure the connections between this type of violence and the system of apartheid.

Finally, once vigilantes have produced a cowed and disorganized community, a political vacuum is created which may be filled by a community council or a homeland political party, and which in turn allows these bodies to impose their will on a community with relative ease. This is so particularly for communities who, without access to direct political power, have collective organization as their only weapon.

Countering vigilantes: A case study of Edendale

Communities victimized by vigilante action are faced with a dilemma as to how they can best resist. Should residents go on the offensive and commit a pre-emptive violent assault on the vigilantes? There is no doubt that they would, in such an event, face the full might of the same security forces who were failing to protect them from vigilante violence. Furthermore, vigilantes are in most cases better armed and their defence against an attack could prove fatal for residents. In the final analysis, vigilantes may create their own causes and wage their own wars, but they do so guaranteed by the state's resources. Just how effective the vigilante phenomenon is, and how difficult it is to counter a spiral of vigilante violence, is evident in the events that have taken place in the Pietermaritzburg township of Edendale.

Since 1987 the Edendale valley near Pietermaritzburg has become the site of bloody and violent clashes between residents who are supporters of Inkatha and those who are perceived to be its opponents. By March 1988, nearly two-thirds of those killed nation-wide in unrest-related events had been killed in the Pietermaritzburg district and by March 1989, over 1 200 persons had been killed (Van Zyl Slabbert, 1989: 7). This means that by 1989 vigilante violence and counter-vigilante violence in Pietermaritzburg had become the single most important cause of death in South Africa under the State of Emergency. Inkatha spokes-men have attributed this violence to *structural poverty*. This is inadequate, for it does not explain why conflict erupted in Pietermaritzburg, nor why it erupted when it did.

There had been occasional violent clashes between supporters and opponents of Inkatha in Natal since 1980, but these did not extend to the Pietermaritzburg district until after 1985. In 1985 the situation in Pietermaritzburg began to change. UDF-affiliated youth congresses began to establish themselves in the Pietermaritzburg district and a series of minor skirmishes, involving Inkatha supporters and these youth groups, opened hostilities. A significant number of residents in the Greater Pietermaritzburg area took solidarity action in support of SARMCOL[4] workers in nearby Howick. Inkatha began to lose ground.

In 1986, the United Workers' Union of South Africa (UWUSA) was formed as the trade-union wing of Inkatha and competition between UWUSA and other trade unions gradually increased. In particular, physical attacks were made on members of COSATU, UWUSA's rival union confederation. For example, in December 1986 in Howick, a mob led by nine Inkatha members dragged two COSATU worker-leaders and a young woman out of a car and executed them. To this day, the nine members identified by an inquest magistrate as the culprits have been neither charged nor prosecuted (Haysom, 1986).

On 5 and 6 May 1987, the UDF and COSATU called a stayaway in protest against the parliamentary elections. Although the stayaway was opposed by Inkatha, it was successful. Inkatha attributed this success to the solidarity action of bus drivers who were members of the COSATU-affiliated Transport and General Worker's Union. Thereafter, Inkatha commenced a recruitment campaign in earnest. Threats of violence and actual violence were employed. UWUSA then mounted a campaign to pressurize bus drivers to resign their membership from the Transport and General Workers' Union and in the course of this campaign four drivers were killed. According to court papers, residents of the area known as Vulindela were ordered to join Inkatha by 4 October 1987 (*Zondo v Inkatha*, 1988). By January 1988 the resultant conflict had reached its bloodiest level. The monthly death rate was 162, more than three times higher than the average rate since 1987 (Aitcheson, 1988: 24).

In some cases, violent recriminations have been aimed at the oppo-

---

4. These workers are members of the National Union of Metal Workers of South Africa, which is an affiliate of the Congress of South African Trade Unions (COSATU).

sition faction. In general, however, much of the violence has been indiscriminate and regionally-based. As the conflict has escalated, so Pietermaritzburg has become politically and geographically divided. If one lives in an Inkatha area, one is deemed to be a member of Inkatha. It is not surprising then that many so-called members are ignorant of the policies of the group to which they allegedly belong. Certainly, many of those who claim to be UDF members are not aware of the organization's policies, have never attended political meetings, and can cite no affiliate to which they belong.

Undoubtedly, the central catalyst for the violence is conflict over political control of the region. Inkatha blames the UDF for *attempting to render the area ungovernable* and the UDF and COSATU allege that the conflict is a result of Inkatha's determination to root out the alternative political presence of the UDF. The intensity and scale of the violence, however, can only be adequately explained by reference to the role played by the SAP. At first, COSATU tried to force the police to intervene, to arrest, charge, and prosecute perpetrators of vigilante violence. They believed that police passivity had encouraged the brazen violence perpetrated by Inkatha supporters. COSATU maintained that if the police had mounted four or five vigorous and effective prosecutions in September, October, or November 1987, well over a thousand lives might have been saved (COSATU, 1989). To this end COSATU rendered legal assistance by taking statements, tracing witnesses, delivering potential witnesses to SAP charge offices and identification parades, and by providing the Attorney General with research data.

By March 1988, COSATU had become disillusioned with this strategy and accused the police of siding with Inkatha. In January 1989 COSATU attorneys, believing that their informants' statements revealed a pattern of police collaboration with Inkatha warlords, researched twenty-nine incidents of violence in the Imbali township. As part of this research, police responses to these incidents were recorded and this showed that although the majority of reported attacks had been perpetrated by Inkatha members, most of those who had been arrested were UDF supporters (COSATU, 1989). In many investigations of these incidents, the first step the police had taken was to identify whether a suspect was a member of the UDF/COSATU or of Inkatha. The police had also used Inkatha members to assist them in identifying the *trouble-makers*. Furthermore, since 1987 the police had detained well over 1 076 UDF/COSATU members, in contrast to only a handful of Inkatha members, yet they claimed that all of these detentions were related to the unrest (Merritt, 1988). The COSATU research also suggests that even when Inkatha members were apprehended, they were less likely to be held in custody (COSATU, 1989). As was mentioned earlier, the police sanctioned the carrying of arms by Inkatha members, but continued to raid non-Inkatha communities to search for illegal firearms.

COSATU lawyers have cited numerous incidents in which the police have tried to discourage UDF members from laying charges, as well as cases in which charges have been laid, but the investigations have failed, inexplicably, to proceed to any finality. It has also been pointed out that the investigation and lack-lustre prosecution of the alleged perpetrators of violence in Pietermaritzburg contrast sharply with the vigorous and zealous prosecution of UDF activists in the same area. The fact that only a handful of people have been prosecuted for 1 200 murders speaks for itself. It is significant that the same personalities reappear in statements describing the violence (COSATU, 1989 ;and Dontzin, 1989).

COSATU spokesmen have insisted that police abuse of power in Pietermaritzburg should not be attributed to lazy or rogue policemen, but to an actual police policy. The claim made by the Minister of Law and Order that Inkatha is innocent and that COSATU is to blame for the conflict, illustrates, in COSATU's eyes, that the police are biased (*The Weekly Mail*, 15 June 1989). The fact that senior police officers have attempted to create a positive image of Inkatha when it has been criticized indicates that a policy attitude to Inkatha has been adopted at the highest levels of the SAP. President Botha's refusal to accede to requests made by Lawyers for Human Rights to appoint a commission of inquiry into the role of the police in conflict in the townships provides added support for COSATU's contentions. On 23 May 1989 a final order was granted restraining the police from unlawfully assaulting and from failing to protect the residents of the Mpophomeni township, a COSATU stronghold, from the attacks of nearby Inkatha communities (*Mabambo v Minister of Law and Order*, 1989).

The second attempt by COSATU to limit the violence was the launching of nine urgent interdicts in the Supreme Court. In this way COSATU tried to use the civil courts to police vigilantes. Five applicants, or witnesses, to these proceedings have since been killed or assassinated and to date none of the culprits have been prosecuted. The lawyers were left in the unenviable position of persuading witnesses and applicants to come forward, knowing that legal proceedings could expose such applicants to violent retaliation, against which COSATU could provide no protection.

By August 1988, the situation was so serious that lawyers had come to doubt whether the courts could offer any effective protection to persons seeking their assistance (COSATU, 1989). The following example illustrates this dilemma: In late 1987, Johannes Mthembu and his four sons, who lived in Imbali, clashed with local Inkatha members. In January 1988 one of Mthembu's sons was shot in a confrontation with Inkatha. Mthembu then brought interdict proceedings against Inkatha and after the court papers were served, one of the Inkatha leaders cited in the interdict arrived at Mthembu's home. In the violent clash which followed, two of Mthembu's sons were shot and one of them died. In July 1988 before the latter case, *Mthembu v Zuma* (1988), was due to reopen for oral evidence, Mthembu's fourth son was shot dead by an unknown assassin when he opened the front door of his home (*The Natal Witness*, 5 July 1988). In consequence the family was forced to flee the area. It is certainly possible that the legal steps taken by Mthembu served to aggravate his position and exposed both him and his family to danger.

In September 1988 COSATU entered into a peace pact with Inkatha, in which both organizations committed themselves to a public acknowledgement of the right to freedom of association. The declaration was to be enforced by an informal, expedited arbitration procedure whereby a Complaints Adjudication Board, chaired by former Supreme Court judges, would determine whether members of the respective organizations had breached the code. It would then be left to the organizations to discipline their own members in accordance with the findings of the Board. The Complaints Adjudication Board's stratagem was based on the recognition that the courts and the police were incapable of restraining the violence. It was thus decided that the organizations that did have effective power to control the residents of Pietermaritzburg's townships should shoulder this responsibility. Inkatha members have since refused to participate in inquiries of the Complaints Adjudication Board because they claim that their testimony may be used against them in subsequent criminal proceedings. In May 1989 a COSATU witness, Nicholas Duma, was assassinated three days after having testified against an Inkatha member. In the same month Jabulani Ndlovu, a NUMSA shop steward who publicly alleged police collusion with Inkatha warlords had her house fire-bombed. Her husband and daughter were killed during the attack and she herself died several days later. COSATU has now suspended its participation in the Complaints Adjudication Board (Haysom, 1986).

COSATU has stressed that even if Inkatha and the UDF have the political will to embark upon genuine peace initiatives, partisan policing will undermine such efforts (COSATU, 1989). Indeed, the police have been accused of directly subverting the peace process on seven occasions (*The Weekly Mail*, 15 June 1989). This has been manifest in police attempts to discourage negotiations and in the restriction under emergency regulations of UDF members who have participated in peace talks. Mr. Adriaan Vlok, the current Minister of Law and Order, has openly condemned peace initiatives.

From vigilantes to community guards

A national trend which has raised concern amongst human rights activists and victim communities alike is the induction of vigilantes into the state's formal law-and-order machinery. The incorporation of many of the Queenstown vigilantes into the Queenstown Commando is one such example. A more prevalent form of this process is taking place through the appointment of community guards, a form of municipal police under the control of community councillors (Black Sash, 1988; and CIIR, 1988). It has been reported that erstwhile vigilantes have made applications to join the community guards and that in some areas the guards have simply taken over the role of the vigilantes (CIIR, 1988).

The municipal police or *greenflies* and special constables or *kitskonstabels* have indeed made a special contribution to converting the mood of the townships from protest to fear. Human rights groups from the Eastern Cape to the Transvaal have reported numerous incidents in which the municipal police have assumed vigilante methods. Complaints include torture, beatings, thefts, and forcible evictions. Thus, their responsibility seems to be pacification rather than crime prevention[5] (Black Sash, 1988; and CIIR, 1988). More importantly, increased involvement by the municipal police in policing the townships has gone hand in hand with the withdrawal of the security forces from these areas. The use of municipal police and special constables is part of the strategy of militarizing township society, while appearing to de-militarize local government.

Vigilantes and repression

It remains to place the vigilante phenomena within the state's overall strategy of repression and reform, particularly in the context of the current imperative to reconstitute black politics, dependent on and amenable to, government policies. Vigilantism operates in tandem with other repressive practices, it is part of a multi-faceted stratagem to create moderate black politics. The state of emergency '… provides a legal regime in terms of which the black townships can be pacified' (Haysom, 1987: 145).

The mass detention of leaders and members of popular organizations

---

5. See Chapter 10 for further details.

and intense police control over freedom of assembly and expression produces an organizational stasis or vacuum in black areas. Vigilantes attack popular organizations that manage to survive. Thereafter, they combine forces with community councillors, the municipal police, the special constables, or organizations such as Mbokhoto, and take charge of the townships by filling the vacuum that has been created. Activists who return to such conditions are isolated and victimized.

In this context, Black Local Authorities (BLAs) are given both the financial and policing resources to administer or upgrade their areas. The Joint Management Centres (JMCs), convened and chaired by members of the SADF, play a crucial role in co-ordinating resources to win the hearts and minds of township residents. It is equally clear that the JMCs not only co-ordinate the upgrading of townships, but also their *downgrading*. Devolution of power is frequently made dependent on the existence of vigilantes (Phillips & Swilling, 1988).

Paradoxically, the very withdrawal of troops and police from the townships and their replacement by vigilantes, municipal police, planners, and engineers is directly in line with increasing military influence over civil society. The new military theory stresses the manipulative, but invisible, role of the military in co-ordinating a comprehensive strategy involving economic, political, psychological, and social factors. The logic of modern counter-insurgency strategy requires that the opposition be destroyed, without alienating township residents and without the security forces being seen as directly involved in a war on the masses.

Conclusion

The prospect of the state's comprehensive stratagem actually winning the hearts and minds of township residents is, however, remote. The vigilantes have not been able to create popular support for their politics. Instead, they have created communities which are either sullenly cowed or violently vengeful. These communities are destined to remain in a state of violent stability. While there are certainly short-term gains for the state, in the long term the vigilante phenomenon will erode any possibility of a *popular rights discourse*. Township residents will, with good reason, understand only the language of power. Even for vigilante organizations, the gains are short-term. As a commentator on the vigilante phenomenon in the Philippines has pointed out:

... [t]he campaign of the [vigilantes] may bring some short term results but eventually it must only redown to the gain of the [insurgents] and considerably help their recruitment and propaganda campaigns. Pointing to a [vigilante stronghold] they ask the people is this the type of government you want? ... Vigilantes are themselves victims and objects of an inequitable society. They cannot be the solution. If indeed they are a formula for peace then my country can only be headed for more war (Dionko, 1988: 41).

Bibliography

Books and articles

Aitcheson, J. (1988). Numbering the Dead: Political Violence in the Pietermaritzburg Region. Unpublished paper. Pietermaritzburg: Centre for Adult Education, University of Natal.

Beaufre, A. (1963). *Introduction to Strategy*. London: Faber & Faber.

Black Sash (1988). *Greenflies: The Municipal Police in the Eastern Cape*. Cape Town: Black Sash.

Caceres, G. (1988). Violence, National Security and Democratisation in Central America. Unpublished paper. London: Catholic Institute for International Relations (CIIR).

Catholic Institute for International Relations (CIIR) (1988). *Now Everyone is Afraid: The Changing Face of Policing in South Africa*. Cape Town: CIIR.

Cawthra, G. (1988). *Brutal Force*. London: International Defence Aid Fund (IDAF).

Centre for Adult Education (1989). *Pietermaritzburg Briefing*. Pietermaritzburg: Centre for Adult Education, University of Natal.

Congress of South African Trade Unions (COSATU) (1989). *The Role of the Police in Vigilante Violence in the Pietermaritzburg Area. Report on Mbali Stage I*. Pietermaritzburg: COSATU.

Detainee's Parents Support Committee (DPSC) (1986). *Review of 1985*. Pietermaritzburg: DPSC.

Dionko, M. S. (1988). Self Styled Guardians of Democracy: Vigilantes in the Philippines. Unpublished paper. London: CIIR.

Dontzin, M. S. (1989). Crisis in the Administration in South Africa: Prosecutorial Incompetence in Pietermaritzburg. Unpublished paper.

Pietermaritzburg: University of Natal.

Gwala, N. (1988). Inkatha, Political Violence and the Struggle for Control in Pietermaritzburg. Unpublished paper. Pietermaritzburg: Centre for Adult Education, University of Natal.

Haysom, N. (1984). *Ruling with the Whip*. Johannesburg: Centre for Applied Legal Studies (CALS).

Haysom, N. (1985). 'Human Rights Index'. *South African Journal on Human Rights* 1: 80–91.

Haysom, N. (1986). 'Mabangalala: The Rise of the Right Wing Vigilantes in South Africa', *Occasional Paper* (10). Johannesburg: Centre for Applied Legal Studies (CALS), University of the Witwatersrand.

Haysom, N. (1987). 'Editorial Comment'. *South African Journal on Human Rights* 3: 145–6.

Haysom, N., Smuts, D., Plasket, C. & Murphy, J. (1986). *Human Rights Index* 2: 108–37.

Hansard (House of Assembly Debates) (1986). April 1986. Pretoria: Government Printer.

Human Rights Trust (1988). *Monitor*. June.

Lakob, M. (1984). *Human Rights in South Africa's Homelands: The Delegation of Repression*. New York: Fund for Free Expression.

Lawyer's Committee for Human Rights (1987). *Crisis in Crossroads*. New York: Lawyer's Committee for Human Rights.

Lund, J. (1988). The Law and its Limitations. Unpublished seminar paper. Pietermaritzburg: Centre for Adult Education, University of Natal.

Mare, G. & Hamilton, G. (1988). Liberation Politics. Unpublished seminar paper. Pietermaritzburg: Centre for Adult Education, University of Natal.

McCuen, J. J. (1966). *The Art of Counter-Revolutionary War*. London: Faber & Faber.

Merritt, N. (1988). *Detentions and the Crisis in the Pietermaritzburg Area, 1987–1988*. Pietermaritzburg: Centre for Adult Education, University of Natal.

Miles, S. (1986). Low Intensity Conflict in South America. *NACLA Report on the Americas*.

Phillips, M. and Swilling, M. (1988). The Politics of State Power in the 1980s. Unpublished paper. Johannesburg: Centre for Policy Studies, University of Witwatersrand.

Seekings, J. (1986). 'Probing the Links. Vigilantes and the State'. *Work in Progress* 40: 26–9.

South African Institute for Race Relations (SAIRR) (1984–5). *Race Relations Survey*. Johannesburg: SAIRR.

Tomaselli, R. (1988). Restoring the Dignity of the Local Community: A Case Study of Impartiality, SABC style. Unpublished Paper. Pietermaritzburg: Centre for Adult Education, University of Natal.

Van Zyl Slabbert, F. (1989). 'Towards New Strategy Guidelines: Evaluating Conflict Data'. In *An Overview of "Political Conflict in South Africa" — Data Trends 1984–1988. Indicator South Africa*. Natal: Indicator South Africa.

Newspaper articles

The Natal Witness (5 July 1988).

The Star (23 May 1989).

The Star (10 November 1988).

The Star (10 November 1989).

The Sunday Tribune (31 August 1986).

The Weekly Mail (15 June 1989).

The Weekly Mail (23 June 1989).

Legal cases

Mbambo v Minister of Law and Order May 1989. unrep. (NPD).

Mthembu v Zuma July 1988. unrep. (NPD).

Zondo v Inkatha September 1988. unrep. (NPD).

CHAPTER FOUR

Political discourse and the history of the South African Police

Elrena van der Spuy

Introduction

Until recently the institution of the South African Police (SAP) has remained somewhat obscured from the inquiring thrust of academia. During the eighties, however, the increasingly political role played by the SAP as guardians of *law and order* has fuelled both public and academic interest. In several recent papers critical attention is paid to the SAP and its various auxiliaries (e.g. Fine, 1989; and Hansson, 1989). Descriptive in aim, such articles tend to focus on police misconduct as an instance of crisis politics. Important though such explorations might be, the emerging body of writing on South African policing lacks an analysis of the SAP in a broader socio-historical context. The aim of this chapter then, is to provide such a context as a background to a consideration of actual police practice in Chapters 5 and 10. Dippenaar's recently published book, *The History of the South African Police, 1913–1988* (Dippenaar, 1988), which is the subject of this chapter, is to be appreciated against the background of a relatively sparse police historiography. This dense chronological account contains a wealth of information on specific incidents, broader social and political processes, and individual police personalities that have shaped, sometimes in curious ways, the development of the institution of policing in South Africa. The broad scope of this work makes it a pioneering piece of research.

Dippenaar's account is not only interesting, it is contentious. Written by a policeman as a commemorative album in celebration of the seventy-fifth anniversary of the SAP, the volume can best be described as a *police history of the police*. In the spirit of a true commemoration, the album is largely self-congratulatory, for it focuses on the institutional development of the police force (Dippenaar, 1988). Dippenaar conducts his historical venture from the vantage point of an insider who has enviable access to documentary sources and classified information. Few scholars have enjoyed similar access. Police forces rarely admit scholars to the institutional corridors where coercive power resides. In the South African context, particularly since the advent of Nationalist Party rule, the SAP has systematically insulated itself from the probing eyes of both journalists and scholars. Dippenaar's *History*, written from the belly of the beast itself, is thus worthy of serious academic attention. There is simply no other comparable piece of police historiography. In writing a self-congratulatory police history, however, Dippenaar does not, of course, indulge in a frank analysis of the ills of the institution, nor does he reflect critically on the complexity of policing in a heterogeneous society such as our own. What he does, however, is provide crucial insights into *state perceptions* of the interplay between broader socio-political processes and the development of the police force as an institution.

It is the specific intention of this chapter to provide a sociological review of Dippenaar's History. The main themes around which his historical venture is structured are described. This history is then assessed critically and the critique is used to consider the impact of the state's political discourse on, what Dippenaar considers to be, a historical and political analysis. The book is a political discourse, informed by the ideologies of Afrikaner nationalism and of total strategy, which shape, dictate and, in the end, distort this analysis of the police institution.

Themes and content

Comment

No review can do justice to the richness of detail in Dippenaar's 883-page treatise. It is possible, however, to capture in the broadest of outlines the major themes around which his analysis is organized. The discussion that follows provides a brief exposition of these themes. The four topics that have been identified are:

1. the organizational development of the police institution;

2. ethnic politics and policing;

3. black politics, resistance, and policing; and

4. the notion of total onslaught and policing.

The organizational development of the SAP

Prior to the formation of a national police force in 1913, the SAP, the history of policing is dealt with only briefly. There are various comments pointing to the legacy of *militarism* (shaped by the exigencies of colonial society, frontier wars, and the Anglo-Boer War in particular) to which the SAP was heir after Union. Official thinking on the organizational structure of a national police force was clearly influenced by the long-standing tradition of *policeman-cum-soldier*, so characteristic of nineteenth-century policing. In later years, a variety of factors contributed to the strengthening of the military ethos: the emphasis on military discipline at training depots; the actual experience of soldiering, gained through the participation of the police in both World Wars; the confrontational thrust of public-order policing during this century; and, from the seventies onwards, the shift toward extensive paramilitary training in riot control and counter-insurgency in response to armed insurgency and political resistance.

What also emerges from Dippenaar's account is the persistence of *occupational problems* in the police force, such as manpower short-ages, low salaries, and adverse working conditions, and their destructive effects on both the public image of the force and on the internal morale of the police. Dissatisfaction among the rank and file culminated in a police strike in 1917. In the years that followed, economic recession and the depletion of financial resources aggravated grievances. The appoint-ment of two commissions of inquiry reflected the extent of the problems with morale and public image. The Te Water Commission was ap-pointed in 1936 to investigate the administrative structure, the subdivi-sion of the force, and its finances, and the Lansdown Commission was appointed in 1947 to investigate matters of training, remuneration, and promotion. The persistence of insufficient numbers in the police force required creative ingenuity on the part of the police. Resources were augmented in various ways. In 1961 the Reserve Police Force, a civilian unit, was introduced to assist the police with their *ordinary* duties. In 1972 for the first time, white women were admitted to the force, and in 1973 black women were included. In 1973 a Police Reserve was created consisting of ex-members of the force, and a Junior Reserve Police Force comprising youth was set up in 1981. More recently, surrogate police forces, including the municipal police, or *greenflies*, and the special constables, or *kitskonstabels*, have been introduced to increase the number of bodies of armed police, particularly those operating in black townships. To this day there remains amongst the rank and file a smouldering discontent over working conditions. Although Dippenaar conveniently glosses over the endemic nature of such discontent, the annual discrepancy between approved and actual police strength does suggest, of course, that the police force has remained understaffed, underpaid, and overworked (The Commissioner of the South African Police, 1988).

The sweeping changes induced by technology are related in detail; from the mechanization of transport after the thirties, through to the development of advanced forensic techniques utilized in criminal investigations, and the introduction of a computer-based data system in the seventies. The unarmed, mounted police of the twenties have been replaced by a modern sibling, aggressive in posture and equipped with the most advanced and technologically-sophisticated of weaponry. Dippenaar's exposition of the cumulative deployment of technological hardware remains at the level of mere description. One searches in vain for a critical assessment of the broader political effects of technological hardware, such as riot technology and sophisticated surveillance systems, on the content and form of policing itself. The absence of such an assessment is noteworthy, given that comparable international literature has remained deeply concerned with the encroaching intrusion on the private domain and the disruptive effect of a military style of policing on police–community relations.

Regarding matters of *specialization,* or what can perhaps more aptly be described as *institutional differentiation,* the reader is again confronted with much relevant detail. Starting in 1920 with the amalgamation of the SAP and the South African Mounted Riflemen[1], the reader is taken through to the 1986 amalgamation of the SAP and the South African Railway and Harbour Police as part of the drive toward the rationalization of the civil service. From Dippenaar's account one can trace the gradual evolution of a complex police bureaucracy and its present day organizational structure. The emergence of the subdivisions of Uniform, Detective, Security, and Criminalistic Branches, the creation of a Special Branch in 1929, and the formation of a Security Branch in 1947, with its eventual rise to dominance from the sixties onwards, are all suitably contextualized. Throughout the seventies, a process of specialization resulted in the formation of a series of specialist task forces, geared toward the paramilitary policing demands of a state perceived to be *under siege.* Much attention is also paid to the recent

---

1. In terms of the Police Act 14 of 1912, they were primarily responsible for the policing of rural districts.

streamlining of administrative structures within the force, in accordance with modern managerial strategies. The formation of a public relations section, responsible for all liaison with the news media in order that 'the truth' (Dippenaar, 1988: 545) be told, is documented against a background of long-standing antagonism between the police and the press.

Concerning the *professionalization* of the force, Dippenaar focuses on recent attempts to place policing on an academic basis. The introduction of stricter entry qualifications as a means of upgrading the general standard of education of the force was slow in the making. The National Senior Certificate examination of 1961, however, did provide some opportunity for educational advancement within the force. In the years that followed much talk of *academization* is to be found. The institutionalization of a Diploma in Police Science and later, in 1971, a Bachelor of Arts Degree in Police Administration are portrayed as important manifestations of a commitment within the force to a more *academic* and *scientific* approach to policing. The formation of the Division of Training and Manpower Development in 1983, with the aim of 'planning, co-ordinating and controlling all training and man-power development in the force, except security and counter-insurgency training' (Dippenaar, 1988: 759) points to the continuing importance of in-house training. Although there may be a commitment to a professional police force in the upper echelons, Dippenaar seems to exaggerate the impact this has had on the force as a whole. There is little substantive evidence to show that a more nuanced approach to policing is taking root among the ordinary rank and file. The latter remain locked into a policing style characterized by the use of *crude maximum force*, undaunted by the effects of higher learning (Cawthra, 1986). There is, however, an acute appreciation of the fact that raising academic standards was essential for improving the public image of the police force. As the Minister of Law and Order was to explain:

> .... [it] should provide a conclusive answer to persons who may be inclined to regard the South African Police as a source of livelihood for pupils who are mentally retarded or backward and who lack the intellectual ability to study (Vlok, cited in Dippenaar, 1988: 296).

Dippenaar's *History* provides interesting biographical notes on the impact of particular personalities on the development of the force. His exposition is a useful reminder that the study of *individual biographies* is an important approach to understanding the institutional development of the police force. In search of the impact of ordinary human beings on the institution, Dippenaar captures the influence of successive Commissioners of Police. For example, he examines the influence of the youthful and unrelenting disciplinarian I. V. F. de Villiers, between 1928 and 1945, and the impact, between 1945 and 1951, of the colourful Major-General Palmer, whose 'loyalties were divided between a soldier and a professional police officer' (Dippenaar, 1988: 191). He considers Major-General Rademeyer[2], who was responsible for formulating a standing order regarding the use of the mother-tongue by police in the execution of their duties. Much is also said of the appointment of Mr. B. J. Vorster as Minister of Justice and his close working relations with General Van den Bergh. B. J. Vorster, an erstwhile Koffiefontein detainee, is described as 'the one man to whom every policeman was totally dedicated' (Dippenaar, 1988: 344). Furthermore, Dippenaar furnishes biographical details on contemporary personalities like General Coetzee, the 'expert on Communism', whose appointment from the Security Branch 'was a sure sign of the radical times the Republic was entering' (Dippenaar, 1988: 643).

Ethnic politics and policing

The 1914–15 Rebellion fuelled the emergent ethnic and political mobilization of Afrikaner nationalism. From the thirties onward, the course of South African history was to be shaped irrevocably by Afrikaner nationalism and few institutions were to escape its political effects. Dippenaar details those aspects of white political history that affected the SAP in particular. This use of archival material gives the reader a close-up view of the impact of those incidents considered to be beacons in Afrikaner political history, on the public image and organizational development of the police. By way of illustration, the briefest of reviews must suffice. During the twenties the public image of the force was an embattled one. Shortages of staff, poor working conditions, and inadequate training depressed the morale of the force. Among Afrikaners the political stigmatization of the police as an instrument of British colonial rule dated back to the Anglo-Boer War and was exacerbated by the role that the largely British police force was to play in the Rebellion. The bloody skirmishes between the police and the rebels, the defeat of the rebels, and the eventual capture of the legendary Commandant Jopie Fourie and his execution merely exacerbated the alienation of Afrikaners from the police. As Dippenaar concludes:

---

2. The first member of the Detective Branch to become Commissioner of Police. In his early years he refused to take the Oath of Africa and objected to the interrogation of fellow Afrikaner colleagues, who were suspected of involvement in the military wing of the Ossewabrandwag (Visser, 1976).

Although Fourie's death officially marked the end of the Rebellion, the anguish which his death caused in the hearts of the Afrikaner nation would never be entirely forgotten. Moreover, the image of the Police Force, which had already been damaged by General De la Rey's death and Police involvement in quelling the rebellion, was dealt yet another severe blow by the trial and fusillation [sic] of Jopie Fourie (Dippenaar, 1988: 28).

Against this background of ethnic strife, the question of divided loyalties within the police force was to appear with far greater consequence in the years after 1939. The foothold gained within the force for matters relating to ethnic politics was itself a function of the changing composition of the white section of the SAP. From the late twenties onwards, the majority of the rank and file were drawn from the homes of rural Afrikaners. Both economic circumstances and public policy seemed to have contributed to this process of the *verafrikanisering*[3] of the police force, which had definite political consequences. The decision of General Smuts to enter the Second World War as an ally of the British colonial power was to have vast repercussions for the white community as a whole, as well as for the SAP. Dippenaar documents, in considerable detail, how the organizational loyalty and internal cohesion of the SAP were to be severely strained by police participation in the war. Cohesion was also affected by police support for emerging militant right-wing, extra-parliamentary organizations, such as the Ossewabrandwag[4] and its military wing, the Stormjaers[5]. Furthermore, the changing composition of the force ensured that cultural forms of struggle entered into the institutional politics of the police force. One of the core issues was the use of the Afrikaans language and, before long, Afrikaner policemen were to insist on the usage of Afrikaans for administrative purposes within the force.

Much of Dippenaar's narrative on the political events of the times makes for exciting police drama.[6] The tales told here are also useful reminders of the potential vulnerability of the armed forces to political tensions in ethnic states. In the following quotation, reference is made to the destructive potential of the political strife of the forties on police cohesion:

---

3. Translated as Afrikanerization.
4. Translated as the Oxwagon-Guard.
5. Translated as The Storm Chasers.
6. For example, Dippenaar's discussion of the political manœuvering of Robby Leibbrandt and Johannes van der Walt, and in particular Leibbrandt's pamphlet addressed to the SAP and entitled 'Robby Leibbrandt prepared to die for his Fatherland' (Dippenaar, 1988: 161–78).

> The factor which eventually saved the police force of South Africa from total destruction was undoubtedly the unpopular policy of absolute discipline which Commissioner De Villiers insisted in instilling into policemen at that time. … [Thus] the SAP managed to survive as an intact and disciplined body of men prepared to serve South Africa (Dippenaar, 1988: 145).

It is with much sensitivity and an engaging frankness that Dippenaar thus examines the content and impact of political conflicts in white society on the policing institution of the day. He does, however, foreclose debate on the matter of ethnic politics far too soon. By relegating the importance of ethnic politics to the annals of an earlier history, Dippenaar hardly does justice to the persistence of communal politics in the decades after 1948. The monopolization of political power by Afrikaners in 1948 did not, as Dippenaar seems to suggest, make ethnic politics redundant. On the contrary, an ethnic state has since been systematically and ruthlessly entrenched in accordance with the political doctrine of apartheid. In fact, after 1948, state, government, and police merged effortlessly into one ethnocentric universe. As a constituent member of that universe, Dippenaar seems singularly incapable of examining this reality objectively.

Black politics, resistance, and policing

However, the history of this land was not shaped by the forces of ethnic mobilization alone. Excluded on the grounds of race, the majority of this country's people were to become the political subjects ruled over by a white minority. Black resistance to this system of rule was to dictate the course of our history. For those interested in the historical evolution of policing in this country, it is vital to examine the effect of black politics and black resistance on the institution itself. How far then does Dippenaar's *History* take us in this regard?

In Dippenaar's review of the evolution of the police in South Africa one is indeed struck by the extent to which the subjects to be policed, both historically and in contemporary times, have invariably been black. Furthermore, it is a history of the policing of large *collectivities* of black people, such as black industrial strikers, tribal groups at war, factions on the mines, and *fanatical* crowds of black *uprisers*, demonstrators, and protestors.

The image of policing that emerges is that of large contingents of police faced by large collectivities of blacks. The form their policing takes *vis-à-vis* blacks, therefore, has essentially been that of *public-order policing*. One concludes from Dippenaar's account, that such policing has invariably taken on a *confrontational* thrust. Violence, in a suggestive or concrete form, seems to have been ever present in this history of public-order policing. What Dippenaar captures, implicitly and unintentionally, is the very stuff of *colonial* policing. For in the colonial context it is the police who wield the coercive power of the colonial state over large *mobs of unruly* indigenous people. Such power is wielded not sporadically, but continuously. Thus, what emerges with striking clarity is the central role of the police in the defence of the colonial status quo and the essentially *military* character of this policing. The long and bloody history of public-order policing is interspersed briefly with sensational reports on the exploits of *real hard criminals*, of *daring robbers*, and *psychopathic murderers*. It is extraordinary how little Dippenaar has to say about the relative importance of crime control in relation to other SAP duties.

Dippenaar is largely oblivious to the essentially *colonial* character of public-order policing. The preponderance of rebellious crowds, *uprisers*, and demonstrators is not explained by reference to the colonial character of the racist state, with its political and economic inequality. Instead, his political analysis of the roots of black criminality and public disorder is informed by two other conceptions. The first is a somewhat cheap version of a *modernization* approach to criminality. The second, is drawn from a *conspiratorial* understanding of politics.

From the modernization perspective, policing a heterogeneous society is considered to be an extraordinarily difficult and somewhat unpleasant task. Society is seen to be comprised of two centrifugal components locked in cultural-normative conflict with one another. The *civilized* component, we are told, is naturally endowed with respect for the law. Members of the *primitive, uncivilized* sector, however, are unaccustomed to the rules and obligations embedded in the modern *civilized* sector. As B. J. Vorster, the Minister of Police at the time, explained:

> Had our country been inhabited by a homogeneous population subscribing to a uniform political philosophy with a traditional appreciation of the norms of civilized white society and a thorough knowledge of and strict adherence to the laws of the country, the task of the Police would probably have been far more pleasant. However, as we do not live in such a country, the task of the Police is more difficult. The multiracial composition of our population should be borne in mind. This results in the Police having to persuade people who fundamentally differ from the white man and even from each other and who respect their own distinct norms, to obey laws they do not understand and maintain a kind of order which is foreign to their nature (Vorster, cited in Dippenaar, 1988: 314–15).

In terms of the conspiracy theory of politics, the actions of groups are to be explained in terms of the grand, subverting designs of external forces. In Dippenaar's words, we are told that the *mobs* are inspired by *agitators* in general and by *communist agitators* in particular. This approach deprives political action of any inherent meaningfulness, for the *mob* has no rational faculty of mind or emotional core. It is simply a collectivity of puppets orchestrated from the outside. The ideological imagery spawned by a conspiratorial understanding of politics and policing was, as Dippenaar's analysis confirms, to proliferate under conditions of total onslaught.

In her analysis of state discourse on violence, Posel (1989) has argued that the 'unruly mob' as an image is 'deeply entrenched in this country's ideological history' (Posel, 1989: 272). Dippenaar's account also testifies to the powerful ideological imagery of the *mob*. From the mid-seventies onwards, the confrontational interaction between the racist state and its subordinates is described in graphic detail. In Dippenaar's *History* the forces of *law and order* are juxtaposed sharply with the forces of *anarchy*. Protesters, demonstrators, and rioters are all given to *vandalism* and to *orgies of violence* (Dippenaar, 1988). In an attempt to capture their subversive logic, Dippenaar is forced into an expansive usage of superlatives. Reference is thus made to 'the unjustified allegations' (Dippenaar, 1988: 526) 'blatant lies [and] flagrant distortions of facts' (Dippenaar, 1988: 529) espoused by the *forces of anarchy*. Apart from the amorphous *mob*, Dippenaar also indulges in more specific descriptions of *trouble-makers* who are in possession of *diabolical* plans. A wide range of groups are lumped together as subverters of the 'lawful, democratic and constitutional political order' (Dippenaar, 1988: 723). Special mention is made of the English press and clerics, as well as academics and students on English-speaking campuses, as groupings that participate in a subversive process that aims at 'delegitimating the democratic State' (Dippenaar, 1988: 739). For example, Dippenaar provides a running commentary on the *liberalistic* leanings of the English press which he accuses adamantly of publishing a continuous stream of 'unjustified criticism and verbal attacks' on the police and of grossly 'inaccurate, one-sided and biased ... reportage on the uprisings' (Dippenaar, 1988: 530). English clerics are considered to be responsible for spreading 'the grossest of allegations against the Police' (Dippenaar, 1988: 526), whilst academics at the University of Cape Town are said to have compiled a 'subjective, unscientific and prejudiced' report on the alleged torturing of detainees[7] (Dippenaar, 1988: 779). Dippenaar warns

---

7. This is apparently a reference to Foster et al. (1987).

emphatically against the political manœuvers of '[W]hite leftist liberal radicals' (Dippenaar, 1988: 723). For Dippenaar the integrity of the opponent is never above suspicion. For example, he laments that Braam Fischer never showed the 'slightest intimation of conscience or regret' (Dippenaar, 1988: 340). Reflecting on the deplorable conduct of students involved in a campaign of the National Union of South African Students (NUSAS) for free and fair education in 1972, he writes:

> The Police Force nevertheless took careful note of the slovenly, badly clothed, dirty and foul-mouthed student whose appearance and filthy colloquial usage imbued the concept of "academic freedom" with a totally new meaning. The expletives used by English-speaking students shocked the Afrikaans-speaking policemen who had generally grown up in homes where swearing and discourtesy was not tolerated (Dippenaar, 1988: 441).

It is against this hyperbolic background of *hysterical* protest politics that Dippenaar then presents a *sanitized* view of police action. The police, with their 'unblemished image and excellent record' (Dippenaar, 1988: 402) are responsible for the 'complicated and delicate task' (Dippenaar, 1988: 443) of maintaining law and order in a 'calm [and] disciplined' manner (Dippenaar, 1988: 511), and always maintain a policy of 'firm but non-violent action' (Dippenaar, 1988: 512). With bare clinical precision Dippenaar elaborates on police operational conduct amidst the messy confusion of *mob* politics. From this account the police enter the stage, set by rioters and demonstrators, as benign catalysts and not as alleged aggressive provocateurs. They always restore order where disorder once prevailed. In his sanitized version of police conduct, operational tactics are justified *ex post facto*. In the heat of the Soweto conflict, as Dippenaar explains, the police were *obliged* to fire, and in order 'to bring the situation under control 23 people [had to] be shot dead' (Dippenaar, 1988: 517). Elsewhere, Koevoet is described as having been *obliged* to employ 'unorthodox methods' to counteract the 'cowardly tactics' employed by the South West African Peoples' Organization (SWAPO), who were 'murdering defenceless civilians in cold blood' (Dippenaar, 1988: 696). The responsibility for death and destruction is thus effectively shifted onto the shoulders of *instigators*, as in the case of the bloody events of Soweto:

> ... Tsietsi Mashinini, with his shattered grandiose dreams of a general disruption of the economy of the Republic and the eventual overthrow of the Government ... had been responsible for the death of at least 238 people. Nevertheless abroad he presented a glorified picture of his supposed self-importance (Dippenaar, 1988: 517).

It would be somewhat misleading to suggest that the history of the policing of blacks, related by Dippenaar, is denied any political content. In the conspiratorial-type understanding of the *causes* of black resistance and of the policing strategies considered appropriate for containing such resistance, *communists* and *agitators* were to become the central analytical categories. Dippenaar's *History* is, in fact, proof of the pervasive and obsessive pre-occupation with communism among the political élite of the racist state. Reflecting on the political situation after 1945, the Commissioner of Police at the time warned that:

> … [a] totally new pattern was emerging in the country and a completely new world awaited the policemen returning from the war and the concentration camps — a world of radicalised politics and expanding Communism (Dippenaar, 1988: 191).

There was also an anticipation that the African National Congress (ANC) would influence the course of South African history and its police force in the years to follow. Where Dippenaar's *History* does provide a brief political analysis of the ANC, it is described as being pervaded by the influence of communism. Since the theory of conspiracy arising out of a belief in *die rooi gevaar*[8] is devoid of any subtlety, Dippenaar is able to discard the rather complex history of ideological differences *within* black politics without much ado. The history of black politics is simply reduced to the whims of communist imperialism. Since it inception, the ANC Youth League is alleged to have embraced communism *in toto* and by 1950 the ANC is said to have been taken over and effectively controlled by communists. At times there is a brief recognition of the particular frustrations, including the extension of passes to women and increases in taxes and transport fares, that fuelled the political actions of large numbers of people in the fifties. In the final analysis, however, the political content of black resistance is lost in Dippenaar's conspiratorial understanding of politics. The tendency toward the *criminalization* of more and more aspects of black political behaviour so characteristic of the fifties effectively drains any *political* content from such action. In the police terminology of the times Wolpe, Goldreich, and others were destined to be dealt with simply as political *criminals*. In the years to come, this process of criminalizing and consequently depoliticizing black political action was to become more marked.

What, we may ask, are the effects of this form of confrontational policing of black collectivities on the police force and the task of policing? Earlier in the book Dippenaar captures with considerable skill, the effect of policing in the context of ethnic strife on the very *soul* of

---

8. Translated as the red peril, a reference to communism.

the force itself. He shows the ease with which political loyalties can interfere with the occupational duties of the police. By contrast, this account negates the existence of a soul in the matter of colonial policing. The *agitator agitates*; the *mob mobilizes*; police confront the mob; there is a struggle for time and for space; and decisions are made either to negotiate, to drop teargas bombs, or to shoot. This is only the briefest reflection on the broader political effects of public-order policing and it refers to a much earlier history. For example, during the black miners' strike of 1946, the then Commissioner of Police expressed some concern about the potential effects of increasing police contact with strikers. It was feared that under stressful and dangerous working conditions police 'could react negatively and this would lead to unnecessarily severe and harsh action' (Dippenaar, 1988: 186). Few other examples of such a critical self-appraisal are forthcoming in Dippenaar's *History*. The only other example of an assessment of police and black community relations dates back to 1936. A section of the final report submitted by the Lansdown Commission of Inquiry into the Police (1947), deals with the hostile attitude of blacks towards the police. In the report, restrictive regulations to which blacks alone were subjected are suggested as underlying reasons for this hostility. It is thus noteworthy that the Lansdown Commission is the *sole* example of an investigation into black community perceptions of the police to be found in Dippenaar's review of the historical development of the police. This Commission is of further importance because it recognized that the image of the police would be compromised by the discriminatory rules and regulations to which blacks were to be increasingly subjected after 1948. Sparse as such self-assessments may be, they do suggest a critical faculty of mind and a politically informed understanding of policing within the force of the thirties, which seems to have disappeared in subsequent decades. That critical faculty of mind stands in sharp contrast to the racist assumptions of the explanations of black criminality espoused by prominent Afrikaner politicians some three decades later.

Total onslaught and policing

Proportionally speaking, much of Dippenaar's analysis of the evolution of the SAP is situated in the post-1960 political events of South African history. As the central themes of the post-1960 period came to be those of mass resistance to minority rule and political repression, the police, as primary instruments of state power and guardians of law and order, were to occupy a central place in the political events of the time.

Dippenaar does attend to the impact of socio-political events on the task of policing in the period after 1960. He documents in detail the far-reaching effects of armed insurgency and terrorism on the form and content of policing in the post-Sharpeville era. It is with hindsight that he concludes that the combating of terrorism 'proved to be a prolonged and enduring Police duty' (Dippenaar, 1988: 349). The need for more expansive legal powers to strengthen the hand of police against the *subversive designs of the onslaught* is clearly articulated. The extensive reference to the promulgation of security legislation allows for a detailed view of the process of criminalization of political activity and the streamlining of the coercive power of the state, from the early sixties onwards. Dippenaar's discussion itself is indicative of an *instrumentalist* conception of the law, that is, the unproblematic usurpation of legal powers by bodies of armed people. He thus applauds the power bestowed upon the police by the Terrorism Act 83 of 1967, describing it as,

> ... a very handy legal lever for the South African Police ... allowing them to ... act as if the country were in a state of war, that is to say, to eliminate armed infiltrators (Dippenaar, 1988: 369).

With the SAP locked into combat with the *forces of terrorism*, first in the Rhodesian Bush War and later on the Namibian borders, a reorganization of police training was undertaken. The combat role of the police, however, suggested no deviation from the primary task of policing, since 'Police action against terrorists was simply equated with combating crime' (Dippenaar, 1988: 372). From 1976 onwards, the new era of urban mass-resistance necessitated the processing of ever larger numbers of police through lengthy courses on crowd control and counter-insurgency. After 1976, policing was no longer to be viewed in the one-dimensional light of a decade earlier. The Commissioner of Police at the time explained:

> To many people the notion of "police work" might conjure up a kind of dramatic struggle between a policeman and a criminal ... Traditionally this might have been the case; at present this is only one facet of a policeman's daily task. With the emergence of terrorism ... a very important additional duty fell to the Police, which in recent years has made, and continues to make great demands on the Force (The Commissioner of the SAP, cited in Dippenaar, 1988: 493).

By the late seventies, the now familiar theme of *communist agitation* had been welded into a more cohesive notion. In emerging state security terminology, South Africa was described as being subjected to a *total communist onslaught*. To a large extent total onslaught merely merges and moulds old fears and political concerns into a more comprehensive framework. As a holistic construct, total onslaught advances a closed world view in terms of which South Africa is besieged by a multi-dimensional onslaught, orchestrated by communist imperialist powers and enacted by terrorist front organizations. The aim of this onslaught is the violent overthrow of the South African democratic state, and the destruction of Christian values and the capitalist economy. In Dippenaar's *History* one searches in vain for the sophisticated version of total strategy which has been alleged to have dominated thinking on counter-revolutionary state strategy. What is presented here is a crude version of total strategy based on a simplistic and uncompromising vision of *us versus them* and of *law and order versus anarchy*. The complexity of South Africa's internal political problems is thus reduced to 'a few easy graspable and stereotyped formulae' (Frankel, 1984: 69). Dippenaar thus merely documents the impact of the prevailing national security ideology on the political consciousness of the men in uniform, a *hawkish* vision of politics and of policing a state under siege.

Concerning the announcement of a national State of Emergency and the extension of police powers in June 1986, Dippenaar captures the response of the police as follows:

> The Government of the Republic which had been democratically elected by the inhabitants of the country, decided to stand by its decision [regarding the declared national state of emergency], despite the fact that this would inevitably lead to international isolation, a weakened economy and the inevitable car bomb attacks. The South African Police understood and supported the views of the Government ... (Dippenaar, 1988: 734).

It is against this troubled political background of a continued State of Emergency that Dippenaar finally concludes his dense and detailed historical analysis:

> It is the history of an institution founded from the community for the community with the objective of preserving the internal security of the Republic of South Africa, maintaining law and order, investigating every offense or alleged offense and preventing crime. It is not a perfect organisation. ... However, the Police Force is the best of its kind that, over decades, could be created to meet South Africa's unique needs (Dippenaar, 1988: 854).

A critique of political discourse and police history

In the previous section themes central to Dippenaar's historical analysis of the SAP have been identified. In this section an attempt is made to reflect critically on the descriptive and interpretative aspects of that history. In short, the argument advanced here is that Dippenaar presents us with an *organizational, apologist,* and *ethnocentric* history of the SAP which, because of its selective nature, ultimately distorts that history. The writer himself, one may add, appears curiously unconscious of the political parameters of the history that he presents.

Dippenaar's *History* can be described as a police history of the organizational development of the institution itself. It is largely *inward-looking* and reflects a fascination with the institutional evolution of the police into a technologically advanced, internally complex, bureaucratic machine geared toward the demands of policing a modern, conflict-ridden society. Comparatively speaking, the SAP is considered to be a formidable machine, a force which can hold its own among the best in the world. For those interested in the details of the institutional differentiation, increasing specialization, and professionalization of the SAP, Dippenaar's *History* has much to commend it. As interesting as such a *technicist* history may be, it is also fundamentally *apolitical,* for it fails to reflect the socio-political processes that have influenced the organizational development of the force. There is an absence of contemplation about the preponderance of public-order policing in this country. As such, Dippenaar exhibits a tendency toward the unproblematic *normalization* of public-order policing. This technicist history is seemingly oblivious of the extent to which policing in this country has been, and still is, primarily concerned with the *security* of the state, that is, with political policing. It also fails to assess the consequences of the totalitarian subordination of the society to the state and of the individual to the society.

In the second instance, Dippenaar's *History* can best be described as an *apologist* history. It is, in short, a systematic argument in *defence* of the police institution and of the policy in terms of which it has operated, throughout history. In such an apologist history, there is no analytical or critical assessment of the state of policing. Dippenaar appears singularly unable or unwilling to adopt anything but self-congratulatory approval. It is interesting to note how he fails to mention or reflect on the abiding importance of brute force, *the naked iron fist*, in the daily execution of police law enforcement. No Steve Biko, no Minister of Police who is *left cold* by his death, and no police violence are to be found in this history of the police. Allegations of police misconduct are rejected *in toto* as part and parcel of the ideological warfare waged by revolutionary forces against the state. It is thus argued that '[p]olice brutality [is a] Communist-coined term' (Pike, 1975: 17). On the whole, there are but brief glimpses into the violent spin-offs of a militarized policing function:

> To rub salt in the wounds of the ANC the Police cracked down on a shack in the Soweto township of Port Elizabeth, where a terrorist was reputedly hiding … One policeman drove a Casspir vehicle right over the tin shack without any further ado. Inside the shack, or what remained of it, the bodies of a trained terrorist and two sympathizers were found … The incident in Soweto, Port Elizabeth, should have served to demonstrate to the terrorist organization that policemen are not without initiative when it comes to the elimination of terrorists (Dippenaar, 1988: 818).

How then is one to interpret the absence of police misconduct and of police abuse of power in the history conveyed by Dippenaar? In part, this silence on police abuse of power should be understood as a function of the occupational rules that operate within the police subculture, in particular the rule of *absolute secrecy*.[9] Would a police history of the police dare to violate this code of secrecy? Within police subcultural literature it is well-known that the siege mentality, induced by a hostile outside world, creates a sacred brotherhood among armed men. When the force becomes a target of *terrorist* attacks and then *revolutionary onslaught*, such a *siege mentality* is merely reinforced. Dippenaar captures this drift toward an occupational solidarity under conditions of onslaught very effectively. This closing of ranks hardly permits a public acknowledgement of institutional strains and political conflicts within the force, or of the reality of *panel beating* cops. The heroes to be saluted in a police history of the police are the Vorster's of this world, men who understood the collective psyche embedded within the police subculture, and who created conditions for the unfettered application of police power. The revolutionary onslaught itself becomes a powerful justificatory device for whatever powers the police succeed in accumulating. In Dippenaar's *History* there is little regard for the role of constitutional checks and balances in curtailing the excesses that lurk in the cracks of any secretive institution. In fact, there is no recognition that absolute power may eat away at the moral fabric of the police culture itself and open the door for indiscriminate abuse.

Turning to the accusation of *ethnocentrism*, the fact that the political conflict in a divided society like our own is also manifested in the conflict over history should be considered. It is symptomatic of the polarization of our society that history becomes *a stray dog with two very different masters*. The ethnocentric historian carefully assembles the history of that which is his own, capturing the pulsing heart of that historical matter. In the glorification of one's own, the *opponent* is dehumanized and has neither heroes nor a history. Dippenaar's ethnocentric analysis

---

9. For further details, see Chapter 5.

re-affirms the politically partisan role of the police and is indicative of a political schizophrenia bred by, what Van den Berghe (1965) would call, a *Herrenvolk Democracy*, a parliamentary democracy for privileged insiders, and a colonial tyranny for those who are subordinated. Political dualism is nakedly duplicated within the police force. From Dippenaar's account one concludes just how squarely and comfortably the police force is situated within the womb of the Herrenvolk. The *consensual* nature of relations between police and the volk[10] stand in sharp contrast to the *military* style of policing to which subordinates are exposed. The force participates in the festivities of the volk, 'because of its close ties with the nation' (Dippenaar, 1988: 436). By taking part in the Republic festivities, Bloodriver, Berg en Dal, and the Battle of Amajuba commemorations, the force 'contributes to the cultural heritage of South Africa' (Dippenaar, 1988: 674). Stating the argument for the formation of a cultural organization within the police, Dippenaar explains:

> The Force was regarded as an important component of the nation which supplied its manpower and it was believed that policemen felt called upon to contribute, as individuals and as a unit, to the maintenance and expansion of the nation's common spiritual concerns (Dippenaar, 1988: 246).

In 1955 the Afrikaanse Kultuurvereeniging van die Suid-Afrikaanse Polisie[11] (AKPOL) was officially established, with its membership exclusive to white Afrikaner policemen. An analysis of AKPOL found in *Servamus*, the official SAP magazine, re-affirms its explicitly ethnocentric concern with Afrikaans as a language and with aspects of Afrikaner culture. The institutionalization of a Chaplain Service within the force was instrumental in tying the force to the dictates of Christian nationalism. In an ethnocentric history of the police, it is the ethnically dominant section of the force that constitutes the police and little mention is made of those sections of the force consisting of members of the subordinate groups in society. They are simply *not important* for such a history.

An organizationally *inward-looking, apologist* and *ethnocentric* history of the police does not ultimately make for good history. Its selectiveness produces a distortion of whatever history is presented. It is useful to divide Dippenaar's *History* into two parts: 1913 to 1945 and post-1945. Such a division seems useful not only for reasons of political chronology, but also because it correlates with important shifts in Dippenaar's analysis. The impact of broader political developments on

---

10. Translated as the people.
11. Translated as the Afrikaans Cultural Organization of the South African Police.

the police in the period 1913 to 1945 is dealt with in a far more substantive and sociologically respectable manner than the analysis which follows. Post-1945 politics are analysed in typically conspiratorial terms. It is communism which is considered to be the motor of the history that Dippenaar recounts. One forceful case in point for the selectivity of Dippenaar's analysis concerns the absence of any explicit consideration of the policy of apartheid, its impact on society, and, ultimately, on its police force. To omit the politics of apartheid from a historical analysis of the SAP is simply intellectually inexcusable. There can be no adequate history of the police if a historical analysis fails to examine the impact of the prevailing political structure and culture of a society on its police force. Perhaps Dippenaar's *History* is a crucial testimony of the extent to which the political discourse of Afrikaner nationalism has become so institutionalized in peoples' minds, that they do not appear aware of the distorting effects of such discourse on the historical analyses they so energetically attempt. In a review such as this, one cannot but reflect on the extent to which Afrikaner nationalism, as ideology and as political discourse, has in an important sense become *invisible*. Herein I would suppose lies its importance. As a political analysis, Dippenaar's *History* will eventually be relegated to the *rubbish heap* of historical analysis, or cherished for the banality spawned by the inclusive ideology of total-onslaught/total-strategy politics. By reducing all extra-parliamentary political activity to *stereotyped revolutionary ideology*, Dippenaar puts up his own straw dog, a *stereotyped, counter-revolutionary* view of politics and of policing.

Conclusion

Perhaps it is as a work of fiction that Dippenaar's *History* should be appreciated. A fictionalized account of the history of the police would be little concerned with a neat demarcation between the real and the imagined. In the true tradition of fictitious history the distortion of historical facts occurs, not through deliberate falsification, but through popular tradition. In this case state security ideology has spawned a powerful popular discourse through which reality is mediated. For it is only as fiction that one can suitably appreciate this assessment of the police force by the then Minister of Law and Order:

> ... it can only justly be claimed that the Force has, in the principles on which its duty has been performed, always maintained Christian norms and civilised standards. The Force has ensured the acknowledgement and maintenance of the individual freedom of faith and worship and has ensured the inviolability of freedom in our country. The Force has at all

times ensured the independence of the judiciary and equality in the eyes of the law as well as maintaining law and order and promoted the spiritual and material prosperity of all its people (Vlok, cited in Dippenaar, 1988: v).

Bibliography

Books and articles

Cawthra, S. (1986). *Brutal Force: The Apartheid War Machine*. London: International Defence Aid Fund (IDAF).

Dippenaar, M. (1988). *Die Geskiedenis van die Suid Afrikaanse Polisie, 1913–1988*. (*The History of The South African Police, 1913–1988*). Silverton: Promedia.

Fine, D. (1989). 'Kitskonstabels: A Case Study in Black on Black Policing'. *Acta Juridica*: 44–85.

Foster, D., Davis, D. & Sandler, D. (1987). *Detention and Torture in South Africa: Psychological, Legal, and Historical Studies*. Cape Town: David Philip.

Frankel, P. (1984). *Pretoria's Pretorians: Civil–Military Relations in South Africa*. Cambridge: Cambridge University Press.

Hansson, D. S. (1989). 'Trigger Happy? An Evaluation of Fatal Police Shootings in the Greater Cape Town Area from 1984 to 1986'. *Acta Juridica*: 118–38.

Pike, H. R. (1975). 'Communism and the Police'. *Servamus* October.

Posel, D. (1989). 'A "Battlefield of Perceptions": State Discourse on Political Violence, 1985–1988'. In *War and Society: The Militarisation of South Africa*. (Ed.) Cock, J. & Nathan, L. Cape Town: David Philip.

The Commissioner of the South African Police (1988). *Annual Report*. Pretoria: Government Printer.

The Lansdown Commission (1947). *Report of the Commission of Inquiry*. Pretoria: Government Printer.

The Te Water Commission (1936). *Report of the Commission of Inquiry*. Pretoria: Government Printer.

Van den Berghe, P. L. (1965). *South Africa: A Study in Conflict*. Middletown: Weslyan University Press.

Visser, G. C. (1976). *OB: Traitors or Patriots?* Johannesburg: MacMillan.

Acts

The Police Act 14 of 1912.

The Terrorism Act 83 of 1967.

CHAPTER FIVE

Policing political opponents: Death squads and cop culture

Nico Steytler

Introduction

The principal question to answer with regard to understanding police conduct is,

> ... how policemen act together so that their joint action systematically contributes to the reproduction of relations of subordination and dominance (Shearing, 1981a: 284).

This question pertains to both legal and illegal police actions, because the latter type of action is often taken in pursuit of organizational objectives and results in so-called organizational police deviance (Shearing, 1981b). This chapter focuses on organizational police deviance and, in particular, on death squads. The latter are defined as organized units within a police force whose actions include assassinations and other clandestine acts of violence against persons and property in the pursuance of organizational objectives.

Police conduct is often understood in terms of police subculture or *cop culture*, as it is commonly called, because of 'the powerful controlling effect of those norms and values of the occupational subculture' (Brogden et al., 1988: 44). The question of police deviance is thus approached in terms of social determinants rather than in terms of the motivations or actions of individual officers (e.g. Hagan & Morden, 1981). Reiner defines cop culture as 'the values, norms, perspectives and craft rules which inform their conduct' (Reiner, 1985: 86). In liberal democracies, most studies of cop culture have focused on the conduct of a sub-group within a police force, the *working* police officers, often emphasizing how an occupational subculture is produced by street encounters. Only the relatively powerless police officers have thus been studied, while senior officers have remain unexamined (Brogden et al., 1988: 46). These studies do not reveal how

> … the law, formal organizational policy or senior officers, impinge on this world and this renders existing accounts of cop culture "partial at best" (Brogden et al., 1988: 47).

The focus on *low* policing or street policing has stood in the way of a broader picture of cop culture, where low policing is not the sole or even dominant form of policing (Brodeur, 1983). A different picture may emerge from an examination of *high* policing or *political* policing, which may be the product of a different set of norms that have other origins. For cop culture to be an adequate and useful analytical tool, it must also account for the norms created by, mediated through, and protected by, 'the law, formal organizational policy [and] senior officers' (Brogden et al., 1988: 47).

The concept of cop culture, the norms and values that inform a group of actors, form a valuable part of any explanation of the existence of state-sponsored death squads. However, previous theses on the formation and content of cop culture have to be re-assessed and must include the motivating role of political discourse, the organizational policy determining both the foci and methods of policing, and the *user-friendly* legal framework. It is suggested that the incorporation of these features into the concept of cop culture will produce a fuller understanding of the motivation, methods, and framework underlying organizational police deviance.

Death squads: The available evidence

The difficulties surrounding the assessment of organizational police deviance, when it involves high policing, are notorious. With secrecy being the norm in security organizations, the verification of allegations of organizational police deviance is problematic and knowledge does not necessarily amount to legal proof (Brodeur, 1983; and Turk, 1981). As Turk remarks:

> … [w]hen deviance can be plausibly denied by insiders [police], and even more when denial is politically useful to powerful outsiders [politicians], substantiation of reported deviance becomes virtually impossible (Turk, 1981: 114).

The few sources of information that do exist include the disclosures of disaffected former officers and the occasional court case (Turk, 1981).

In South Africa, the existence of death squads and *dirty tricks units* operating against anti-apartheid activists is suggested by the high number of violent incidents. It is reported that since 1978, sixty people have been assassinated in South Africa, and a further sixty-one people who had links with South Africa have been killed outside the country. Numerous others have simply disappeared (*The Weekly Mail*, 5 May 1989). Although the assassinations of David Webster, an academic and community worker, and Anton Lubowski, a prominent white member of the South West African Peoples' Organization (SWAPO), in 1989 focused attention once again on death squads, these events represent the mere apex of the pyramid of illegal, clandestine acts against anti-apartheid activists. A report of the Independent Board of Inquiry into Informal Repression (IBIIR) gives some indication of the extent of these activities over the past three years, but notes that the figures are likely to be an underestimation (IBIIR, 1989a). It is alleged that since 1985, 165 houses, offices, clinics, churches, and vehicles have been destroyed by fire that has been started by various incendiary devices. There have been seventeen alleged incidents of petty vandalism, including the slashing of tyres, the placing of dead animals on door steps, and the firing of gunshots through the windows of parked cars. Six incidents of teargas being fired into homes have been alleged, as well as two grenade attacks on homes, thirteen cases of homes being stoned, thirty-seven burglaries, fifteen bombings of offices and homes, plus a host of incidents of obscene phone calls, bomb threats, death threats, and, more recently, the use of poisonous substances to deter left-wing activists[1] (IBIIR, 1986b).

The unifying feature of all these events is the singular failure of the South African Police (SAP) to arrest, let alone prosecute, a single perpetrator in respect of any of these cases; despite the fact that the most senior detective of the SAP, Major-General Joubert, has taken charge of investigations into so-called right-wing violence. The lamentable failure of police investigations has exacerbated the fear that it is members of the SAP who have been implicated in these clandestine acts of terror. This of course, suggests state complicity.

While the South African Defence Force (SADF) has admitted that it was involved in a dirty tricks campaign against members of the End Conscription Campaign (ECC) (*End Conscription Campaign v Minister of Defence*, 1989), the SAP has adamantly denied any complicity in such

---

1. For example, church leader, the Reverend Frank Chikane, had to be hospitalized after his clothes had been covertly impregnated with a poisonous substance.

activities. A few hours before Butana Almond Nofomela was to be executed for murder, at 7 a.m. on 20 October 1989, the first direct evidence of police complicity came to light. In an affidavit, Nofomela stated the following:

> During the period of my service in the Security Branch, I served under station commander Brig Schoon. In 1981 I was appointed a member of the security branch's assassination squad, and I served under Capt Johannes Dirk Coetzee, who was my commanding officer. ... I was the leader of this group that was to eliminate [Griffiths] Mxenge. ... I was involved in approximately eight other assassinations during my stint in the assassination squad, and also numerous kidnappings (IBIIR, 1989a: Annexure A).

In November the Afrikaans weekly paper, *Vrye Weekblad*, published an extensive interview with Captain Coetzee, which confirmed and expanded on Nofomela's allegations of the existence and operation of a death squad within the Security Branch (*Vrye Weekblad*, 17 November 1989). A third member of the alleged death squad, David (Spyker[2]) Tshikalange, further corroborated the allegations. The IBIIR's investigation found 'important corroboration of certain of the incidents so far detailed by Nofomela' (IBIIR, 1989a: 18).

A number of important features of death squads emerge from the reports made by ex-members: (1) It was a specialist unit which commanded considerable financial, technical, and intelligence resources; (2) the direction of and assistance to death squads came from high-ranking officers; (3) the initial objective was the elimination of suspected ANC targets and personnel both inside and outside the country; (4) as the political conflict deepened internally, the focus was extended to the assassination and harassment of anti-apartheid activists in the townships; (5) detainees whose continued detention proved problematic were killed for reasons of expediency; and (6) the unit made extensive use of ex-ANC-guerrillas to conduct assassinations.

The weight of the evidence is such that the existence of a specialized death squad within the police force cannot be refuted easily. It must be emphasized that the accounts of death squad activities used as illustrative material in this chapter are based on allegations made by three ex-policemen.[3] Whether or not these allegations are found to be substantially true, the argument in this chapter is concerned more with the structures within which the police force operates and with the condi-

---

2. Translated as Nailer.
3. This chapter is based on information available at 3 February 1990. The evidence advanced to the Harms Commission has not been included.

tions that make it possible for death squads to exist and function, than with individual events and allegations. Valid observations may thus be made and preliminary conclusions drawn. More specifically, it is argued that this extreme form of organizational police deviance can be best understood in terms of a cop culture which reflects and perpetuates dominant social structures. Cop culture is characterized by factors that function as prerequisites for this type of occupational deviance. It is argued further that: (1) Political discourse, at least in part, provides motivation and justification for organizational police deviance; (2) the military methods that are employed are products of organizational policy and structure; (3) the contradiction that arises when the uphol-ders of law and order transgress the law is managed using the skill of hypocrisy; and (4) organizational police deviance functions within a legal system that is user-friendly, one that facilitates such behaviour and that protects those who engage in such conduct.

The dominant political discourse

Reiner (1985) identifies a sense of *mission* as a central feature of cop culture, namely:

> … a feeling that policing is not just a job but a way of life with a worthwhile purpose, at least in principle. … The purpose is not conceived of as a political enterprise, but as the preservation of a valued way of life and the protection of the weak against the predatory. The core justification of policing is a victim centred perspective (Reiner, 1985: 88).

The question thus arises as to the set of beliefs that lend substance to this sense of mission. It has been maintained that cop culture also reflects the norms and values of the social structure which is being policed (Brogden et al., 1988; Jakubs, 1977; and Reiner, 1985). Cop culture thus aligns the police with the dominant group in a society, against outsider groups, variously called 'troublemakers, scum, dregs [or] third and fourth class citizens' (Shearing, 1981a: 285–6). In the police perception the public is divided into those the police should serve and protect and the *scum* from whom the latter should be protected.

This sense of mission is easily identifiable among the norms that underpin the existence of death squads in South Africa. It has involved a belief in 'the preservation of a valued way of life' but, in contrast to Reiner's suggestion, it has also been a 'political enterprise' (Reiner, 1985: 88). In this regard the government-propagated political theory on *ideological crime* has been of particular importance. In response to increasing black resistance and militancy, coupled with increasing international isolation and pressure, the state formulated the political discourse of *total onslaught* and, more recently, *revolutionary war*. It called for a total strategy and counter-revolutionary warfare to eliminate the enemy, who was identified as being the communist-expansionist threat in the guise of the African National Congress/South African Communist Party (ANC/SACP) alliance[4] (Swilling & Phillips, 1989).

It is argued here that this overtly political discourse has been assimilated by the SAP, that it has informed their sense of mission, and has created conditions that could produce and support the activities of death squads. The very position of the police force within the governing structure has accorded it an overtly political role, for the SAP has functioned as one of the essential instruments for maintaining white domination (Sachs 1975; Steytler 1987a; and Van der Spuy, 1988). This truism has been articulated more obliquely by the former Police Commissioner, General De Witt:

> ... the history of South Africa has ... mirrored the history of the South African Police. The two have been, and still are, inextricably interlaced (De Witt, in Dippenaar, 1988: xi).

The discourse of total strategy and counter-revolutionary warfare, which is the product of the 'military mind' (Grundy, 1986: 1), has been incorporated into the institutional thinking of the police force. It is clear from official police publications[5] that this dominant police discourse 'provides an overarching political framework within which the police as an institution reviews its annual position' (Van der Spuy, 1988: 11).

Black police, who now comprise half of the force, have been described as 'soldiers without politics' (Grundy, 1983: 1). Yet years of political socialization experienced in police college training and in policing the apartheid system, have had a profound impact. Moreover, the experience of being a target of ANC attacks would be neatly accounted for by the proffered political theory. For rank-and-file police the result may thus be that 'total strategy merges and moulds rather old fears and political concerns into a more comprehensive format' (Van der Spuy, 1988: 133). However, no cop culture is uniformly distributed across all ranks or within ranks in a police force, nor does it remain unchanged over time (Brogden et al., 1988; and Shearing, 1981b). This

---

4. The unbanning of the ANC, the Pan African Congress (PAC), and the SACP on 2 February 1990 will have a profound effect on cop culture, but does not affect the present analysis, as the conduct that is examined here falls under the old dispensation.
5. Such as Parliamentary White Papers, the Annual Report of the Commissioner of Police, and the police journal, *Servamus*.

is certainly true of the SAP. The recent dissent in the ranks of coloured police officers, articulated by Lieutenant Rockman in his objections to the political nature of police duties, is evidence of contradictory opinions and responses to the official political theory.

Available evidence about death squads also suggests that it would be too simplistic to see the dominant political discourse as sufficient reason for their existence. Political discourse works together with professional and career interests, which may operate independently of political discourse. Captain Coetzee describes his participation in a death squad as being preceded by a rapid promotion through the ranks to the position of a commissioned officer, followed by his admission to the Security Branch, the *élite* unit of the force:

> I was even more honoured when, on top of it all, they selected me to lead the murder squad. My bosses like me, I thought and my country needs me, a terrible task rests on me. There are people who want to take the country and who must be killed[6] (*Vrye Weekblad*, 17 November 1989).

Coetzee's career ambition and the confidence of his senior officers strongly influenced his conduct. Coetzee's brother observed that, 'the praise which his senior officers gave him was an inspiration for him and, I think, determined his direction'[7] (*Vrye Weekblad*, 24 November 1989). The professional demands made by the organizational structure of the police were not on their own a sufficient reason, but were reinforced and legitimated by Coetzee's sense of mission. Furthermore, the direction of this mission was definitively moulded by the dominant political theory. Coetzee had a clear perception of the enemy, *the terrorists*, and of how to deal with them: 'Let the bastards burn at the stake'[8] (*Vrye Weekblad*, 17 November 1989). He believed that it was right for Griffiths Mxenge to have been murdered, because Coetzee had been informed by the Security Police in Durban that the ANC were channelling money through Mxenge, although this could not be proven. What is important is that Coetzee's beliefs were not antithetical to the dominant ideology, but reflected it accurately. Coetzee's brother described him as 'a staunch patriot with an image of the fatherland and the nation based on the traditional and prevailing perceptions'[9] (*Vrye Weekblad*, 24 November 1989). When the mission to kill Marius Schoon was cancelled, Coetzee was disappointed: 'I believed he should die. Such a white man among

---

6. Editors' translation of Afrikaans original.
7. Editors' translation of Afrikaans original.
8. Editors' translation of Afrikaans original.
9. Editors' translation of Afrikaans original.

the terrorists, I thought'[10] (*Vrye Weekblad*, 17 November 1989). The idea that a *white*, anti-apartheid activist represents double deviancy is not unique to Coetzee. Mr. Justice Van der Walt expressed a similar sentiment when he sentenced Marion Sparg, a white member of Umkhonto we Sizwe, the armed wing of the ANC, to twenty-five years imprisonment.

> If a black South African were in your position his or her acts could be understood although not excused. The fact that as a white South African you have espoused the cause of revolution I regard as an aggravating factor (*S v Sparg*, 1986).

Because Coetzee shared, and acted upon, the dominant political discourse of total onslaught, it is understandable that he still does not view his past conduct as immoral, but rather considers it to be a waste. At the time of talks about negotiations between the government and the ANC, Coetzee remarked: 'How could I have involved myself in such futility'[11] (*Vrye Weekblad*, 17 November 1989). The recent unbanning of the ANC and SACP can only compound his sense of waste.

It has been noted above that cop culture is not necessarily accepted uniformly within the force. For the effective execution of policy, however, it may not be necessary for the norms of political discourse to infiltrate the *whole* force, for where political theory fails to motivate rank-and-file members, the organizational structure may well compensate. Coetzee regarded loyalty of the death squad's turned ANC cadres, called *Askaris*, with skepticism. It has been reported that at least ten Askaris have defected from the police and returned to the ANC (*Vrye Weekblad*, 8 December 1989). The organizational structure of the police has had to have an iron grip to ensure the commitment of Askaris in assassinations by death squads. The hopeless position of captured ANC cadres combined with financial incentives, has helped to secure some degree of compliance. To illustrate, Coetzee claimed that after two ANC members had been abducted by the SADF from Mozambique in 1980, one decided to join the Security Police, while the other adopted an attitude of charge me or shoot me. The latter was later shot in the head, his body burnt, and his ashes thrown in the Komati River (*Vrye Weekblad*, 17 November 1989). Furthermore, the Askaris who were involved in the assassination of Mxenge, an alleged ANC member, were rewarded with a bonus of R1 000 (IBIIR, 1989a: Annexure A). Thus, as long as the dominant political discourse is mediated by commanding

---

10. Editors' translation of Afrikaans original.
11. Editors' translation of Afrikaans original.

officers, death squads can operate as highly organized units that use hired assassins to do their dirty work.

Military methodology

A political theory that espouses the elimination of the enemy does not translate automatically into action. As Boraine (1989) has argued, state counter-revolutionary warfare may require systematic repression in order to bolster reform, which makes assassinations and abductions essential components of upgrading initiatives. What is then required is the translation of these requirements into practice. Where political discourse calls for the elimination of the enemy, not only must there be a determination of the methods of destruction, but these methods must themselves be normalized by a further set of enabling norms. It is at this level that military discourse and methods provide the necessary mechanism for the police to translate structure into action. The state's policy of militarizing the SAP to counter military insurgency by the ANC and the Pan African Congress (PAC) has made it possible to imbue cop culture with military methodology, namely, military techniques and methods and the norms that support these methods.

The emergence of death squads tends to coincide closely with the rise to dominance of the military in national politics. In Central and South America this trend has been particularly pronounced. Death squads within the security forces have served to obscure military regimes' responsibility for the systematic elimination of political opponents. The practice of simply making people *disappear* avoids the negative attention that results from overt killing, and this eases international pressure on regimes by lowering the number of those who can be defined as prisoners (Petras, 1987).

In Brazil the advent of military authoritarian rule in 1964 and the suspension of all constitutional safeguards also saw the formation of death squads, with the approval of the regime, to combat urban guerrillas (Bowden, 1978; Jakubs, 1977; and Petras, 1987). Soon after the demise of the urban guerrillas, the police shifted the activities of the death squads, the *esquadrão da morte*, to a general policing function and used them to systematically exterminate common criminals (Jakubs, 1977). In Argentina the military coup of 1976 brought the federal police under the direction of the army. In joint actions the armed forces conducted a *dirty war* in the language of a *holy war* against 'subversion and communism and foreign ideologies which threatened the Argentinean way of life' (Shank & Talamente, 1987: 105). In this dirty war, which lasted until 1982, more than 10 000 people disappeared (the Argentinean Commission, 1986). From 1973 onward in Chile, the Pinochet military regime attempted the destruction of social movements and the depoliticization of the population by making local grassroots opinion leaders 'disappear' (Petras, 1987: 93). In the first two months after the coup, approximately 5 000 people were executed and about 1 000 more were subsequently eliminated by the Security Police (Dinges, 1983: 16). Since 1980 more than 60 000 people have been killed by death squads and security forces in the military dictatorship in San Salvador (Amaya et al., 1987: 13). The dominance of the military over all aspects of state administration ensures a 'penal system for the disappeared', which is complemented by a 'counter-penal system that operates to *not* punish the guilty', with the result that 60 000 homicides remain uninvestigated (Amaya et al., 1987: 15).

The reference to South American death squads is not made to suggest that General Geldenhuys[12] and Brigadier Wandrag's[13] secret visit to Argentina and Chile in 1981 had anything to do with the formation of death squads in South Africa. However, these two parties did think they had much in common, for in a discussion between General Geldenhuys and his Argentinean counterpart, it was

... explained that both Police Forces were fighting a mutual enemy, Communism, and that the exchange of knowledge was absolutely essential (Dippenaar, 1988: 621).

A similar rapport was evident with the Chilean police authorities. After a visit by the Chilean Commissioner of Police to South Africa in 1982, General Geldenhuys took the following decision:

Both organizations would exchange information of mutual interest and priority should be given to training and information concerning terrorist organizations (Dippenaar, 1988: 622).

What is of importance is the similarity between these countries in the way they view the common enemy, communism, and in the military way in which they have responded.

The link between military regimes and death squads lies in the very absoluteness of military actions. The aim of military operations is the destruction of the enemy, its total annihilation. Military targets are destroyed, the enemy is eliminated. In contrast to the limited function of ordinary policing, namely, the investigation and apprehension of suspects, the essence of the military method is to collapse all of the

---

12. Then Commissioner of the SAP.
13. The new head of the Riot Police.

elements of the criminal justice process into one, namely, the identification of the enemy, their apprehension, arraignment, prosecution, sentencing, and execution. In contrast to the basic principle of policing, the minimum use of force, the military exalts in being a *killing machine*. Where political problems can no longer be dealt with using normal police practices, the military method becomes an attractive option and the militarization of the police the consequence (Steytler, 1987b).

Police forces the world over are frequently described as quasi-military organizations. From their outset they have been paramilitary in structure and discipline (Bowden, 1978: 31). However, the military character is more pronounced in police forces that are colonial in origin (Brogden, 1983). Political violence, such as that encountered in Northern Ireland, has contributed towards the Royal Ulster Constabulary adopting a 'highly militarised repressive form of "crime control" while lessening officers' adherence to "due process" concerns' (Weitzer, 1985: 47). The SAP exemplifies all these elements in the extreme. With its roots firmly in colonial policing, its strong paramilitary character has been increased by the many threats to public order (Brewer et al., 1988; and Grundy, 1986). Police training has included military skills which are put into practice during periods of obligatory service by the police in the operational military areas. Furthermore, in the blending of military and police operations in the townships, traditional distinctions have become obsolete.

Police training has included a strong military component in response to guerrilla incursions[14] in Namibia and Zimbabwe, and later terror attacks in the urban areas in which the police were identified as a particular target. Counter-insurgency training has for many years 'been built into the making of a South African policeman' (*Servamus*, 1981: 10). At the Police Centre for Intensive Training in Maleoskop, the syllabus covers:

> … patrolling, battle craft, ambushes, counter-ambushing, road movement, attack on enemy bases, follow-up and mopping-up operations, internal security operations, appreciations, briefing, forward air control, anti-riot procedures, urban terrorism and terrorist tactics' (*Servamus*, 1981: 10).

This training is reinforced by active military-type service. From 1967 to 1975 the SAP did active military service in what was then Rhodesia, and from 1967 to 1985 they fought in the bush war in Namibia (Brewer et al., 1988; and Dippenaar, 1988).

---

14. By the ANC, PAC, and SWAPO.

During this time paramilitary units were also formed in or under the direction of the SAP. In Namibia, Unit-K, later known as *Koevoet*, was established in 1976. In 1981 other policing duties were transferred to the South West African Police and the SAP retained control over Koevoet, which concentrated on 'offensive action [in] the tracking and eradication of terrorists' (Dippenaar, 1988: 696). In 1984 Koevoet was described by Lieutenant General Verster as, 'a cold, calculated, effective and ruthless unit and the major thorn in the flesh of the SWAPO terrorists' (Verster, in Dippenaar, 1988: 696).

The criticism of Koevoet for its notorious brutality was dismissed by the police, although they admitted that controversy over this unit had arisen 'for the simple reason that it was obliged to employ unorthodox methods' (Dippenaar, 1988: 698). The police claimed as late as 1988 that Koevoet 'reduced SWAPO to one of the world's most irrelevant terrorist organisations' (Dippenaar, 1988: 695). However, Koevoet has since been disbanded in terms of the 1989 peace plan, which paved the way for the Namibian elections and the eventual electoral victory by SWAPO.

In South Africa counter-insurgency units have been formed within the Security Branch of the SAP. The existence of Group C-1 came to light in a number of trials and inquests. This unit, commanded by Brigadier Schoon, made widespread use of Askaris. The operations and the discourse in terms of which the unit was conducted, have strong military characteristics. In the trials of *S v Forbes & Others* (1987) and *S v Yengeni & Another* (1989), for example, the operations of the *Terroriste Opsporingseenheid*[15] suggested military objectives and methods. The unit would track down and confront ANC cadres to extract information about the operation of underground networks, in order to destroy them. When suspects were apprehended, a different team of security police would be responsible for obtaining incriminating evidence for the purposes of a possible prosecution (Hope, 1989). The operations of the Security Police were conducted in military fashion and couched in military language (Hope, 1989).

Since 1985 the 'fuzzy and overlapping division of labour' between the police and the defence force has been extended with the deployment of the SADF in black townships (Grundy, 1983: 136). Their high level of interaction and co-operation has been co-ordinated by the State Security Council (SSC) and the National Management System (NMS) (Grundy, 1986). The alleged activities of the death squads proximate traditional military operations. The 1983 raid into Swaziland, in which a transit house was destroyed and three people were killed, differs from

---

15. Translated as Terrorist Detection Unit.

previous SADF raids into neighbouring states,[16] only because it was conducted covertly[17] (Luyt, 1989). The effect was the same: Physical structures thought to house ANC operatives were destroyed and their occupants were killed. An open raid on ANC targets, violating the territorial integrity of Swaziland, would certainly have placed international pressure on Swaziland to discontinue the good relations that existed between Pretoria and King Sobhuza II at the time. In South Africa, the same military methodology was applied. Coetzee disclosed that,

> I was in civvies [civilian clothes] with an arsenal of weapons in the back boot of my car, ready to make terrible war[18] (*Vrye Weekblad*, 17 November 1989).

Coetzee's weapons included forty kilograms of Russian explosives, a suitcase full of offensive and defensive Russian hand-grenades, and five hand machine guns and Russian pistols, which are hardly the weaponry of a civilian policeman! Many of the officers who have been named in connection with the alleged South African death squads have also been operatives in Koevoet in Namibia. The alleged commanders of a death squad, Brigadier Schoon and Major De Kock, have both held positions of leadership in Koevoet (*Vrye Weekblad*, 24 November 1989).

A military discourse provides a comfortable way of legitimating operations like the raid into Swaziland. '[L]aundered language' in which terms such as kill and murder are replaced with words like eliminate and neutralize enable death squads to conceive of and execute their missions with clinical precision (Brodeur, 1983: 509). For Captain Coetzee, the persons who were killed remained anonymous military targets. However, the alleged activities of the death squads have not been limited to traditional military operations. The bulk of the activities that have been reported were directed against non-military targets, that is, individuals have been assassinated. A critical disjunction occurs when military methods, which are usually deployed against groups of people and physical structures, are employed in police work that is traditionally concerned with individuals and their conduct.

According to Captain Coetzee, when traditional police methods failed to prove that Mxenge was channelling money for the ANC, the police opted for a military solution, that is, the elimination of the enemy. By

---

16. Such as Mozambique, Botswana, Zimbabwe, Zambia, and Lesotho.
17. See IBIIR (1989a: 6) for important new corroboratory evidence about the raid into Swaziland.
18. Editors' translation of Afrikaans original.

this action, the police took military methods into an entirely new terrain as a response to the requirements of the dominant political discourse. This was facilitated by the militarization of the SAP.

Such a shift has important effects on perceptions of this mode of conduct. Captain Coetzee expressed one such perception in his claim that he had found it difficult to participate in *eliminations* when he had known the faces of the victims (*Vrye Weekblad*, 17 November 1989). Even for trained killers, the military method of the public killing of a *faceless enemy* is not easily transferred to clandestine operations against *known* persons. Of greater significance is the public's reaction to this type of illegal conduct on the part of the police. All illegal police conduct involves an inherent contradiction, because of the role that the police are meant to play as *upholders of law and order*. It should be noted, however, that different degrees of deviance evoke different levels of reaction to such contradictions. The public is most concerned when the contradiction is sharpest. The probability of such behaviour being labelled deviant depends on whether police conduct involves assassinations, maimings, or the use of methods that are generally repugnant, such as, germ warfare, poison, and letter bombs.[19] If action is taken abroad, it is usually regarded as being less serious than if it happens at home. In addition, actions taken at home against minority-status groups are likely to attract less negative attention than actions taken against persons of majority status. Finally, actions taken against organizations are less likely to be viewed as deviant than those taken against individuals (Turk, 1981).

The skill of hypocrisy

Where the police indulge in illegal behaviour there must be a means of managing, at least for public consumption, the inevitable contradiction that arises when upholders of law and order act *outside* the law. Indeed, a prerequisite for the continued operation of a death squad and the subsequent preservation of a positive image of the police is the ability to mask illegal activities. The skill of hypocrisy is thus essential.

All South American military regimes have used the justification that national wars are being waged for the 'survival of Western Civilization' (Petras, 1987: 94). Even when a dominant section of the Brazilian population supported death squads, it was important for Brazil's international relations that it was seen to be a civilized country (Jakubs,

---

19. These are known as Geneva offences, that is, contraventions of the Geneva Convention (1949).

1977). This set of moral values, which are loosely grouped under the all-embracing rubric of Western civilization, comes into play when a certain image of the state has to be protected and reinforced. When a regime's governance comes under attack, it often seeks to legitimize its own power interests in the name of orderly and civilized government. But,

> ... the regime which allows, or indeed encourages, its policemen to move beyond the limits of the law, does so at the cost of discrediting the very law they are struggling to defend and uphold (Bowden, 1978: 15).

Where the upholders of law and order are involved in illegal conduct, the management of the resulting contradiction occurs at the level of both senior officers and rank-and-file members. Without the latter managing hypocrisy successfully at the street level, attempts by those in the upper echelons to present the image of a law-abiding force cannot succeed. Where the norms of cop culture authorize or direct police deviance, various strategies are employed to secure such hypocrisy. First, secrecy is all important. The central rule is to keep those rules that promote deviance hidden.

> The only rule to keep in mind when bending others is that one should take every precaution to avoid being found out (Ericson, 1981: 89).

The rule of secrecy may be enforced negatively through internal disciplinary procedures (Ericson, 1981), or positively by rewarding the successful maintenance of organizational hypocrisy. A study in Canada revealed that officers perceived 'those who were most adept at sustaining the official hypocrisy of police work ... as having the best career prospects' (Shearing, 1981b: 31). Where the existence of the contradiction becomes visible, a simple strategy of denial is often employed. Lying thus becomes 'a routine tactic whose use evidently is limited only by considerations of expediency' (Turk, 1981: 112). Since there is great difficulty involved in establishing facts, denial of wrongdoing becomes standard fare.

Where illegal actions can no longer be denied plausibly, blame is attached routinely to a few 'rotten apples', who deviate from the norm by being overly zealous (Turk, 1981: 113). In Brazil a few trials of 'token suspects' did take place, particularly where the victims were *not* 'marginals' (Jakubs, 1977: 102). In such cases the conduct of suspects represented 'an overstepping of the extended boundaries of acceptability' (Jakubs, 1977: 102).

The preservation of Western civilization also underpins the South African government's commitment to the dominant political discourse. In executing the duty to preserve this order, the SAP's conduct is also presented in terms of that moral standard. In the words of the current Minister of Law and Order, Mr. Adriaan Vlok,

> ... it can also justly be claimed that the Force has, in the principles on which its duty has been performed, always maintained Christian norms and civilized standards (Vlok, cited in Dippenaar, 1988: v).

Set against this standard, the SAP is well aware of the dire consequences that result when a contradiction comes to the surface. Steve Biko's death in detention, at the hands of the Security Police, damaged the image of the police locally and abroad. Captain Coetzee alleged that the SAP attempted to make the Mxenge assassination appear to be a robbery, because they 'did not feel like another Biko incident'[20] (*Vrye Weekblad*, 17 November 1989).

The depth of the contradiction suggested by allegations of death squads is well illustrated in the defamation claim that was brought by the Assistant Commissioner of the Police and Head of the Police Forensic Laboratory, Lieutenant-General Neethling, against the newspaper, *Vrye Weekblad*. In claiming one million rand damages, the plaintiff argued that readers of the *Vrye Weekblad* would interpret the reports as meaning that, 'he was the leader of an illegal criminal organization which murders or attempts to murder people'[21] (*Vrye Weekblad*, 8 December 1989). He also maintained that the reports suggested that he was 'guilty [of] very serious criminal infringements because he [had] provided poison with which people were murdered'[22] (*Vrye Weekblad*, 8 December 1989).

If the death squad allegations are fully substantiated, then the success with which this phenomenon has been hidden for almost a decade is evidence in itself that the practice of hypocrisy is both pervasive and effective. Only when Nofomela was faced with execution did he breach the rule of police secrecy. His allegations, and those of Coetzee and Tshikalange, direct attention to the skill with which senior officers managed the alleged contradiction.

SAP responses to death squad allegations

Brief attention is now paid to a few events that have followed the disclosure of death squads. The police response to allegations has involved denial, pointing to rotten apples, and the discovery of new

---

20. Editors' translation of Afrikaans original.
21. Editors' translation of Afrikaans original.
22. Editors' translation of Afrikaans original.

enemies. All of these strategies are part of a predictable pattern of conflict management that occurs irrespective of whether allegations are in fact true. The SAP's first reaction to allegations of death squads was categorical denial. This was followed by the rotten apple approach. Captain Coetzee underwent a character assassination and it was said that if the allegations made by Coetzee, Nofomela, and Tshikalange were true, then they had acted for their *own* motives in defiance of official police policy (*The Argus*, 20 November 1989). Attention was soon deflected away from the SAP by the discovery of a right-wing terror group. Instead of focusing on the few rotten apples in the SAP, it was found that the assassination of anti-apartheid activists was a right-wing strategy against the government. The arrest and detention of Ferdie Barnard and another right-wing activist were cast in this mould. In a replying affidavit to a court application for Barnard's release from detention under Section 29, the Commander of the Murder and Robbery Unit, Brigadier Mostert, said that the assassinations of David Webster and Anton Lubowski[23], as well as other attacks on left-wing political activists, were aimed at disrupting the government's attempts at reconciliation (*Rapport*, 3 December 1989). Soon after this, five members of the extreme right wing were arrested and a large number of arms were seized. A death list was also found, which included the State President, F. W. de Klerk, three cabinet ministers, and the leader of the Afrikaner Weerstandsbeweging[24] (AWB), Eugene Terre'Blanche. A communiqué by Major-General Stadler stated that five detainees would be questioned on a whole spectrum of issues pertaining to death squads and specific acts of terror that had been alleged by Coetzee and Nofomela.[25] The police added tellingly that the link, if any, between this group of detainees and the assassinations of Dr. Webster and Advocate Lubowski, was not clear (*Die Burger*, 6 December 1989).

The discovery of such an ultra-right-wing group lent substance to the idea that death squads were groups that had the means to commit assassinations. More importantly, it provided a plausible explanation of

23. It is interesting that the Defence Force has now adopted a different strategy with regard to Anton Lubowski. On 26 February 1990, the Minister of Defence, General Magnus Malan, announced that it was illogical to suggest that Lubowski had been assassinated by the state, because he had been an undercover agent for the Defence Force (South African Broadcasting Company (SABC), 26 February 1990).

24. Translated as the Afrikaner Resistance Movement.

25. Eventually this group was charged with the murder of a black taxi-driver, the illegal possession of explosives, and the bombing of the apartment of Mr. Terre'Blanche's alleged lover, Ms Allen (*The Argus*, 2 February 1990).

the motive behind such activities, while simultaneously exonerating the government. The creation of a link between this right-wing group and the alleged death squads has, to some extent, diverted attention away from the real issue of the original allegations, that is, police deviance.

The legal framework for organizational police deviance

A cop culture that motivates and conceals organizational police deviance should *not* be seen as the mere antithesis of the legal order. Such a culture flourishes in a legal framework within which rules *allow* conduct that is usually untenable and a system which inhibits the effective control of police conduct. The culture incorporates an awareness of a user-friendly framework of enabling rules and a protective legal system. It has been argued that 'legal rules are *for* police deviance' (McBarnet 1979: 39). Perceived deviance is none other than lawful behaviour which appears deviant, because the letter of the law[26] permits conduct that runs contrary to an ideology of law that is based on liberal, democratic norms, such as, equality and legality.

Although such an analysis is useful for understanding conduct which is deviant from the ideology of law, it does *not* address the problem of conduct that is manifestly unlawful, even in terms of the letter of the law. Brodeur (1983) has taken McBarnet's 1979 analysis a step further by arguing that illegal police practices are, to a significant extent, grounded in the law. In cases of operational necessity, or what is perceived as such, specific legal enactments allow the general rules of law to be transgressed. The general rule against murder is circumvented by allowing, where operational necessity demands it, the use of deadly force.[27] It is easy then for the concept of operational necessity to lead to operational deviance, such as executions conducted by the police. The difference between operational necessity and deviance, then, is simply a matter of different 'scores on a legal scale' and this makes it difficult to categorize police conduct (Brodeur, 1983: 138). It is clear from this argument that the wider and more nebulous the legal ambit of operational necessity, the easier is the drift into operational deviance.

The permissive quality of law in relation to policing has often been emphasized. For example, Reiner (1985) has argued that law does not direct or motivate police action. Instead it leaves considerable leeway

---

26. Legislation and judicial decisions.
27. For example to effect an arrest. See Hansson (1989) for further details.

for other forces to shape and direct police activities in accordance with situational demands. This is particularly true where the law has an open texture and is intentionally vague and ambiguous about police powers (Ericson, 1981; and Hagan & Morden, 1981). Where 'legal rules, as well as other organizational rules, enable an enormous range of practices … [such] rules are for police deviance' (Ericson, 1981: 86).

The emphasis here is on law as rules which command, permit, or can be used to justify actions that are taken. This analysis of law should be seen together with and in the context of a wider view of law, namely, law as a system of rule application. The law does not facilitate deviant behaviour only because some legal rules are worded ambiguously or defined broadly. The legal process itself also allows conduct that falls outside the letter of the law, however vaguely that law is worded. Since the police are assigned the pivotal position in investigating and reconstructing *facts*, the skill of hypocrisy can operate to mask illegalities in police work successfully. It is in such a legal process that the police

> … have fundamental control over the construction of "facts" for a case, and all other actors (the prosecutor, the judge, the defence lawyer) must work within the framework of facts as constructed by the police (Ericson, 1981: 96).

This notion of law as a system underlies the analysis of the penal system in El Salvador by Amaya et al. (1987). In addition to the common penal system, they identify 'the penal system for the disappeared [and] the penal system for immunity' (Amaya et al., 1987: 14). The latter is described as

> … a counter-penal system that operates to *not* punish the guilty [which comprises] a whole body of unwritten rules [that] designate untouchable procedures and persons (Amaya et al., 1987: 14).

This penal system is located outside of the legal order in a set of unwritten rules. Here, however, it is argued to the contrary, that the penal system for immunity may operate within a legal system that comprises legal rules which permit the guilty to go unpunished. A cop culture that directs organizational deviance is likely to flourish within a legal order of permissive rules and a penal system for immunity.

The South African legal order has an abundance of permissive rules and a protective legal system which has produced a penal system of immunity. The almost unlimited powers of the SAP in terms of the repressive security legislation are already well documented[28] (e.g. Dugard, 1978; and Mathews, 1985). The police have exploited this 'freedom to act in a relatively unrestrained capacity' consistently (Brewer et al.,

---

28. Powers of arrest, detention, interrogation, search, and seizure.

1988: 181). The Supreme Court's failure to curtail the police through statutory interpretation and in practical application is equally well known and has given rise to the accusation of the dereliction of judicial duty (Mathews, 1986). These powers have breached the traditional principle of policing, the limited function of investigation and apprehension, and in effect have bestowed the judicial function of safeguarding individual freedom on the police (Steytler, 1987b).

It is of equal importance, however, to examine how conduct which is not executed in terms of established legislation remains unpunished. It is argued in this regard that the structure of the criminal justice process, namely, the extent to which its control lies in the hands of the police, may account for the fact that no one has been convicted of the murder of any of the sixty anti-apartheid activists who have been assassinated since 1978. The legal duty to investigate any unnatural death, including political assassinations, rests with the police. The police face a dilemma when they do investigate such incidents only to find that their own colleagues have been involved. Where death has been the outcome of an official policy, the dilemma is more apparent than real. The events surrounding the death squad allegations illustrate this point well. Perhaps the reaction of the police to these allegations revealed more than was intended. The Head of Police Public Relations and former ANC expert for the Security Branch, Major-General Stadler, denied categorically that there was an organized police hit squad that was responsible for assassinations.[29] Allegations of organizational police deviance were thus dismissed before an investigation was lodged and the standard police duty and practice to investigate all allegations before coming to a conclusion was ignored. Police investigations premised on the assumption that there is nothing to investigate can only reach this conclusion. The centrality of police discretion in the decisions regarding whether to investigate, the nature and depth of investigation, and the scope of enquiries is abundantly clear.

In the *mopping-up* operations that take place after an unnatural death, inquest procedures further entrench the penal system of immunity. The inquest of Griffiths Mxenge, held in August 1982, was characterized by poor police work (*Vrye Weekblad*, 24 November 1989). A detective-sergeant and a lieutenant who investigated the case confessed in court that their notebooks had disappeared. Furthermore, the deceased's shirt, for which there was a signed police receipt, also went missing. In finding

---

29. He admitted, however, the existence of Askari units, but pointed out that they were not instructed to commit political murders, but rather to apprehend living suspects (*Rapport*, 3 December 1989).

that Mxenge was murdered by unknown persons, the magistrate commented that the police did try, but that they might have done more had they known that their investigations were to be subjected to cross-examination (*Vrye Weekblad*, 24 November 1989). In response to the complaint by counsel about the poor quality of the police investigation, the magistrate suggested that if counsel wished, he could complain to the Minister of Law and Order (*Vrye Weekblad*, 24 November 1989). In this way the magistrate emphasized ironically, but correctly, an all important aspect of the legal structure of the criminal process, namely, the political responsibility for the police.

Inquest procedure can obscure the nature of investigations even more completely. After the murder of Victoria Mxenge, Griffith's wife, in 1985, the magistrate decided to hold an informal inquest. Although the magistrate was legally entitled to adopt this course of action, it meant that the police had to submit only written statements to the court and could thus avoid scrutiny of their investigation (*Vrye Weekblad*, 24 November 989).

At the level of governmental responsibility, the penal system for immunity receives final imprimatur. When the control of a troublesome group proves to be difficult, political authorities often cede title of that group to the police. Such groups then become *police property* and as long as the police effectively control them without attracting adverse publicity, the police are left to their own devices (Jakubs, 1977; and Lee, 1981). In this context, members of the government have, 'neither the interest nor inclination to seek confirmation of what they suspect or have been "confidentially" told' (Brodeur, 1983: 510).

The more knowledgeable government members are, the more vulnerable and accountable they become. Consequently, 'they immunize themselves from detailed knowledge of police wrongdoing' (Brodeur, 1983: 510). The willingness of political élites to remain conveniently ignorant and to overlook violent shortcuts contributes to police immunity and allows police deviance to flourish (Hughes, 1964; and Jacobs & Britt, 1979).

When the recent allegations of death squads called the South African government to account, the dominant position of the police within the legal structure of criminal investigation remained intact. After the Nofomela affidavit, the Minister of Justice, Mr. Kobie Coetzee, appointed a board of inquiry comprising the Attorney-General of the Orange Free State, Mr. Terence McNally, and Lieutenant-General Conradie of the Central Investigations Division of the SAP. This was hardly an independent or public investigation, but merely an internal board of inquiry headed by a senior police officer and an attorney-general, who by the very nature of his position had worked closely with the police (*Vrye Weekblad*, 24 November 1989). The investigations of this board have been described as 'very poor' (*Vrye Weekblad*, 24 November 1989). For example, the SAP did not take a statement from Captain Coetzee in the three weeks prior to his departure from South Africa. Although the state failed to even locate the third member of the alleged death squad, Tshikalange, a newspaper reporter managed to secure an interview with him (*Vrye Weekblad*, 24 November 1989). The report of the Independent Board of Inquiry into Informal Repression (IBIIR), which provided substantial corroboration for some of Nofomela's allegations and which was presented to the McNally Inquiry, would have been sufficient to compel the government to act positively.

At first the government decided not to appoint a judicial commission of inquiry, which would have secured an investigation by a body independent of the police. Instead, it opted to prosecute three individuals who confessed their complicity in a death squad, namely, Nofomela, Coetzee, and Tshikalange. The Minister of Law and Order, Mr. Adriaan Vlok, gave an assurance that a list had been compiled of the names of people, both on the left and on the right, who had been murdered for political reasons and that these cases were being investigated anew. He concluded that,

> ... [we] want to charge the culprits. They must be brought before the courts to answer and be judged. I have confidence in the courts of this country (Vlok, cited in *The Argus*, 9 December 1989).

The effect of the Minister's approach was to divert attention away from the central issue, a judicial commission of inquiry into the existence of police death squads that target left-wing activists. By introducing the issue of violence against right-wingers, whose identities were not disclosed, he undercut the specificity of the allegations, and by placing the courts in the spotlight, he fudged the central role the police play in any apprehension and prosecution. His confidence in the courts is shared by many, but that is precisely not the issue. On the contrary, it is the confidence in the police, on whom any criminal case depends, that has been shaken profoundly. The prosecution of Nofomela and the warrants for the arrests of Coetzee and Tshikalange involved an abdication of responsibility. Attention was shifted away from organizational structures, including senior police officials, organizational policy, and law, that produce death squads, to a few policemen who have become the 'fall guys' of the system (McBarnet, 1979: 39).

It is submitted that the recent surprise announcement of a judicial inquiry into political murders with Mr. Justice Harms as its sole member is a precursor of the effective abandonment of the political discourse of total onslaught (*The Argus*, 1 February 1990). A few days later, this change of direction was underlined by the unbanning of the ANC, the SACP, and the PAC, in preparation for negotiations with these organizations (*The Argus*, 2 February 1990). The essence of this new discourse is summed up in the following statement by President F. W. de Klerk:

> Our country and all its people have been embroiled in conflict, tension and violent struggle for decades. It is time for us to break out of the cycle of violence and break through to peace and reconciliation (*The Argus*, 3 February 1990).

It is now possible for the state to allow the investigation and exposure of state-sponsored violence, which will serve to emphasize the break with the past and heralds the new South Africa. The terms of reference of the Harms Commission reflect concretely this new political discourse. The objective of this Commission is to,

> … inquire into and report on the alleged murders and other unlawful acts of violence committed in South Africa (including the self-governing territories) to achieve, effect or promote constitutional or political aims in South Africa (*The Argus*, 3 February 1990).

The inquiry is thus not limited to allegations of death squads, but concerns incidents of political violence, including necklace murders (*The Argus*, 1 February 1990). Within the new political discourse, the perniciousness of the past in begetting violence on all sides can thus be exposed. At one and the same time, a justification is provided for the state's new policy.

Conclusion

In analysing organizational police deviance, in particular death squads, the concept of cop culture defined as a set of norms and practices that inform police conduct is a useful analytical construct. However, this concept acquires its full explanatory utility with regard to high policing only when it is broadened to include: (1) the dominant political discourse which motivates and gives direction to action; (2) a methodology which is justifiable in its own terms; (3) a means of managing the inevitable contradiction that arises when those who are meant to uphold the law conduct themselves outside of the law; and (4) an awareness of a user-friendly legal framework within which rules allow conduct that is usually untenable and within which the system blocks effective control of police conduct. These are the elements of a cop culture in South Africa that may have provided the conditions for the existence of death squads. It re-affirms the observation that cop culture 'both reflects and perpetuates the power differences within the social structure it polices' (Reiner, 1985: 87).

This analysis has important implications for the control of organizational police deviance. If the argument, that cop culture plays a determining role in organizational deviance has substance, then attempts at controlling illegal behaviour should be directed at changing the very norms and values that inform policing. Thus, changes in the dominant political discourse, operational methodology, and law would be of particular importance.

The recent abandonment of the discourse of total onslaught will have a profound impact on policing in general. Welcoming the enemy back must undercut the *raison d'être* of death squads. Senior officers will play a critical role in mediating this altered discourse. In January 1990, F. W. de Klerk addressed 500 senior police officers and exhorted them to adjust to and to implement a new depoliticized style of policing (*Die Burger*, 29 January 1990). A police force divorced from the social structure it polices is inconceivable, but making policing less of a political enterprise may be possible. The dilemma the government now faces is that a *rapid* change in discourse will not take place within the force. Total onslaught has become central to cop culture and continues to shape police officers' views of the political aspirations of blacks and, hence, police responses. Instead of death squads sponsored by the state, it is likely that right-wing factions within the police will continue this *work* outside of their office hours.

The demilitarization of the SAP would do much to counter the pervasiveness of military methodology in cop culture. With the cessation of armed conflict between the state and the ANC now dependent on the outcome of negotiations, rather than being a pre-condition for their commencement, the process of demilitarization may still be far off (Mandela, cited in *The Argus*, 26 January 1990). Nevertheless, there has been some movement in this direction. In January 1990 the police announced the withdrawal of Casspirs[30] as patrol vehicles in Soweto in the Transvaal. It should be emphasized again that more than twenty years of militarization will not be rapidly eradicated from cop culture. However, a change in the political discourse may reduce the need to resort to military methods to resolve political issues. Removing the mandate to the police to eliminate the enemy will ease the pressure on the SAP to achieve specific results by illegal means, if

---

30. A tank-like vehicle for riot control.

… the mandate to prevent radical changes in the distribution of power and privilege is incompatible with the idea of a legally or ethically limited effort to do so (Turk, 1981: 118).

Finally, the elements in the legal framework that allow organizational deviance to flourish should be addressed. Legal rules that not only grant the police wide powers, but also give them the assurance, grounded in their experience of the application of such rules, that they are *above* the law, should be abolished. A drastic curtailment of police powers would limit their actions and may remould their perceptions regarding their place in the legal order. A legal system that eschews accountability, both on legal and political levels, must be replaced by one that instils the value of accountability in cop culture.

The central and decisive role that the police play in the investigation and production of evidence in criminal proceedings opens the system to gross manipulation. To counter the successful management of the contradiction that results from organizational deviance, the police monopoly on investigation must be challenged by introducing independent judicial investigation. This is not a novel idea; there is a tradition of judicial commissions having been appointed where police conduct has been at issue, to ensure the independence of investigations. This has again been confirmed by the recent appointment of the Harms Commission of Inquiry. The principle of independent investigation can, and should, be applied on a routine basis in criminal investigations. The office of an independent investigator[31] to investigate inquiries may change the image of the criminal justice system as a set of rules that can be manipulated by those skilled in hypocrisy.

Bibliography

Books and articles

Amaya, A. R., Amaya, M. A., Avilez, C. A., Ramirez, J. & Reyes, M. A. (1987). 'Justice and the Penal system in El Salvador'. *Crime and Social Justice* 30: 1–27.

Boraine, A. (1989). 'The Militarisation of Urban Control: The Security Management System in Mamelodi, 1986–1988'. In *War and Society: The Militarisation of South Africa*. (Eds.) Cock, J. & Nathan, L. Cape Town: David Philip.

Bowden, T. (1978). *Beyond the Limits of the Law.* Harmondsworth: Penguin.

---

31. Such as that of the French Investigating Magistrate.

Brewer, J. D., Guelke, A., Hyme, I., Moxon-Browne, E. & Wilford, R. (1988). *The Police, Public Order and the State*. London: MacMillan.

Brodeur, J. P. (1983). 'High Policing and Low Policing: Remarks about the Policing of Political Activities'. *Social Problems* 30: 507–34.

Brogden, M. (1983). 'The Emergence of the Police: the Colonial Dimension'. *British Journal of Criminology* 27: 4–14.

Brogden, M., Jefferson, T. & Walklate, S. (1988). *Introducing Poliwork*. London: Unwin Hyman.

Dinges, J. (1983). 'The Rise of the Opposition'. *NACLA Report on the Americas* 17: 15–26.

Dippenaar, M. D. (1988). *Die Geskiedenis van die Suid Afrikaanse Polisie.* (*The History of the South African Police 1913–1988*). Silverton: Promedia.

Dugard, J. (1978). *Human Rights and the South African Legal Order*. Princeton: Princeton University Press.

Ericson, R. W. (1981). 'Rules for Police Deviance'. In *Organizational Police Deviance*. (Ed.) Shearing, C. D. Toronto: Butterworths.

Grundy, K. W. (1983). *Soldiers without Politics: Blacks in the South African Armed Forces*. Berkeley: University of California Press.

Grundy, K. W. (1986). *The Militarisation of South African Politics*. Bloomingdale: Indiana University Press.

Hagan, J. & Morden, C. P. (1981). 'The Police Decision to Detain: A Study of Legal Labelling and Police Deviance'. In *Organizational Police Deviance*. (Ed.) Shearing, C. D. Toronto: Butterworths.

Hansson, D. S. (1989). 'Trigger Happy? An Evaluation of Fatal Police Shootings in the Greater Cape Town Area from 1984 to 1986'. *Acta Juridica*: 118–38.

Hope, P. J. (1989). Who are the Terrorists? An Account of Security Police Operations in the Forbes and Yengeni Trials. Unpublished paper. Cape Town: Faculty of Law, University of Cape Town.

Hughes, E. C. (1964). 'Good People and Dirty Work'. In *The Other Side: Perspectives on Deviance*. (Ed.) Becker, H. S. New York: Free Press.

Jacobs, D. & Britt, D. (1979). 'Inequality and Police Use of Deadly Force: An Empirical Assessment of a Conflict Hypothesis'. *Social Problems* 26: 403–12.

Jakubs, D. L. (1977). 'Police Violence in Times of Political Tension: The Case of Brazil 1968–1971'. In *Police and Society*. (Ed.) Bayley, D. H. London: Sage.

Lee, J. A. (1981). 'Substructural Aspects of Police Deviance in Relations with Minority Groups'. In *Organizational Deviance*. (Ed.) Shearing, C. D. Toronto: Butterworths.

Luyt, C. (1989). 'The Killing Fields: South Africa's Human Rights Record in Southern Africa'. *Social Justice* 16: 89–115.

Mathews, A. S. (1985). 'The South African Judiciary and the Security System'. *South African Journal on Human Rights* 1: 199–209.

Mathews, A. S. (1986). *Freedom, State Security and the Rule of Law*. Kenwyn: Juta.

McBarnet, D. J. (1979). 'Arrest: the Legal Context of Policing'. In *The British Police*. (Ed.) Holdaway, S. London: Edward Arnold.

Petras, J. (1987). 'Political Economy of State Terror: Chile, El Salvador and Brazil'. *Crime and Social Justice* 27/8: 88–109.

Reiner, R. (1985). *The Politics of the Police*. Sussex: Wheatsheaf Books.

Sachs, A. (1975). 'The Instruments of Domination in South Africa'. In *Change in Contemporary South Africa*. (Eds.) Thompson, L. & Butler, J. Berkeley: University of California Press.

Shank, G. & Talamente, O. (1987). 'Introduction to Terror in Argentina'. *Crime and Social Justice* 30: 104–8.

Shearing, C. D. (1981a). 'Subterranean Processes in the Maintenance of Power: An Examination of the Mechanisms Coordinating Police Action'. *Canadian Review of Sociology and Anthropology* 18: 283–98.

Shearing, C. D. (1981b). 'Deviance and Conformity in the Reproduction of Order'. In *Organizational Police Deviance*. (Ed.) Shearing, C. D. Toronto: Butterworths.

Steytler, N. C. (1987a). 'Criminal Justice and the Apartheid State'. In *Race and Law*. (Ed.) Rycroft, A. Kenwyn: Juta.

Steytler, N. C. (1987b). State Terrorism and the Limits of the Criminal Sanction. Unpublished paper. Durban: Society of University Teachers of Law.

Swilling, M. & Phillips, M. (1989). 'State Power in the 1980s: From "Total Strategy" to "Counter-revolutionary Warfare"'. In *War and Society: the*

Militarisation of South Africa. (Eds.) Cock, J. & Nathan, L. Cape Town: David Philip.

The Argentinean Commission (1986). *Nunca Mas: The Report of the Argentinean Commission into the Disappeared*. New York: Farrar, Straus & Giroux.

The Independent Board of Inquiry into Informal Repression (IBIIR) (1989a). 'Allegations of the Existence of a Death Squad within the South African Police'. *IBIIR Report*.

The Independent Board of Inquiry into Informal Repression (IBIIR) (1989b). 'A Preliminary Investigation into Attacks against Community Leaders and Organisations from 20 May 1985 to mid-September 1989'. *IBIIR Memorandum*.

Turk, A. T. (1981). 'Organizational Deviance and Political Policing'. In *Organizational Police Deviance*. (Ed.) Shearing, C. D. Toronto: Butterworths.

Van der Spuy, E. (1988). Policing the Eighties: Servamus et Servimus? Unpublished paper. Durban: The Association of Sociologists of Southern Africa (ASSA).

Weitzer, R. (1985). 'Policing a Divided Society: Obstacles to Normalization in Northern Ireland'. *Social Problems* 33: 41–55.

Newspaper articles and television programmes

Die Burger (6 December 1989).

Die Burger (29 January 1990).

Rapport (3 December 1989).

SABC (The South African Broadcasting Company). Television News. (26 February 1990).

Servamus (November 1981).

The Argus (20 November 1989).

The Argus (9 December 1989).

The Argus (26 January 1990).

The Argus (1 February 1990).

The Argus (2 February 1990).

The Argus (3 February 1990).

The Weekly Mail (5 May 1989).

The Weekly Mail (17 November 1989).

The Weekly Mail (24 November 1989).

Vrye Weekblad (17 November 1989).

Vrye Weekblad (24 November 1989).

Vrye Weekblad (8 December 1989).

Legal cases and conventions

End Conscription Campaign v Minister of Defence 1989 (2) SA 80 (CPD).

S v Forbes & Others 1987 FS 621/88 unrep. (CPD).

S v Sparg 1986 unrep. 166 (WLD).

S v Yengeni & Another 1989 FS 1/89 unrep. (CPD).

The Geneva Convention of 1949.

CHAPTER SIX

Capital punishment and the politics of the doctrine of common purpose

Dennis Davis

Introduction

Despite international protest against the use of the death penalty in South Africa during the late seventies and early eighties, South Africans themselves remained relatively disinterested in the issue of capital punishment, until the case of the Sharpeville Six in 1987 (*S v Safatsa & Five Others*, 1988). This case was significant for a number of reasons, among these was the fact that it was the *first political* trial in which the doctrine of *common purpose* was applied. The essence of this doctrine has been described as follows:

> [Where] two or more people associate in a joint unlawful enterprise, each will be responsible for acts of his fellows which fall within their common design or object (Snyman, 1989: 258).

In other words, a person may be convicted of an offence as serious as murder, merely by virtue of the fact that that person *actively associated* with those who actually killed. The focus of this chapter is on the way in which the doctrine of common purpose has been used by the South African state.

Setting the scene

It was the execution of Solomon Mahlangu, an African National Congress (ANC) guerrilla who was convicted of murder in 1978, that drew *international* attention to the South African system of capital punishment in *political* cases (The South African Institute for Race Relations (SAIRR), 1986). A number of international leaders, including President Carter of the United States of America, appealed to the South African government to exercise clemency in this case. Mahlangu, however, was executed. Then, in 1985, the attention of the world was focused on the case of Benjamin Moloise (SAIRR, 1985). Moloise was sentenced to death in 1983 for the murder of a Mamelodi security policeman, Phillipus Sepe. A 28-month legal battle ensued. Appeals for clemency were made by the British government, the European Economic Community (EEC), and the Secretary General of the United Nations, Mr. Pérez de Cuellar. Nevertheless, Moloise was hanged and the refusal to accede to pleas for clemency was justified as follows:

> Moloise was convicted of the common law crime of murder for which the supreme penalty is imposed if no extenuating circumstances are found (Van der Merwe, cited in *The Cape Times*, 18 October 1985).

At this time in South Africa, more crimes had been made punishable by death[1] and capital punishment was being imposed more frequently than ever before (Currin, 1989). There were, however, no organizations actively campaigning against the death penalty. The Society for the Abolition of the Death Penalty (SADP), an organization which had been extremely active during the sixties and early seventies, had all but disbanded by the early eighties. This was indicative of the general climate of apathy regarding the death penalty that permeated South African society at this stage.

The political conflict, known as the *unrest*, began in 1984 and gave rise to a new category of condemned prisoners, namely, those convicted of *unrest-related* murders in which the victims were police officers, community councillors, and alleged informers. In 1986, the South African Youth Congress (SAYCO) led a campaign to save the lives of the thirty-two people who had been sentenced to death for their involvement in killings that had occurred during the 1984 protests against rent increases, in the Vaal Triangle area. Significantly, the campaign also incorporated the demand that all people captured after taking up arms against the South African government be given prisoner-of-war (POW)

---

1. Section 277 of the Criminal Procedure Act 51 of 1977 lists the offences for which the sentence of death is a competent sentence. These include not only murder but also treason, kidnapping, child stealing, rape, and robbery or housebreaking if the court finds aggravating circumstances to be present. Other legislation such as the Internal Security Act 74 of 1982 also allows for the imposition of the death penalty.

status in terms of Protocol 1 of the 1949 Geneva Convention. This Protocol extends the protection applicable to POWs to,

> … armed conflicts in which peoples are fighting against colonial domination and alien occupation and against racist regimes in the exercise of their right of self-determination (cited in SAIRR, 1988: 552).

So began the *Save the Patriots Campaign.*

The early eighties also saw an escalation in ANC-guerrilla activity. Between 1979 and 1986, eight ANC guerrillas were executed. Apart from Mahlangu and Moloise, Thelle Mogoerane, Jerry Mosoloti, and Marcus Motaung were hanged in June 1983 for killing four police officers during a number of attacks on police stations in Pretoria and Soweto (SAIRR, 1986). Zondo was executed after being convicted of planting a limpet mine in an Amanzimtoti[2] shopping centre (SAIRR, 1986). Clarence Payi and Sipho Xulu were hanged for the murder of Benjamin Langa (SAIRR, 1986). Such cases heightened interest in the use of capital punishment, particularly in political trials. The *political* nature of these capital cases is well illustrated in the trial of Robert McBride (*S v McBride*, 1988). He was sentenced to death in 1987 for the bombing of a bar in which three women were killed. During cross-examination. David Gordon SC, the leader of the defence team, maintained that the ANC perceived the South African Government as a violent body as it begot violence. The following exchange then took place between Brigadier Stadler, of the Security Branch of the South African Police (SAP), and Gordon:

> *Stadler:* That is absurd. The State does not initiate violence, but reacts to violence. If people throw petrol bombs the police must act. The police do not act to terrorize, but try to protect people.
> *Gordon:* Some of the people described by the Government as terrorists see themselves involved in a war.
> *Stadler:* The ANC constantly tries to move away from the perception as a terrorist organization. The ANC does so because it relies on outside help.
> *Gordon:* Many authorities from Cabinet level down describe people fighting what they perceive as an unjust society, as soldiers of freedom fighters striving for a just society.
> *Stadler:* A person who uses violence to terrorize, and that is the aim of the ANC, is a terrorist.
> *Gordon:* If that is your definition of a terrorist, then many in the townships may regard the Defence Force and police as terrorists.
> *Stadler:* No. Although the ANC has a military capability it launches cowardly attacks with weapons on innocents (*The Sowetan*, 4 February 1987).

It took until 1987 for a *sustained* campaign against the death penalty to be mounted. This was also the year in which a *record* number of

---

2. A suburb on the South Coast of Natal.

164 people went to the gallows (Milton, 1989: 135). Consider the United States as a comparison. In 1987 it had a population more than ten times that of South Africa, yet only twenty-five people were executed (Currin, 1989).

It was the use of the doctrine of common purpose in a number of unrest-related murder trials, however, that brought the issue of capital punishment to the front pages of newspapers. Here the *political* nature of the use of capital punishment in South Africa was highlighted. A controversy began with the case of the Sharpeville Six, in which a woman and five men were sentenced to death for the murder of the Deputy Mayor of Lekoa (*S v Safatsa & Five Others*, 1988). When the Appellate Division dismissed an appeal for clemency in this case, the anti-apartheid movement launched an international campaign to save the Sharpeville Six. Domestically and internationally this campaign focused attention, as *never before*, on the system of capital punishment in South Africa. In response, the South African government maintained that it could not concede to politically-motivated requests to commute the death sentences of the six people, as this would undermine the country's legal system (SAIRR, 1988: 553). Ironically, however, it was the *legal outcome* of the case that had this effect. An eminent, English barrister, Louis Blom-Cooper QC, commented:

> Why the judges involved in the case of the Sharpeville-Six did not use the power (to find extenuating circumstances) seems inexplicable. Granted even the instinctive judicial restraint in trespassing upon the Executive's prerogative of mercy, the failure to find extenuating circumstances lends credence to the claim that the judgement on the Sharpeville-Six is a charade, designed to serve the purposes of the state through intimidation (*The Pretoria News*, 17 March 1988).

It is noteworthy that the publication of this article culminated in the successful prosecution of the *Pretoria News* for contempt of court. Criticism was also levelled by South African lawyers. For example, the judgment of the Appellate Division was described by Edwin Cameron of the Centre for Applied Legal Studies[3], as 'an unwarranted extension of the doctrine of common purpose' (*The Sunday Times*, 21 February 1988). Subsequently Cameron suggested that it represented '[a] widening of the doctrine of criminal liability in response to evidence of township revolt' (Cameron, cited in *The Times* (London), 9 June 1988).

Acting Chief Justice Rabie responded angrily to these criticisms. In particular he referred to an editorial in which it had been suggested that the dismissal of the application to appeal had been a result of disgraceful

---

3. At the University of Witwatersrand.

chicanery and that the judiciary 'had created a doctrine which established the death penalty for merely being present at a riot where death occurs' (*The Times* (London), 9 June 1988). The Acting Chief Justice described this claim as follows:

> This is of course a shocking and disgraceful statement and anyone who knows anything of our judicial system will reject these remarks about it with scorn (Rabie, cited in *The Times* (London), 9 June 1988).

The doctrine of common purpose before 1988

Within a year the common purpose doctrine had become, arguably, the legal concept best known to the South African public. If the sudden application of the doctrine of common purpose in political trials was in fact a response by the state to civil unrest, then the implications for a criminal justice system operating within a divided society are serious. It is to this issue that the discussion is now turned.

Common purpose is a doctrine that originated in English case law. In the English case of *R v Maclin, Murphy & Others* (1838), the court defined the doctrine as follows:

> It is a principle of law, that if several persons act together in pursuance of a common intent every act done in furtherance of such intent by each of them is, in law, done by all (cited in Rabie, 1971: 229).

The doctrine was introduced into South African law via the Native Territories Penal Code G24 of 1886. Section 78 of this Code provided that:

> … if several persons form a common intention to prosecute any unlawful purpose, and to assist each other therein, each of them is a party to every offence committed by any one of them in the prosecution of such common purpose, the commission of which offence was, or ought to have been, known to be a probable consequence of the prosecution of such common purpose (cited in Rabie, 1971: 229).

Subsequently, the Appellate Division considered the matter of common purpose in the civil case of *McKenzie v Van der Merwe* (1917). From the evidence in this case it appeared that the defendant was the Assistant Commandant of a commando of rebels who operated in the Orange Free State under the command of General De Wet during the 1914 Rebellion. The plaintiff claimed that certain stock had been removed from his farm and that his wire fence had been damaged by rebels. There was, however, no evidence showing that the defendant had been associated with these acts in any way, or that the acts had been committed by the men in his commando. What became apparent, was that one of the defendant's veld-cornets had lent a cart to two rebels from another commando, although he had known that it was to be used to carry off sheep that belonged to the plaintiff. After losing his case, the plaintiff appealed to the Appellate Division using the argument that:

> ... every person who joins in rebellion is party to a common unlawful purpose; the taking of stock and the cutting of wire are incidents which must be taken as likely to happen during the execution of that purpose; and therefore every rebel is liable for all acts of that kind committed by other rebels in prosecution of the rebellion (*McKenzie v Van der Merwe*, 1917).

Chief Justice Innes dismissed this argument on the following grounds:

> Now that rule has not been deduced from general principles, but rests upon certain old decisions. The terms in which it is expressed and the limitations to which it is subject would seem to indicate that the principle which underlies it is that of agency. However that may be, its place in our law must be that of an application of the doctrine of implied mandate. There is none other upon which it can be grounded; and its operation in our practice must be confined within the limits of that doctrine. Indeed a reference to the old English decisions shows that there were cases in which the person convicted was present, in pursuance of the common purpose, at the commission of the crime charged. Under such circumstances the inference of authority to do the deed would probably not be a strained one (*McKenzie v Van der Merwe*, 1917).

Thus, although the doctrine of common purpose became part of South African law over seventy years ago, at first it was defined *narrowly*. The Appellate Division did, however, extend the initial definition, prior to the case of the Sharpeville Six. In 1982 Judges Hoexter and Botha held that in cases of common purpose to murder, association in the common design renders the act of the perpetrator the act of all the participants. Furthermore, the act of each participant need not contribute *causally* to the death of the victim (*S v Khoza*, 1982). The position on common purpose at this time was set out in a leading textbook on criminal law as follows:

> Proof, whether by evidence of words or conduct, of agreement to participate in the criminal design, added to proof of participation, and directly or by necessary implication of contemplation of (possible) consequences, irrespective of the particular means by which they were attained (coupled with recklessness as to whether those consequences occur or not), provides the proper test in law of the liability of parties to a common purpose (Burchell & Hunt, 1983: 434–5).

It should be noted that at this stage the courts had dealt with very few cases of the kind they were to confront during the mid-eighties in township murder trials. In his judgment in the case of the Sharpeville Six, Mr. Justice Botha referred to only two cases which he suggested were similar to the facts of the case at hand. The first of these was the case of *R v Mgxwiti* in 1954, in which eight persons were accused of murder. According to the evidence, a large group of people, including Mgxwiti, assaulted the victim in her motor car. Stones were thrown at her and she was beaten with a stick. Mgxwiti's contribution consisted of assaulting the victim with a knife through the open window or door of the car. Eventually the car, with the victim inside, was set alight. The district surgeon reported the cause of death to have been extensive burns. He added, however, that the deceased's remains had been reduced to a charred mass by incineration, making it impossible to ascertain whether she had already been fatally wounded *before* the car had been set alight. The majority of the court agreed that Mgxwiti had been seen walking in the direction of the victim's car with a knife in his hand, before the victim was fatally wounded. Mgxwiti's appeal was rejected and his conviction for murder was confirmed.

The second case to which Mr. Justice Botha referred was *R v Dladla & Others* (1962), in which a crowd was found to have chased two police officers out of a township by having stoned one of them, whom they had then pursued and killed. The accused had been in the vanguard of this crowd. He had then joined another crowd which had chased and killed the second police officer. In convicting the accused of murder, the court found that he had been in the vanguard of the party that had chased the first police officer, so he must have seen the ferocity of the killing, the deceased having suffered more than fifty injuries. From this observation, the accused must have realized the crowd's murderous intent against the police. Furthermore, the accused had also been in the crowd that had chased the second police officer, and he must have known that the specific purpose of the crowd had been to kill this officer. Additionally, the accused had been in the party that had besieged the second police officer when he had tried to hide in a cottage and the accused had been in the party that had attacked and killed the second officer when he had run from this cottage. The accused had been armed with two sticks and had given no explanation to the effect that his role was merely that of an observer.

Although both of these cases concern group violence in which the accused were not charged with administering the fatal blow to the victim, the evidence shows a *considerable measure of participation* by the accused in the events that led up to the death of the victims. These two cases *differ* from the case of the Sharpeville Six. In neither case was the court required to decide upon the guilt of *part* of a large crowd in which *collective anger* had set events in motion that had led to the death of a victim. Until the case of *S v Safatsa & Five Others* (1988), the vast majority of cases that had involved common purpose had concerned two types of situations. The first had been that in which the accused had been part of a group that had set out to commit a robbery, the commission of which had ended in the death of the victim (e.g. *S v Malinga & Others*, 1963; *S v Nkomo*, 1966; and *S v Nkumbani*, 1964). The second had been that in which the accused had participated actively in an attack, made by another member of the group, which had resulted in the death of the victim (e.g. *S v Khoza*, 1982; and *S v Thomo & Others*, 1969).

The common purpose doctrine had thus been recognized in South African law for many years before the case of the Sharpeville Six. The Appellate Division had applied the doctrine in cases of crowd violence (e.g. *R v Dladla & Others*, 1962), and the accused had been found guilty of murder by reason of common purpose with a group, despite the absence of proof of causal connection between the accused's conduct and the death of the deceased (e.g. *S v Khoza*, 1982; and *S v Nkwenza & Another*, 1985). Thus, if Cameron's (*The Times* (London), 9 June 1988) submission was that the judgment in the case of the Sharpeville Six widened the scope of criminal liability in response to the unrest in the townships, then he was *incorrect*. However, if his claim was merely that the doctrine had *never* been employed in cases of township violence of the kind experienced during the mid-eighties, then he was *correct*. For this reason, Cameron's proposition needs to be *clarified*, rather than *rejected*. Arguments like the following, however, completely ignore the differences between the factual context of cases in which the doctrine was applied previously and those characterizing subsequent cases of township violence.

> It would be wholly inaccurate to suggest (as was done in certain newspaper reports) that the case widens the ambit of criminal liability ... for it cannot be said that the case heralds new developments in the law of common purpose (Matzukis, 1988: 227).

The doctrine of common purpose after 1988

The case of the Sharpeville Six

Having examined the nature of the common purpose doctrine, it is now possible to explore the effect of its application in cases of township violence during the eighties. The case of *S v Safatsa & Five Others* (1988) rapidly became the leading case of the application of common purpose to township violence. Briefly the facts were as follows: On 3 September 1984, the Deputy Mayor of the Town Council of Lekoa was murdered outside his home. The accused were part of a crowd of about 100 people that attacked the victim's home with stones and petrol bombs, setting it on fire. The victim fled the house, armed with a pistol, but before he was able to reach his neighbour's house, he was disarmed by members of the crowd, stoned, assaulted, and then dragged into the street, where he was doused with petrol and set alight. Each of the accused had acted against the victim and in the context of the actions taken against him by other members of the crowd. The first and third accused had wrestled with the victim for possession of his pistol and the third had succeeded in gaining possession. The eighth accused had constructed and distributed petrol bombs with instructions to use such bombs on the victim's house. Others among the accused had played minor roles. The fourth accused had exhorted the crowd to kill the victim and had slapped the face of a woman who remonstrated with the crowd not to burn him. The second accused had thrown stones at the deceased and his house.

It was assumed, in favour of the accused, that there was *no* proven causal link between the actions of the accused and the death of the deceased. The court found, however, that there was *no need* for the state to prove the existence of a causal connection between the actions of the accused and the death of the victim. Mr. Justice Botha analysed the previous cases which had involved common purpose and held that to find in favour of the accused on the question of the requirement of causation would constitute a drastic departure from a firmly established practice. The court thus appeared to consider this case to be an *ordinary* criminal case in which the doctrine of common purpose was applicable. In confirming the conviction Mr. Justice Botha held:

> ... there can be no doubt, in my judgment, that the individual acts of each of the six accused convicted of murder manifested an active association with the acts of the mob which caused the death of the deceased. These accused shared a common purpose with the crowd to kill the deceased and each of them had the requite *dolus* in respect of his death. Consequently the acts of the mob which caused the deceased's death must be imputed to each of these accused (*S v Safatsa & Five Others*, 1988: 901).

One searches the judgment in vain for some recognition that the case involved a crowd of 100 angry people who had surrounded the home of the victim, in a context of *extreme political turbulence*. Indeed, in finding no extenuating circumstances, Mr. Justice Human employed similar language to that used by the judge in *S v Maarman & Others*

(1981) to describe the attitude of a gang that had used violence, murder, and robbery to terrorize the inhabitants of a township. Mr. Justice Human said:

> The spirit of the crowd including the accused was one of violence, of disregard for the peaceful existence in which people can expect to live in mutual protection, of disregard for the law and the personal rights of other individuals. It surely cannot be an extenuating circumstance that people who have political or social grievances may air those grievances by sowing death and destruction. They assaulted the deceased an elected member of the Lekoa town council, who had been linked with the increased service charges and killed him in a gruesome, medieval and barbaric manner. Such actions cannot be tolerated in a modern state[4] (*S v Safatsa & Five Others*, 1988: 1495).

The Appellate Divisions' *only* recognition of possible differences between *common law thieves* and *township dwellers* caught up in major political turmoil is to be found in a reference to the criticism of the cases of *R v Mgxwiti*, (1954) and *R v Dladla & Others* (1962),

> … on the basis that it would be arguable whether, as a matter of fact, the evidence showed an active association by the accused with the acts of the mob which caused the death of the deceased (S v Safatsa & Five Others, 1988: 901H).

It is noteworthy, however, that the evidence of the accused's association was in fact stronger in these earlier cases than in the case of S v Safatsa & Five Others (1988), in which different members of the crowd might well have had differing versions of, or commitments to, the eventual result. Mr. Justice Botha's failure to consider the particular facts of the Safatsa case and to evaluate the trial court's treatment of the crime as similar to that of a robbery committed by a group has been the subject of trenchant criticism. It has been argued, correctly, that the concept of a mob has no significance for criminal law. A crowd of people can share a purpose, but this is dependent upon the exercise of the individual wills of each member of that crowd. Criminal law accepts the notion of individual will. Collective action is only relevant if derived from a conscious, individual decision and criminal consequences cannot be based on passive attribution from a constructed, collective will (Unterhalter, 1988).

In the Dladla and Mgxwiti cases, the crime was of such a nature that the accused clearly consented to be bound by the collective will, whereas in the case of Safatsa the evidence was far more equivocal. By deriving the existence of an individual *mens rea* from the collective will, the Safatsa judgment provided little reason as to why the entire crowd

---

4. Editors' translation of Afrikaans original. Quote from trial court record.

of 100, if identified, should not have been convicted of murder. It appears as if this criticism of the judgment in the Safatsa case caused the Appellate Division to reconsider. Some ten months later, in the case of *S v Mgedezi & Six Others* (1989), the same judge who had handed down the Safatsa judgment took the opportunity of qualifying the principles he had laid down in the Safatsa case. Mr. Justice Botha noted the trial judge's observation that a mere spectator in a crowd cannot be held liable for the violence of the crowd and commented that:

> … no one has ever suggested the contrary. (I ignore the misguided comments of hysterical politicians masquerading as lawyers, following upon the judgment delivered in the case reported as *S v Safatsa & Five Others*) (*S v Mgedezi & Six Others*, 1989: 702I).

In allowing the appeal, however, the judge held that:

> The trial court was obliged to consider, in relation to each individual accused whose evidence could properly be rejected as false, the facts found proved by the State evidence against that accused, in order to assess whether there was a sufficient basis for holding that accused liable on the ground of active participation in the achievement of a common purpose. The trial Court's failure to undertake this task again constituted a serious misdirection (*S v Mgedezi & Six Others*, 1989: 703J–4A).

The case of the Upington 26

Unfortunately, the last-mentioned attempt by the Appellate Division to narrow the scope of the doctrine amounted to shutting the conceptual stable door after the proverbial horse had bolted! The uncritical application of a legal concept in a novel context was to have horrendous results in the case of the Upington 26 (*S v Khumalo & 25 Others*, 1989).[5]

In convicting twenty-five of the twenty-six accused of murder, Mr. Justice Basson found that:

> The persons who participated in the attack rendered assistance to kill the deceased and they actively associated themselves with the group to bring about the deceased's demise. The first thing which had to be done, was to get the deceased out of the house so that he could be killed. They thus made a contribution to the attainment of this common purpose. The state did not prove that all the accused who attacked the house also participated in the actual killing of the deceased but this is also not necessary. With crowd conduct of this type everybody cannot be at the same place at the same time. The conduct of the person who flees may also determine which members of the group he first makes contact with. If those members kill him, it is to a large extent merely coincidental, as if he had fled in another

---

5. See Chapter 8 for the facts of this case.

direction another person would have killed him. The same could also occur with the pursuit. Those who are nearest to the person in flight, have a better chance of catching him than those who are far away from him. A fit person who runs fast may catch up with him quicker than an unfit weighty person. Similarly the chances of a woman with high heels arriving first at the fleeing person are also slight. It does not really matter which of the crowd killed the deceased. The crowd had the common purpose and each person who made an active contribution to the attainment of the purpose is responsible for his death[6] (*S v Khumalo & 25 Others*, 1989).

In this case, other members of the crowd should consider themselves extremely fortunate that they were not identified and charged together with the twenty-six accused, for here the implications of the Safatsa judgment were taken to their logical, but terrifying conclusion. *All* members of the crowd were found to have had the necessary *mens rea*, owing to the clear collective intention of the *mob*. This is a criminal law concept, designed to cater for the situation where X, Y, and Z associate in a joint unlawful enterprise, so that X and Y are responsible for any crime committed by Z which falls within their common enterprise (Burchell & Hunt, 1983). In this case, however, it was used with little consideration for the different context, namely, township violence caused by a range of social and political factors.

The response of the defence to common purpose: De-individuation as an extenuating circumstance[7]

Defence lawyers have used novel arguments to show extenuating circumstances in response to the state's use of common purpose. If common purpose has been the criminal law's potion to control resistance in the townships, de-individuation has become its antidote. Once the common purpose doctrine introduced the notion of the collective will, defence lawyers began to argue that in crowd situations, individuals become de-individuated and manifest behaviour that is emotional, impulsive, and irrational. Mechanisms that usually regulate social behaviour are weakened and individuals may act violently, without realizing the consequences of their behaviour. This, the defence has claimed, is what happens to the accused in cases of collective violence.

---

6. Author's translation from Afrikaans.
7. This topic is discussed in further detail in the next chapter.

In the Safatsa case this argument failed because evidence was not led to show that any of the accused had undergone the process of de-individuation that was described by the expert witness (*S v Safatsa & Five Others*, 1988). De-individuation was accepted as an extenuating circumstance in the case of *S v Thabetha & Others* (1988). In this regard Mr. Justice Human said the following:

> This process produces behaviour analogous to the behaviour of persons who are hypnotized or under the influence of alcohol. The de-individuated state is one which, depending upon the intensity of the de-individuating process, can prevent people foreseeing the consequences of their actions and from making rational and moral decisions about their actions. If a person loses awareness of the self and all his attention is focused on the environment, he becomes de-individuated. This state hampers a person's ability to self-regulate his behaviour and he becomes more responsive to environmental cues for behavioural direction rather than looking to internal standards of appropriate conduct (*S v Thabetha & Others*, 1988: 280).

The defence opposed the claim that an individual's intention could be derived from that of a crowd, by arguing that the actions of a crowd in a case of collective violence was analogous to that of a group of intoxicated or hypnotized people. This approach to crowd behaviour is part of a *conservative* political discourse in which crowd behaviour is explained in terms of irrational forces that drive such a crowd to commit violent and unnatural actions. This school of thought presents crowd behaviour as a form of *mob psychosis* and ignores the *social context* of, and the *political motivation* behind, such collective action. This theory of de-individuation thus offers a decontextualized, anti-historical construction of what is fundamentally a political event (Du Toit & Mangani, 1990). The politically decontextualized nature of the concept of de-individuation, in which emphasis is placed on the irrationality of acts, is well illustrated in the evidence of Andrew Coleman, a social psychologist whose expert testimony was accepted by the court in *S v Gwebe & Others*, (1989):

> Now it is difficult to imagine how you could create a social event which is more de-individuating than that particular afternoon. You had a very large crowd, a very emotional issue. Probably many of them were sleep-deprived. They were toi-toiing[8], and they were singing and they were chanting, and everything points to a kind of activity and behaviour that, if anything, is going to be de-individuating. I think that it is as de-individuating as it could possibly be. Now all of these social forces, or each of these social forces on its own, as I say, is powerful and can lead people

8. A political dance.

to behave in ways which are not characteristic of their normal behaviour. Taken together in these highly unusual circumstances, they all happened through some horrible combination of circumstances to come together. To have them come together like that I would have thought as a social psychologist is a recipe for trouble (*S v Gwebe & Others*, 1989: 409).

In the Gwebe case, the evidence on de-individuation was accepted and Mr. Justice Jansen held that all the accused were in such a state of de-individuation that they were inclined to do things that they would not normally have done. The Upington 26 were less fortunate, however. The court took account of the political motivation of the crowd, but used this finding to justify its rejection of the argument in favour of extenuation. The court thus presented crowd action as irrational, violent, and unnatural *political* activity.

Unrest, political discourse, and common purpose

The similarity between the court's approach to the events in the Upington 26 case and the dominant political discourse regarding the unrest of the mid-eighties is particularly revealing. The unrest, which began on 3 September 1984 in the Vaal Triangle and which quickly spread throughout South Africa, represented an unprecedented challenge to the apartheid state. The most crude measure of this opposition, namely casualties, shows that South Africa had never before experienced such dimensions of resistance to official authority. Between September 1984 and December 1987, 2 987 deaths related to political conflict were reported, compared to 575 deaths during the previous wave of resistance in 1976. Furthermore, some 45 000 people were detained during this period, compared with 2 500 during 1976 (Du Toit & Mangani, 1990). Thousands more were shot, teargassed, whipped, and tortured.

From the commencement of this political conflict, state discourse presented political violence in terms of the familiar white fear of the *uncontrolled, irrational black mob* constituting a threat to the *civilized* standards which the government was striving to maintain (Posel, 1989). A few examples drawn from the state-run media are illustrative. Television news of the police shootings at Langa in Uitenhage on Sharpeville Day 1985 explained that: 'an unruly mob numbering several thousand ... some armed with petrol bombs and others with weapons, encircled a small group of policemen' (The South African Broadcasting Company (SABC), 21 March 1985). The very existence of a crowd was considered sufficient explanation for the Uitenhage tragedy. No reference was made to the fact that the crowd was proceeding *peacefully* to a funeral and that violence only began *after* police killed a young boy, who raised his fist in a salute whilst cycling past the procession (Posel, 1989). A background report of the unrest was presented as part of a television interview concerning *unrest trends*, with Kobus Neethling of the Department of Information. This contained what has become standard footage, namely, shots of flaming tyres, burning shacks and vehicles, crowds throwing stones, and petrol bombs exploding (SABC, 3 February 1987). Television viewers have been consistently informed of *waves of arson attacks* (SABC, 24 April 1985) and the *latest spurt of violence* (SABC, 9 May 1985). It is the so-called *unrest reports* of the Bureau for Information that provide no context other than *gratuitous mob violence*, often described as being orchestrated by the South African Communist Party (SACP)/ANC alliance. For example:

> The low unrest figure, a tendency which developed during the second half of 1986, continued during the first two months of this year ... This low level of unrest remains very encouraging and it is of cardinal importance that this tendency should continue its downward trend if a meaningful situation of normality is to be attained (*The Citizen*, 12 March 1987).

Crowd, mob, stonethrowers, and *unrest* became the key words in state discourse on violence, each word seemingly possessing an autonomous, decontextualized existence of its own (Posel, 1989). Political trials involving common purpose, such as those of the Sharpeville Six and the Upington 26, should be analysed within this discourse. Whilst the courts did not *invent* the doctrine of common purpose for the purposes of unrest cases, they applied the concept without any reference to history or to the context of the facts which they were required to examine. A sociologist, influenced by the work of Moore (1978), would understand the events that occurred in Upington or in Sharpeville very differently. South Africa of the mid-eighties was a country in turmoil and revolt. Such a sociologist would recognize that these conditions contributed to a changed perception of authority which had a profound social and psychological impact on the hitherto suppressed population. After years of passivity and reluctant acceptance of the prevailing social order, the masses of South Africa finally perceived and defined their situation, as had other suppressed people before them, 'as the consequence of human injustice: a situation that they need not, cannot and ought not endure' (Moore, 1978: 459). With this deep sense of social injustice fueling an unprecedented level of moral outrage, the moral authority of the state collapsed and resistance to the state increased. In many instances this sense of moral outrage culminated in tragic acts of violence, defiance, and rage.

Lawyers, however, do not operate with copies of the work of Moore on their desks or in the courtrooms. Facts are analysed purely in terms of their fit with established legal concepts. Hence, in political cases involving common purpose, the South African courts have performed as could be expected of judicial institutions. Not only did the cases of the Upington 26 and the Sharpeville Six reflect the decontextualized character of judicial procedure, the use of the doctrine of common purpose to criminalize township unrest reinforced state discourse which cast popular resistance as *irrational and senseless violence by unruly black mobs*. Once charged, the accused were confronted with a state that occupied the ideological high-ground. To develop a case for extenuation by emphasizing the *political* nature of crowd violence would have, in all probability, proved counter-productive. To have based legal debate on the history of a township and the meaning of a crowd's behaviour would have, undoubtedly, made such trials explicably political. In turn, the lawyer's task of persuading a conservative, white judge would have been made even more problematic (Du Toit & Mangani, 1990).

Conclusion

During the past decade, criminology has developed a far more sophisticated understanding of crime and punishment (Garland & Young, 1983). The conviction of township residents from Lekoa and Paballelo, their depiction as murderers, and the consequent imposition of the death penalty show that the entire criminal justice system is an institution through which political, ideological, economic, and legal relations operate and in which their impacts are materially inscribed (Garland & Young, 1983).

Despite the fact that the state occupied the ideological high-ground initially, cases involving common purpose have become sites of political struggle for the anti-apartheid movement, often more outside than inside the courtroom. For this reason, more than any other, the death penalty has become an important political issue in a country which, in earlier years, managed to execute hundreds of its citizens without much opposition. It is likely that this politicization of capital punishment will herald the eventual demise of the death penalty as a major penal instrument in apartheid South Africa. The State President's recent announcement of changes to the law relating to the death penalty (*The

Cape Times, 2 February 1990) represents, at least to some extent, a response to this process. At the time of writing it would appear that extenuation is to be replaced by the doctrine of aggravation, so that the death penalty cannot be imposed by a court unless that state discharges the onus of proving the existence of aggravating circumstances. Doubtless this change will reduce the number of death sentences, which will make it easier to campaign for the *complete* abolition of the death penalty.

Bibliography

Books and articles

Burchell, E. M. & Hunt, P. M. A. (1983). *South African Criminal Law and Procedure* (Vol. I). Cape Town: Juta.

Currin, B. (1989). The Application of Capital Punishment in South Africa. Unpublished paper. Cape Town.

Du Toit, A. & Mangani, C. (1990). *The Time of the Comrades*. London: MacMillan.

Garland, D. & Young, P. (1983). *The Power to Punish: Contemporary Penalty and Social Analysis*. London: Heineman.

Matzukis, N. A. (1988). 'The Nature and Scope of Common Purpose'. *South African Journal of Criminal Justice* 1: 226–34.

Milton, J. (1989). 'Editorial Comment'. *South African Journal of Criminal Justice* 2: 135–6.

Moore, B. (1978). *Injustice: The Social Bases of Obedience and Revolt*. London: MacMillan.

Posel, D. (1989). 'A "Battlefield of Perceptions": State Discourses on Political Violence'. In *War and Society: The Militarisation of South Africa*. (Eds.) Cock, J. & Nathan, L. Cape Town: David Philip.

Rabie, M. A. (1971). 'The Doctrine of Common Purpose in Criminal Law'. *South African Law Journal* 88: 227–45.

SAIRR (South African Institute for Race Relations). (1985). *Survey of Race Relations*. Johannesburg: SAIRR.

SAIRR. (1986). *Survey of Race Relations*. Johannesburg: SAIRR.

SAIRR. (1988). *Survey of Race Relations*. Johannesburg: SAIRR.

Snyman, C. R. (1989). *Criminal Law*. Durban: Butterworths.

Unterhalter, D. (1988). 'The Doctrine of Common Purpose: What Makes One Person Liable for the Acts of Another?' *South African Law Journal* 105: 671–8.

Newspaper articles and television broadcasts

Cameron, E. (1988). Interview in *The Times* (London) (9 June 1988.)

SABC (The South African Broadcasting Company). Television News (21 March 1985).

SABC. Television Interview (24 April 1985).

SABC. Television News (9 May 1985).

SABC. Television Interview (3 February 1987).

The Cape Times (18 October 1985).

The Cape Times (2 February 1990).

The Citizen (12 March 1987).

The Sowetan (4 February 1987).

The Pretoria News (17 March 1988).

The Sunday Times (21 February 1988).

The Times (London) (9 June 1988).

Acts, codes, and conventions

The Internal Security Act 74 of 1982.

The Geneva Convention of 1949.

The Native Territories Penal Code G24 of 1886

Legal cases

McKenzie v Van der Merwe 1917 SA 41 (AD).

R v Dladla & Others 1962 (10) SA 307 (AD).

R v Maclin, Murphy & Others 1838 (2) 225 Lewin.

R v Mgxwiti 1954 (1) SA 370 (AD)

S v Gwebe December 1989 unrep. (ECD).

S v Khoza 1982 (3) SA 1019 (AD).

S v Khumalo & 25 Others May 1989 unrep. (NCD).

S v Maarman & Others 1981 (4) SA 790 (CPD).

S v Malinga & Others 1963 (1) SA 692 (AD).

S v McBride 1988 (3) SA 10 (AD).

S v Mgedezi & Six Others 1989 (1) SA 687 (AD).

S v Nkomo 1966 (1) SA 831 (AD).

S v Nkumbani 1964 (4) SA 377 (AD).

S v Nkwenza & Another 1985 (2) SA 560 (AD).

S v Safatsa & Five Others 1988 (1) SA 868 (AD).

S v Thabetha & Others 1988 (4) SA 272 (TDO).

S v Thomo & Others 1969 (1) SA 385 (AD).

CHAPTER SEVEN

Expert testimony on collective violence

Don Foster

Introduction

Expert[1] testimony by psychologists and, in particular, psychiatrists on the mental state of persons involved in criminal proceedings has become fairly commonplace in the higher courts of South Africa. However, the testimony of social scientists, more specifically psychologists, in politically-related cases is a phenomenon of the eighties. This perhaps says as much about the desperation of defence lawyers as it does about the maturity and skills of those in the social sciences and humanities.

Although expert testimony in politically-related trials has, in the main, involved psychologists rather than psychiatrists, the past few years have also seen the appearance of experts in various other fields. Dr. Lodge, and the now discredited former state witness Mr. De Vries, both from political studies, have been involved in cases related to the African National Congress (ANC). Professors Du Toit and Degenaar have testified, as philosophers, on the issue of political violence. Testimony has been heard from such varied fields as sociology, history, social anthropology, social work, and criminology. Although such testimony is still relatively rare, there can be no doubt that it has increased considerably during the eighties.

This chapter focuses on *one* class of cases in which expert testimony

---

1. The term *expert* refers to a particular category of witness in a South African trial. It is not intended as a comment on the real or imagined expertise of such persons.

has been heard, namely, cases involving *collective violence*. Trials of public violence, in which expert testimony may well be applicable, but has seldom been heard, have not been included. In general, the politically-related cases which have involved experts have been those in which the accused have been charged with murder. All of these murders have occurred in *collective* situations, with some being committed by the so-called *necklace* method.[2] Expert testimony has usually been called by the defence at the stage of extenuation, that is, after the verdict but prior to sentencing. By this stage, therefore, the accused may already have been found guilty of murder, and under South African law, if extenuating circumstances[3] are not found, the judge is obliged to pass the death sentence (Section 277 of the Criminal Procedure Act 51 of 1977).[4]

In the examination of expert testimony that follows in this chapter, the general arguments put forward in extenuation are considered first. The circumstances and the findings in selected cases are then discussed, along with some of the mythologies surrounding so-called *mob violence*.[5]

Argument in extenuation

The following thirteen cases of collective violence since 1983 demonstrate themes in the testimony of experts for the defence:

- *S v Khumalo & 25 Others* (1989)
- *S v Manginda & Eight Others* (1986)
- *S v Manotsi & Six Others* (1988)
- *S v Matshoba & 14 Others* (1986)
- *S v Molatedi & 11 Others* (1988)
- *S v Motaung & Eight Others* (1987)
- *S v Mpetha & 17 Others* (1983)

2. In which a rubber tyre is placed around the body of the victim, doused with petrol, and then set alight.
3. Factors which reduce the *moral blameworthiness* of the accused.
4. State President F. W. de Klerk recently announced that the mandatory death sentence is to be abolished (*The Argus*, 2 February 1990).
5. The term *mob* is regarded as unacceptable in relation to such events. The terms *collective behaviour* or *collective action* (Reicher, 1987) are preferred, on both scientific and ideological grounds.

- *S v Ngidi* (1988)

- *S v Ngoyi & Eight Others* (1987)

- *S v Nkunda & Mahlalela* (1988)

- *S v Safatsa & Five Others* (1988)

- *S v Sibisi & 17 Others* (1989)

- *S v Thabetha & Six Others* (1988)

The recent retrial of the Matshoba case (1987), is also considered.

In all these cases expert testimony was presented by psychologists[6], usually those with an expertise in social and group psychology. A number of international psychologists[7] have also been called to give expert opinion. In essence, the argument has been that the accused have been subjected to a range of physical and psychological processes common in crowd situations, which in sum have reduced their moral blameworthiness, thus allowing the court to make a finding of extenuation. Such processes include physiological arousal, modelling, conformity, group decision-making and, centrally, the phenomenon of de-individuation. Psychological explanations of this sort have been presented within the particular South African context of social deprivation, poverty, thwarted life-opportunities, widespread township violence, and increasing conditions of *social strain* (e.g. Smelser, 1963).

Precise details of the psychological theories are not the concern here.[8] What is important is the criticism that *situational* circumstances have been *underemphasized* in explaining behaviour. This claim has found empirical support in contemporary research conducted across many and varied situations, which has shown that situational forces are highly pertinent in accounting for individuals' actions. More specifically, it has been shown that the presence of large crowds is likely to *increase* the effect of situational, rather than personal, determinants of behaviour. Processes that effect behaviour in crowd situations have been well described in an extensive literature dating back to Le Bon (1896), although adequate explanation and empirical support has been forthcoming only during the past decade (Diener, 1977; Graumann & Moscovici, 1986; Mann et al., 1982; and Prentice-Dunn & Spivey, 1986).

---

6. Professors Du Preez, Foster, Manganyi, Tyson, Dr. Raath, and Mr. Dawes.
7. Including Professors Diener and Fraser from the United States of America, and Colman from the United Kingdom.
8. For details of such theories see, for example, Diener (1977), Graumann & Moscovici (1986), Mann et al. (1982), and Prentice-Dunn & Spivey (1986).

Alternatively, theories of arousal, frustration, and de-individuation explain it as a process in which the efficacy of the mechanisms which usually inhibit violent behaviour are reduced, thus releasing anti-normative behaviours that are *not* consistent with the character of the person concerned. *Mob* situations are said to increase the probability of these processes, thus enabling members of a group to engage in exaggerated violence (Diener, 1980; and Prentice-Dunn & Rogers, 1982 & 1989).

In cases of collective violence, the state has usually tried to demonstrate planning and intent on the part of the accused, by reference to the events that led up to the murder in question. Alternatively, the state has attempted to attribute violence to the leadership and to political aspirations. Technical arguments used in challenging the defence case have been based on the limited extent to which experimental findings can be generalized to real-life situations, or on methodological flaws in the empirical research from which conclusions have been drawn. The most common argument used by state counsel, however, has been that the defence has failed to demonstrate that the *general* theories of crowd behaviour which have been presented by expert witnesses applied to the particular state of mind of *individual* accused at the time of the event in question.

Court findings

Of the thirteen cases selected for discussion here, the court findings must be regarded as something of a *mixed legal bag*. The cases of Nkunda (1988) and Khumalo (1989) are still under consideration by the Appellate Division. It should be noted that in the latter case the trial court found *no* extenuation. Although extenuation was found in two of the remaining eleven cases, it was *not* derived from expert testimony on crowd behaviour. In the Ngoyi case (1987), extenuation was granted primarily on the grounds of youth and in the Mpetha case (1983), on a range of grounds.

Of the nine remaining cases in which evidence on crowd behaviour *was formally heard*, no extenuation was granted in the six original trial cases of Manginda (1986), Matshoba (1987), Molatedi (1988), Nkabinde (1987), Safatsa (1988), and Sibisi (1989). Two of these cases have already been dealt with by the Appellate Division and the remainder may still be reviewed. In the original Nkabinde (1987) case, only Ngidi was found guilty of murder *without* extenuation and sentenced to death. In *S v Ngidi* (1988), the Appellate Division overturned the trial court's decision and found extenuation on grounds of youth[9] and other circumstances, including the influence of the crowd situation on the accused's behaviour. Accordingly, Ngidi's sentence was commuted to ten years imprisonment. In *S v Matshoba* (1987), popularly known as the case of the *Queenstown Six*, the Appellate Division ordered a retrial on the grounds of a *technicality*, namely, that one assessor had been released from the original trial owing to ill-health. At the recent retrial in East London, Mr. Justice Jansen recognized the defence of de-individuation as an extenuating circumstance (*S v Gqweba & Five Others*, 1989). The death sentences of five of the accused, one of whom had already died on death row, were commuted to effective terms of twenty months (*The Cape Times*, 22 November 1989).

Psychologists' expert testimony on crowd behaviour has been accepted in extenuation by Judges Hartzenberg, Human, and Malherbe, in the cases of Motaung (1987), Thabetha (1988), and Manotsi (1988) respectively.

The three cases where the influence of the crowd situation was *accepted* as a basis for extenuation bear closer examination. In the Motaung (1987) and Thabetha (1988) cases, a video recording of the events constituted part of the evidence, leaving no doubt about the accuseds' participation. This differs from other cases, in which alibis were the basis of the pleas entered by the defence. The significance of this factor will become evident in the discussion that follows. In the Motaung case (1987), Mr. Justice Hartzenberg found extenuation for all nine of the accused by reference to a range of factors, including the intake of liquor, the youthful age of some of the accused, the fact that there was no evidence that the accused had started the attack, and the unusually tense atmosphere in Duduza at the time. The court also found that the accused had been emotionally aroused by speeches, singing, dancing, and the shouting of slogans, and that they had considered the deceased, Maki Skosana, to have been an *impimpi*[10], who had been implicated in the deaths of four young people. In the words of the presiding judge:

> We accept that all these things were foremost in every one of their minds due to the emotion and incitement which accompanied the funeral, the procession and the gathering in the stadium. That these factors subjectively influenced the accused to behave as they did, we think is unquestionable[11] (*S v Motaung & Eight Others*, 1987: 1839).

---

9. Ngidi was eighteen-and-a-half years old at the time of the incident.
10. A traitor or informer.
11. Editors' translation from Afrikaans original.

It is noteworthy that a theory of crowd behaviour was neither formally accepted, nor was it a primary consideration in granting extenuation. However, it does appear as though the evidence of Professor Diener, presented in this case during the hearing of the merits of the case rather than during the extenuation phase of the trial, may have contributed toward this finding (*The Weekly Mail*, 26 June 1987). Three of the accused received life sentences and the remaining six, a total of sixty-two years imprisonment.

In the Transvaal case of Thabetha (1988), in circumstances remarkably similar to those in the Motaung case (1987), Mr. Justice Human accepted Professor Tyson's evidence on de-individuation and other crowd factors as the basis of extenuation for all four accused who had already been found guilty of murder (Skeen, 1989). Their sentences ranged from four to seven years imprisonment at the Leeuwkop Youth Centre. In accepting de-individuation theory, the judge commented as follows:

> The de-individuated state is one which, depending on the intensity of the de-individuating process can prevent people from foreseeing the consequences of their actions and from making rational and moral decisions about their actions. ... [T]his state hampers a person's ability to self regulate his behaviour and he becomes more responsive to environmental cues for behavioural direction rather than looking to internal standards of appropriate conduct. He [Tyson] says de-individuation interferes with the individual's cognitive abilities. There is a decreased ability to engage in rational thought. A person becomes emotional, impulsive, irrational or atypical (*S v Motaung & Eight Others*, 1987: 14)

Note that in this case the accused were interviewed by Professor Tyson, by an honours graduate in psychology, and by a psychiatrist,[12] all three of whom testified for the defence. By contrast, the accused were *not* interviewed in the cases of *S v Safatsa* (1988), and the *Sharpeville Six*, which were also tried by Mr. Justice Human.

Although the acceptance of crowd theory as an extenuating circumstance appears to be more robust in the Thabetha (1988) case as compared with the Motaung case (1987), in the former case the youth of the accused was a significant factor. To illustrate:

> There cannot be the slightest doubt that in each of the cases of the accused they are youthful offenders and that by itself is an extenuating circumstance (*S v Thabetha & Others*, 1988: 25).

Furthermore, in the Thabetha case (1988) the accused pleaded guilty to murder with extenuating circumstances, while in the Motaung (1987)

---

12. Mrs. Makam and Dr. Sevel, respectively.

case, the state did *not* oppose a finding of extenuation. Undoubtedly, such legal differences influenced the outcomes of these cases, quite apart from the expert testimony on the psychology of collectivities.

To date, *S v Manotsi* (1988) is perhaps the *only* case in which crowd theory has been accepted unequivocally as an extenuating circumstance in the original trial court. Here Mr. Justice Malherbe found in favour of the expert testimony which was based on a somewhat wider theoretical perspective than de-individuation (Reicher, 1987). This approach took account of group polarization, social tension, and other events that preceded the incident, as well as behaviour in the crowd situation. The court accepted these antecedent factors as part of the pattern of events. The crux of Judge Malherbe's judgment was as follows:

> … [E]vidence concludes that certain influences emanated from the group which influenced the individual members of the group to such an extent that they behaved differently from the way they would have behaved had they been alone. According to him [the expert] this influence can occur without the individual being aware of it[13] (*S v Manotsi & Six Others*, 1988: 1361).

Judge Malherbe found that the expert testimony in this case corresponded with Hiemstra's descriptions of *mass psychosis:*

> People who are not in their essence violent or murderous, can reveal an unusual tendency to violence when they develop a mass psychosis. The one goads the other along. A gentle soul becomes courageous when he sees others committing violence. It does not have to be a large crowd, as few as four or five can have a mutually inciting effect. In such circumstances, someone who, in the court's opinion, does not have a violent nature, can be spared the highest punishment. The upsurgence of a collective action can be an extenuating circumstance[14] (Hiemstra, 1987: 625).

This explanation was accepted in extenuation for all four accused who had been found guilty of murder, and each was sentenced to twelve years imprisonment. It is interesting that these accused proffered alibis in their defence, and did not change this defence even when interviewed by the expert witnesses. Mr. Justice Malherbe remarked:

> It follows that these witnesses were not in a position to testify on factors which did in fact influence the mental states of the accused concerned[15] (*S v Manotsi & Six Others*, 1988: 1360).

The presiding judge was nevertheless satisfied that the evidence as a

---

13. Editors' translation from Afrikaans original.
14. Editors' translation from Afrikaans original.
15. Editors' translation from Afrikaans original.

whole showed the presence of factors which together qualified as extenuating circumstances.

In those cases in which extenuation was *not* found, the issue of testing the subjective mind and emotion of each accused has been the central issue. In this regard, the classic judgment is that of Mr. Justice Botha in the Safatsa case (1988):

> The views expressed by the witness were of a wholly generalized nature, and unrelated to the individual accused. The generalization of the probability referred to by the witness cannot be specifically related to any individual accused in the absence of any evidence at all regarding the actual motivation and state of mind of such individual accused. No such evidence was placed before the trial Court (*S v Safatsa & Five Others*, 1988: 904F–G).

This approach does not preclude the possibility of crowd factors as grounds for extenuation when proven on a balance of probabilities. It has, however, made it difficult to find extenuation in cases in which accused have originally claimed alibis, or only minor participation. Take for example *common purpose* cases such as the Upington 26 and the lesser known case of the Queenstown Six.[16] Here fourteen and six persons respectively were originally sentenced to death, despite the fact that expert testimony showed a strong probability that the accused had been influenced by the crowd situation. However, Mr. Justice Jansen, on the retrial of the Queenstown Six, accepted crowd theory as grounds for extenuation. More importantly, he acknowledged the fact that all of the accused had already spent up to four years in jail, of which two had been spent on death row. Furthermore, in the retrial the accused pleaded guilty to murder with extenuating circumstances, which was not the case in the original trial, and the factor of their altered plea was also recognized in extenuation.

The notion of the subjective mental state of each accused is again evident in Mr. Justice Lategan's judgment in the Manginda case (1986), in which three accused were sentenced to death:

> I must point out immediately that all three of the accused with whom I am concerned, decided it best not to testify in person about what their mental state was and what motivated them at the time of their participation in the assault on the deceased. We are left totally in the dark about whether each of these accused in fact was carried along by the group psychosis to do what each one individually did[17] (*S v Manginda & Eight Others*, 1986: 991).

---

16. *S v Khumalo & 25 Others* (1989) and *S v Matshoba & 14 Others* (1987), respectively.
17. Editors' translation from Afrikaans original.

Similarly, Mr. Justice Lichtenberg found *no* extenuation and sentenced five of the accused to death in *S v Molatedi & 11 Others* (1988). With the exception of the Manotsi case (1988), it seems clear then that for crowd factors to be accepted in extenuation it is necessary to provide evidence of the accused's subjective state of mind and emotions, either through the accused person's own testimony, or through testimony based on extensive interviews with the accused by expert witnesses.

The investigative procedure for extenuation is described by Mr. Justice Rumpff, in the leading case of *S v Babada* (1961). For extenuation to be found, the following three criteria must be met: first, circumstances must have existed that could have influenced the mental ability or emotions of the accused; secondly, such circumstances must have in fact influenced the accused; and thirdly, the influence must have been such that it reduced the moral blameworthiness of the accused. The judgment in the Manotsi case (1988) seems to imply that inferences made from the cumulative evidence about the events and from expert testimony can serve to meet these criteria adequately. It is not necessary to resort, therefore, either to the accused person's own testimony or to require experts to know the accused person's state of mind at the time of the events. Other judgments, however, contradict this notion. Consider the cases of Manginda (1986), Matshoba (1987), Molatedi (1988), and Safatsa (1988).

The issue of the necessity of leading evidence on subjective mental state has been debated recently at great length in the case of the Upington 26, in which the existence of extenuation was eventually denied by the trial court. This case involved the killing of a municipal policeman during the conflict of 1985, in the township of Paballelo outside Upington, in the northern Cape.[18] The defence in this case introduced two psychologists as experts. Professor Tyson testified on de-individuation in general, without interviewing the accused. Dr. Raath, formerly a psychologist in the South African Prisons Service, testified on personal aspects of each of the accused, which he based on extensive psychometric testing and personal interviews. Since all of the accused used alibis in defence, Dr. Raath was unable to obtain information about each accused's state of mind at the time of the event. Furthermore, he was only called to assist in this matter nearly three years *after* the events. In turn, the state called two expert witnesses, Dr. Fourie, a psychiatrist in private practice in Bloemfontein, and Dr. De Kock, a sociologist employed by the Human Sciences Research Council (HSRC). Apart from other matters, these experts challenged the

---

18. A more detailed account of this case is provided in the next chapter.

defence on the grounds that no evidence of the individual accused's state of mind and emotions at the time of the events had been led. This is the point which makes the judgment on extenuation in this case important, quite apart from the significance of the verdict as another conviction based on the doctrine of common purpose.

In respect of the assessment of the individual accused's state of mind Mr. Justice Basson stated:

> We have already heard authority which suggests that the person who must be evaluated, namely the accused, can usually provide the best information on his mental capacity and his mental and emotional state. The accused is a competent witness and not to give him an opportunity would be totally wrong. Naturally an accused has the right to remain silent, and this must be respected, but if he wants to testify about his emotional or mental state or his mental capacity, the evidence which he provides in very relevant and must enjoy serious attention.
>
> Prof. Tyson has made the point that it is not necessary to question an accused in the current case because, what he says will not affect his diagnosis. There are various reasons provided for this. Dr. Raath's attitude was also that an accused's account would not be helpful to him. It would only lend colour to the picture he had already drawn.
>
> This approach is so obviously in conflict with the approach of our Courts that a person is actually dumbstruck that scientists could try and convince a court of their views[19] (*S v Khumalo & 25 Others*, 1989: 44).

His concluding comments were:

> We come thus to the conclusion that, mainly because of the accuseds' refusal to testify, there is so little information before the Court, that the Court cannot find on a balance of probabilities that any of the accused were de-individuated on 13.11.85[20] (*S v Khumalo & 25 Others*, 1989: 58).

A further point, first raised by Judge Lategan in the Manginda case (1986), was also contested in the Upington 26 case. This is the issue of *free choice* in an individual's decision to join a crowd. At present it is unclear what bearing this theoretical point will have in subsequent cases of collective violence, but it did appear to contribute to Mr. Justice Lategan's judgment:

> Now it strikes us, and Professor Du Preez [the expert witness] also concedes readily, that in the final analysis, any member of a group at least at some stage, some or other time, has a free choice as to whether he will join such a group and whether he will participate in the foreseeable activities of this group[21] (*S v Maginda & Eight Others*, 1986: 990).

---

19. Editors' translation from Afrikaans original.
20. Editors' translation from Afrikaans original.
21. Editors' translation from Afrikaans original.

To summarize at this point: In those cases of collective violence where extenuation has not been found, the central issue has been the absence of evidence on the accused's subjective state during the activities of the crowd.

In a few other cases, argument based on collective psychology did *not* succeed due to *other* factors. In *S v Mpetha & 17 Others* (1983), Mr. Justice Williamson inexplicably failed to comment, in *any* respect, on expert testimony regarding collective psychology, but found extenuation on *other* grounds. Perhaps the fact that this was the first case in which such evidence had been led explains the presiding judge's failure to comment. It does not follow conclusively, however, that the evidence was not taken into consideration in reaching the finding.

In *S v Ngoyi & Eight Others* (1987), a case of necklacing, Mr. Justice Solomon of the Eastern Cape bench rejected expert testimony on crowds. He claimed that experimental findings from the United States of America and those involving students from the University of Cape Town could not be extrapolated to Xhosa-speaking people and were therefore not applicable. Besides this argument, which contains a hint of racial bias, he also raised the issue of subjective state of mind by pointing out that the expert who had interviewed the accused had not been aware that one of the accused had made a confession which showed his intent. Extenuation for the one accused found guilty of murder was found on grounds of youth and a fourteen-year prison sentence was handed down.

In the Nkabinde case (1987) Ngidi, one of the accused, had himself given evidence at the stage of extenuation. As part of his judgment in which he rejected crowd psychology as grounds for extenuation, Mr. Justice Spoelstra said:

> He (Ngidi) voluntarily associated with this crowd and was aware that they were leaving with the intent to kill one or more persons. ... Their conduct as a whole shows that they were actuated by inner vice and that they did not commit indiscretions which may be attributed to youthfulness, lack of experience or immaturity. ... We also reject the suggestion that the accused was swept along by the crowd or that he became excited or aroused by the crowd. He himself did not say so and in our view the conduct of the group from the onset contradicts such a suggestion. In our view this is not a case where psychological influences of a crowd operated on the mind of the accused (*S v Nkabinde, Kwela & Ngidi*, 1987: 567–9).

The Appellate Division subsequently found that the trial court had misdirected itself regarding extenuation and substituted a finding of extenuation and a term of ten years imprisonment for the original sentence (*S v Ngidi*, 1988). In justifying this decision, Mr. Justice Nicholas explained:

[W]hat was important was the psychological make-up and characteristics and the conduct and state of mind of Ngidi. ... For years there has prevailed in Soweto and other townships a climate of violence and a breakdown of law and order. There has ruled a subculture of violence, characterised by armed clashes between rival gangs and attacks on the police. Inevitably the young must have been influenced by the prevailing climate and by the example which they find all about them. ... As a teenager, Ngidi was probably more susceptible to external influences, such as the prevailing climate of violence and lawlessness in Soweto, and the psychology of a violent mob with its pressures and *stimuli* to aggression (*S v Ngidi*, 1988: 17–19).

Two points should be made in summarizing the position thus far. First, it would appear that no court has to date *entirely rejected* expert psychological evidence regarding collective violence. In all cases, with the possible exception of the Upington 26, the evidence itself and the status of the expert witnesses have been accepted. Instead, the evidence on crowd behaviour has been found, for one or other reason, *not* to apply to the *particular* accused in these cases. It may also be suggested, albeit in a tentative fashion, that the courts have been somewhat dubious of and thus cautious in their treatment of such evidence. Whether this is due to the inherent conservatism of the judicial procedure, to the fact that social scientific theory lacks coherence and definitive levels of proof, or to fear of the political implications of certain decisions remains debatable. The second point is that apart from the Khumalo case (1989), crowd psychology as a defence has not been tested particularly stringently by state-led experts. In most cases the state has *not* used experts to testify, although it has become apparent that certain experts have advised the state's legal team. The most stringent test to date occurred in the case of the Upington 26, in which some seven weeks or more of evidence and intense argument took place at the stage of extenuation. It is thus reasonable to predict that in future the state is likely to contest such lines of defence strongly.

Myths about collective violence

Before attempting to show patterns in cases of collective violence, it is important to dispel some of the myths about *mobs* and collective violence which have dominated thinking over the past century. Although a full critique is beyond the scope of this chapter, a few points will be highlighted here.[22]

One consistent theme has permeated thinking, from Le Bon's ideas

---

22. For detailed accounts, see Reicher (1982) and Reicher & Potter (1985).

in 1896, through to some of the contemporary theories of de-individuation. The behaviour of individuals in a crowd is characterized as regressed, primitive, irrational, and barbaric. The underlying assumption
is that crowds somehow remove people from their *civilized* state and
unleash a *pre-civilized* violence. The very term *mob* typifies the exaggerated and gratuitous negativity which is readily attributed to crowds.

Secondly, there is a tendency to remove the *mob* from its social
setting. The causes of violent behaviour are attributed to the inner state
of individual members of a crowd, rather than to aspects of a situation.
In particular, the inter-group dynamics characteristic of most incidents
of collective violence are grossly underemphasized and there is almost
total amnesia regarding the central role played by state authorities,
including the police, in situations of collective violence.

Thirdly, psychology has stereotyped crowd behaviour as a fixed
behavioural pattern of the stimulus-response kind, and has underplayed
the *meaning* that events have for crowd participants as *social actors*. In
so doing, it has unwittingly reduced the political dimension of collective
violence to that of automatic responses by individuals to crowd-stimulus
configurations such as arousal, participant numbers, contagion, conformity, obedience to authority figures, diffusion of responsibility, and
ultimately, to de-individuation as a loss of self-control. If crowd situations automatically produce a loss of self control, then how is it that in
recent incidents of collective crowd violence in South Africa the participants have not gone on general rampages, striking at random targets?
Instead, these crowds and those reported historically,[23] have consistently limited their attacks to objects and agents associated with state control.
The answer is surely that crowd action is as much a *political* as it is a
psychological or sociological phenomenon. Both the courts and expert
testimony have tended to neglect the *political* dimension of crowds in
favour of the *psychological*. Although at times the courts have been
reluctant to accept the testimony of psychological experts law and
psychology have generally reinforced each other by demanding in
reciprocal fashion, the limitation of discourse to the particular, the event,
the facts, and the individual. Both disciplines have encouraged a reifi-
cated and decontexualized analysis of processes. In essence, both wish
to occlude the political, if for different reasons.

---

23. For example, see Graumann & Moscovici (1986), Rude (1959), and Tilly et
al. (1975).

Patterns of events in collective violence

In this section common elements in cases of collective violence have been extracted for discussion. Although this may be useful to social scientists seeking to explain general processes, those in the legal profession may question the validity of an understanding which extends beyond the legally accepted parameters of findings of fact and the analysis of individual cases as unique phenomena. There is merit in pursuing the former course, however, since contextual issues are crucial to the understanding of crowd behaviour and emerge only through such generalized analysis. It may be contended then, that the court limits its understanding of the pertinent dynamics by restricting itself to its justifiable strengths, the facts pertaining to the case before it. This is precisely what may produce findings and interpretations that are unnecessarily cautious and conservative.

It is apparent that the incidents of collective violence discussed earlier in this chapter occur within a context of inter-group relations. The violent event, therefore, is not merely the sudden or spontaneous outburst of a *regressed mob*, but takes place within a framework of escalating group polarization. Although these cases show variations in the group situation across different geographical locations, all reflect the deeper political situation in South Africa. For example, in the Port Elizabeth case of Ngoyi (1987), the conflict was between members of the United Democratic Front (UDF) and the Azanian People's Organization (AZAPO) in a context of heavy police repression within a township. In the case of the Queenstown Six, an anti-apartheid group of youth and a contingent of black police, called *Inkatha*, introduced to replace the local police who had lost control of the situation, were involved. In the majority of recent cases of collective violence in South Africa, the fundamental inter-group conflict has occurred between state authorities, usually the police, and anti-apartheid groups, often the youth. Frequently, inter-group violence has escalated in the period preceding an incident. Murders have often followed immediately after an incident in which people have been killed or attacked either by the authorities or by vigilantes.[24] The authorities, particularly the police, have usually played a significant role in the escalation of violence antecedent to the events. For example, in the Upington 26 case, the police fired teargas after the crowd had knelt to pray and were singing

---

24. For instance, in the cases of Khumalo (1989), Manotsi (1988), Matshoba (1987), Molatedi (1988), Motaung (1987), Ngoyi (1987), Sibisi (1989), and Thabetha (1988).

the anthem. In the Molatedi case (1988), a policeman was killed the day after the police demolished a *people's park* which had been built by the youth. In almost all of the cases cited in this chapter, the deceased were not random targets, but were people perceived to be representative of state authority or traitors. This fact reinforces the notion of inter-group conflict.

There is widespread and quite justified repugnance regarding the *necklacing* method of killing. The brutality of this type of murder is frequently excessive, that is, beyond that required to kill the victim. This is significant with respect to the myth of barbarism. It also suggests a kind of frenzy or disinhibition consistent with the description of de-individuation. However, an equally plausible interpretation is that necklacing is symbolic and the product of political frustration. It is interesting to note that there has been evidence in many cases showing that victims have been killed *before* being set alight.

All of these cases are characterized by large heterogeneous crowds that have engaged in singing, dancing, and the chanting of political slogans. The *riff-raff* theory of crowd violence has long been discredited (Perry & Pugh, 1978), and these South African cases prove no exception. Typically they have involved a wide range of people including well and poorly educated, employed and unemployed, young and old, those who are politically aware and those who are politically naïve.[25] It is suggested that this heterogeneous composition goes against a simplified notion of prior intent and planning. The state has frequently attempted to show that collective violence has been preceded by a *hearing* or meeting of a *people's court,*[26] for example in the cases of Khumalo (1989), Matshoba (1987), Mpetha (1983), Ngoyi (1987), and Nkunda (1988). This notion, however, has *not* been supported, for where there has been evidence of such meetings, it has been unsuccessful in linking these to later incidents of violence. This suggests a degree of *spontaneous* action, although always, as stated above, spontaneity within the context of a polarizing inter-group situation.

In collective violence trials the state has usually stressed the rationality, planning, intent, and political motivations of the accused. In countering this view the defence has tended to argue for irrational, impulsive, spontaneous behaviour that is somewhat *out of control* and has downplayed political and inter-group issues. De-individuation the-

---

25. For example, the case of the Upington 26.
26. Adjudicatory structures set up after 1985 by progressive residents in African townships, as an alternative to the court system which was perceived to be unjust.

ory does not necessarily depict behaviour as irrational. The rational/irrational dimension is largely a construction of the court, but analogies such as alcoholic and hypnotic effects, drawn by experts to assist the court, have reinforced the notion of irrationality. It should be emphasized, however, that this is *not* an attempt to disparage expert testimonies, but a recognition of the fact that the court procedure regarding extenuation, particularly the imperative to account for the individual's state of mind, tends to produce a psychological reductionism. This may be a wise legal strategy, but it is unfortunate both theoretically and politically. It would seem that incidents of collective violence are distorted when reconstructed in the courtroom. The situations are more rational, political, and ordered than the defence case would sometimes have it, yet also more spontaneous, impulsive, non-planned, and *emergent* than the state case would have it. The crux of the matter is that both sides need to recognize the politically contextualized nature of such events and to request the courts to see such actions in historical context.

Collective violence in South Africa constitutes part of the politics of resistance. Nevertheless, in trying to reach a better and more accurate understanding of such events, one need not condone the violence or the brutality. The expert witness faces a distinct dilemma. It would be tragic if the defence expert, in attempting to assist the accused whilst remaining true to a sense of justice, actually reinforced the notion of politically-constructed action as the outcome of a semi-crazed, irrational, and primitive mob. It would be preferable for experts to develop a more appropriate theory, able to incorporate both sides of the structural divide. Reicher (1987) provides such a theory, but it has not yet been aired in South African cases, with the exception of the recent trials of Manotsi (1988) and Nkunda (1988). Detailing such a theory is beyond the scope of this chapter. All that needs to be noted here is that this theory recognizes fully the inter-group and political nature of collective violence. It does postulate a shift in the individual psychological process of crowd participants, but in such a fashion that social, group, or political identities, rather than primitive, regressed mechanisms, become more salient. It is argued that such a crowd process still constitutes grounds for extenuation. Instead of a loss of mind, however, the grounds are political and genuinely social factors.

Conclusion

Collective violence cases, particularly those that have emerged out of the post-1984 crisis period, have become part of the legal and political landscape of South Africa. In handing down the ultimate penalty in many of these cases, the legal system may be seen to be assisting the state in controlling political resistance. In recent years expert witnesses, mainly academic psychologists called by the defence, have become part of this landscape. The aim of the defence has been to release the court from its obligation to pass the death penalty by leading evidence on the psychology of collective behaviour as an extenuating circumstance. The courts have found a number of shortcomings in this approach. In particular, they have rejected this defence as inapplicable when evidence has not been led relating the effects of the crowd situation to the subjective state of mind of individual accused. In only one of the thirteen cases discussed in this chapter was expert testimony on collective action accepted as extenuation.

Experts in such cases face something of a dilemma, because the dominant theories of crowd psychology tend to view crowd behaviour as irrational, regressed, and more primitive than the behaviour of individuals. This conception decontextualizes what is fundamentally an act of political resistance, however repugnant and ill-conceived it may be, and tends towards a psychological reductionism. Further work on the structural nature of such incidents of collective violence is needed if we are to put forward acceptable grounds for extenuation that acknowledge the political form of these actions. The insights thus provided, it is hoped, will facilitate a better form of justice and a more just society.

Bibliography

Books and articles

Diener, E. (1977). 'De-individuation: Causes and Consequences'. *Social Behavior and Personality* 5: 143–55.

Diener, E. (1980). 'De-individuation'. In *The Psychology of Group Influence* 2nd edn. (Ed.) Paulus, P. B. Hillsdale: Erlbaum.

Graumann, C. F. & Moscovici, S. (1986). *Changing Conceptions of Crowd Mind and Behaviour*. New York: Springer-Verlag.

Hiemstra, V. G. (1987). *Suid-Afrikaanse Strafproses* 4th edn. Durban: Butterworths.

Le Bon, G. (1896). *The Crowd*. London: Ernest Benn.

Mann, L.; Newton, J. W. & Innes, J. M. (1982). 'A Test Between De-individuation and Emergent Norm Theories of Crowd Aggression'. *Journal of Personality and Social Psychology* 42: 260–72.

Perry, J. B. & Pugh, M. D. (1978). *Collective Behavior*. St. Paul: West Publishing Company.

Prentice-Dunn, S. & Rogers, R. (1982). 'Effects of Public and Private Self-awareness on De-individuation and Aggression'. *Journal of Personality and Social Psychology* 43: 503–13.

Prentice-Dunn, S. & Rogers, R. (1989). 'De-individuation and the Self-Regulation of Behavior'. In *The Psychology of Group Influence* 2nd edn. (Ed.) Paulus, P. B. Hillsdale: Erlbaum.

Prentice-Dunn, S. & Spivey, C. B. (1986). 'Extreme De-individuation in the Laboratory'. *Personality and Social Psychology Bulletin* 12: 206–15.

Reicher, S. D. (1982). 'The Determination of Collective Behaviour'. In *Social Identity and Inter-group Relations*. (Ed.) Tajfel, H. Cambridge: Cambridge University Press.

Reicher, S. D. (1987). 'Crowd Behaviour as Collective Action'. In *Rediscovering the Social Group*. (Ed.) Turner, J. C. Oxford: Blackwell.

Reicher, S. D. & Potter, J. (1985). 'Psychological Theory as Inter-group Perspective'. *Human Relations* 38: 167–89.

Rude, G. (1959). *The Crowd in the French Revolution*. London: Oxford University Press.

Skeen, A. (1989). 'De-individuation and Extenuating Circumstances: *S v Thabetha*'. *South African Journal on Human Rights* 5: 78–81.

Smelser, N. J. (1963). *Theory of Collective Behavior*. New York: Free Press.

Tilly, C.; Tilly, L. & Tilly, R. (1975). *The Rebellious Century 1830–1930*. London: Dent.

Newspaper articles

The Cape Times (23 November 1989).

The Weekly Mail (26 June 1987).

The Argus (2 February 1990).

Legal cases

S v Babada 1961 (1) SA 26 (AD).

S v Gqweba & Five Others November 1989 unrep. (ECD).

S v Khumalo & 25 Others May 1989 unrep. (NCD).

S v Khumalo & 25 Others 1990 unrep. (AD).

S v Manginda & Eight Others September 1986 unrep. (CPD).

S v Manotsi & Six Others August 1988 unrep. (OPD).

S v Matshoba & 14 Others June 1987 unrep. (ECD).

S v Molatedi & 11 Others August 1988 unrep. (OPD).

S v Mpetha & 17 Others June 1983 unrep. (CPD).

S v Motaung & Eight Others June 1987 unrep. (TPD).

S v Ngidi September 1988 unrep. (AD).

S v Ngoyi & Eight Others March 1987 unrep. (ECD).

S v Nkabinde, Kwela & Ngidi July 1987 unrep. (TPD).

S v Nkunda & Mahlalela July 1988 unrep. (TPD).

S v Safatsa & Five Others 1988 (1) SA 868 (AD).

S v Sibisi & 17 Others February 1989 unrep. (TPD).

S v Thabetha & Others 1988 (4) SA 272 (TPD).

CHAPTER EIGHT

Expert testimony on community attitudes to sentencing: The case of the Upington 26

Desirée Hansson and Derrick Fine[1]

Introduction

The trial of the *Upington 26, S v Khumalo & 25 Others* (1989), is a case of some note. Not only is it the political trial in which the *largest* number[2] of trialists have been convicted of murder in terms of the doctrine of common purpose[3], it is also the *first* such trial in which the defence has attempted to lead expert *evidence* in *mitigation* on community attitudes to sentencing. In South Africa, capital cases, like all other criminal trials, involve a stage during which the guilt of the accused is decided. The difference in a *capital* case, however, is that if the accused is found guilty, the death sentence is mandatory in most cases[4], unless the defence is able to show that circumstances existed at the time of the offence that reduce the 'moral blameworthiness' of the accused (Section 277 of the Criminal Procedure Act 51 of 1977). Such evidence

---

1. The authors wish to thank all those who assisted with this study, particularly Dirk van Zyl Smit. This chapter is based on the report of the survey findings that was prepared for the court (Hansson & Fine, 1989). The full report and a booklet summarizing the study (Fine & Hansson, 1989) are available from the Institute of Criminology at the University of Cape Town.
2. Twenty-five of the twenty-six accused. The remaining accused was found guilty of attempted murder (*S v Khumalo & 25 Others*, 1989).
3. See Chapter 6 for a detailed discussion of this doctrine.
4. The death sentence is not mandatory where a woman is convicted of the murder of her newly born child, or if the person convicted of murder

---

is lead at the *extenuation* stage of the trial. If the court finds extenuation, the death sentence need not be imposed, sentencing follows, and the defence may then lead evidence in mitigation, namely, evidence to justify a lesser sentence.[5] Even where extenuation is found, the court still retains the discretion to impose the sentence of death.

In the previous chapter, an analysis was made of the way in which defence counsel has used expert testimony on de-individuation to show that there have been extenuating circumstances in certain political cases of collective violence. It should be noted that de-individuation was rejected as extenuation in the case of the Upington 26. The judge reasoned that since the accused held to their alibis, there was no evidence to show that any individual accused had in fact experienced de-individuation (*S v Khumalo & 25 Others*, 1989).

The Institute of Criminology at the University of Cape Town conducted an opinion poll or attitudinal survey, at the request of the defence attorneys in this case. Residents of the township in which the offence had occurred were interviewed to ascertain their opinions about sentencing these trialists. By the time this request was made, the twenty-six trialists had already been convicted and the attorneys hoped that such survey findings would assist them in their arguments for mitigation. The expert testimony on crowd behaviour delivered in recent South African political trials differs from the evidence on attitudes to sentencing that was prepared for the case of the Upington 26. The evidence is not only dissimilar in content, it also differs with regard to the *type* of expert who delivers the evidence, the *stage* of the trial at which such testimony is introduced, and its *purpose*. Thus far, expert testimony on crowd behaviour has been presented mainly by psychologists and psychiatrists, at the stage of *extenuation*, to dissuade the court from imposing the death penalty. In contrast, the single instance of expert testimony on attitudes to sentencing in the Upington 26 case was to be delivered by criminologists, at the stage of *mitigation*, in an attempt to persuade the court to impose lesser sentences. Furthermore, in former cases testimony has been based on existing social scientific theories and findings on crowd behaviour, whereas in the latter case it comprised empirical research that was conducted specifically for the case in question.

---

is under eighteen years of age (Section 277(2) of the Criminal Procedure Act 51 of 1977). A court may, however, still use its discretion to impose the death penalty in such cases.

5. Recently, the State President announced that the mandatory death penalty is to be abolished, whereafter the role of extenuation will change (De Klerk, in *The Argus*, 2 February 1990).

In this chapter, the central findings of the opinion poll that was conducted for this case are discussed and the survey methodology is detailed to assist those who may wish to conduct similar surveys. In conclusion, the issue of whether such survey data should be admitted as evidence or rejected as irrelevant is explored briefly.

Background to the case

At the time of the offence, all twenty-six trialists were resident in the African township of Paballelo, in which the incident took place. Paballelo is situated on the outskirts of the rural town of Upington, in the Northern Cape (West & Ramphele, 1988). The township was established in the early sixties in terms of legislation which designates separate *group areas* for different ethnic groups. The initial population consisted of Africans who were forced to leave a neighbouring coloured group area. It now comprises about 10 000 inhabitants, who, like most African township residents, are economically deprived (Rademeyer et al., 1987). Until 1985, Paballelo was *not* a politically active community. During the first half of 1985, however, scholars in Paballelo boycotted the local high school as part of the 1985 nation-wide campaign against the system of African education. In the latter part of 1985, Paballelo youths established the Upington Youth Organization (UYO), a body aligned with the United Democratic Front (UDF) (Bernadt et al., 1988).

S v Khumalo & 25 Others (1989) involved the death of a municipal policeman, Jetta Sethwala, on the 13 November 1985. The following is the pattern of events that has been reconstructed from the survey interview information and the attorneys' summary of the facts (Bernadt et al., 1988). For some time before Jetta's death, Paballelo residents had been concerned about a number of community issues, the most important of these being high rentals, many evictions, no electricity, streetlighting or tarred roads, poor medical services, high rates of unemployment, and abuse by the municipal police, known as *greenflies*.[6] Township residents reported that the greenflies had killed three residents in the first three months of their deployment in Paballelo. In general, people said that the municipal police were a *bad* influence in the community, because they randomly assaulted residents and destroyed their property. Jetta, the victim in the Upington 26 case, was particularly disliked for his violent and abusive behaviour. Some interviewees said that the people of Blikkies[7], the neighbouring coloured township, had

---

6. Due to the dark green trousers they wear as part of their uniform.
7. Translated as little tin cans.

previously threatened to kill Jetta for this reason.

Three days before Jetta was killed, a community meeting was held to discuss grievances. In the two days that followed, the Riot Police were active in Paballelo for the *first time ever*. There were stonings and cars were burnt. The police were said to have teargassed, detained, and shot at residents, and at least one person had been killed. On the morning before Jetta's death, a community meeting was called on the township soccer field.[8] The police used teargas to disperse what residents said was an orderly gathering of about 3 000 people. The crowd fled in all directions to avoid police fire and teargas. Many ran up Pilane Street where Jetta lived, since it was one of the streets closest to the soccer field. Stones were thrown at a police Casspir[9] in the street parallel to Pilane Street. In time, a crowd of 200 to 300 people gathered outside Jetta's house, stones were thrown, people shouted, Jetta shot at the crowd and wounded an eleven-year-old child. Jetta, armed with a shotgun, then emerged from the house, apparently in an attempt to seek help for his family who remained inside. Some of the crowd members chased him to an open area, where he was knocked to the ground, assaulted, killed with the butt of his own gun, and his body set alight. None of the accused were arrested at the scene of the crime and it took between three and four weeks to arrest all twenty-six of the accused.

The pilot study

A pilot study was conducted to assess the feasibility of the survey proposed by the defence attorneys. Consultations were held with the attorneys and the social anthropologists[10] who had been requested to report on the social context of Paballelo. A list of potentially useful areas of investigation were drawn up and used to interview seventy-three Paballelo residents. Although this pilot sample was not randomly selected, but comprised volunteers, it included people of various ages, both sexes, and people with differing attitudes to the accused and the deceased. Relatives of the accused, those closely acquainted with the deceased, and those not acquainted with either party were interviewed.

---

8. It remains uncertain who called the meeting, as twelve of the trialists testified that it was the Riot Police, but the Captain of the Riot Police and the court rejected this claim.
9. A tank-like, riot-control vehicle.
10. Professor Martin West and Dr. Mamphele Ramphele of the Department of Social Anthropology at the University of Cape Town.

The attitudinal survey or opinion poll

The interview schedules

Following the pilot study it was decided that a full-scale survey was feasible and the attorneys gave the go-ahead. The interview schedule and the introduction to respondents presented in Figures 8.1 and 8.2 were constructed and then translated into Xhosa, Sotho, and Afrikaans, the languages understood by the majority of Paballelo residents (Rademeyer et al., 1987).

Questions (1) and (2) on the interview schedule were included to enable checking during the survey. Questions (3) to (7) reflect important demographic characteristics of the respondents. Since it was deemed important to elicit only informed opinion, Question (8a) was included to separate out those residents who did not know about the offence in this case. This meant that respondents who said that they did not know about the incident in which Jetta, the municipal policeman, was killed were not interviewed beyond Question (8a). The purpose of Question (8b) was to distinguish further those with *more direct experience* of the circumstances in Paballelo on the day of the offence, namely, those residents who were present. The following two questions, (9a) and (9b), were included at the instruction of the attorneys, who explained that there had been a lack of clarity in the evidence about who had called the meeting antecedent to the offence. Question (10) aimed to elicit residents' opinions on extenuating and mitigating circumstances.

The next three sets of questions, (11) through to (13), separate the trialists found guilty of murder into the three categories defined by the court: (1) the *accomplices*, or those who were found guilty because they stoned the deceased's house to drive him out so that he could be killed; (2) the *co-perpetrators*, or those who were found guilty because they assaulted the deceased and stoned his house to drive him out so that he could be killed; and (3) the *perpetrator*, or the trialist who was found guilty because he inflicted the fatal injury (Bernadt et al., 1988). Each question was prefaced with a précis of the judge's findings regarding the guilt of the category of trialist concerned, to enable respondents to give *informed* opinions based on *findings of fact*. Questions (11) to (13) each comprise the same three subsections namely, (a), (b), and (c). Subsection (a) pertains to respondents' opinions about *whether to punish* each category of trialist. Subsection (b) deals with respondents' opinions about the *types of punishment* appropriate for each category of trialist. Subsection (c) focuses on respondents' reasons or *justifications for* the opinions they were asked to express about punishment in

Subsections (a) and (b). The final two sets of questions, (14) and (15), concern respondents' feelings with respect to the *most* stringent and the *least* stringent possible punishments for the trialists, namely, hanging versus release, respectively.

FIGURE 8.1: INTERVIEW SCHEDULE

1. Date ....
2. Interviewer ....
3. Respondent
   Householder   Spouse   Elderly adult   Young adult

4a. Home language ....
4b. Interview language
    English   Afrikaans   Xhosa   Sotho

5. Age (in complete years)...
6. Sex
   Female   Male

7. How long have you lived in Paballelo (in complete years)?.................
8a. Do you know about the incident in which Jetta the municipal policeman was killed?

    Yes   No [stop interview here]

8b. Were you here in Paballelo on the day that Jetta was killed (13 November 1985)?
    Yes   No

9a. Do you know about the big meeting that was held early on the morning of the day that Jetta was killed (13 November 1985), on a soccer field in Paballelo?

    Yes   No [go to Question 10]

9b. Who do you think called this meeting?..
    ....

10. Why do you think Jetta was killed? ....
    ....

11a. The judge has found some of the accused guilty of murder because they stormed Jetta's house to drive him out so that he could be killed

    Do you think these accused should be punished?
    Yes   No [go to Question 11c]

11b. How do you think they should be punished?
    Hanged
    Imprisoned   — for over 20 years

                              — for 16 to 20 years

                              — for 11 to 15 years

                              — for 6 to 10 years

                              — for up to 5 years
    Punished in some other way/s. In what way/s? ....
    ....

11c. Why do you think this?...
....

12a. The judge has found some of the accused guilty of murder because they stoned Jetta's house and assaulted him, to kill him.

Do you think these accused should be punished?
Yes   *No* [go to Question 12c]

12b. How do you think they should be punished?

Hanged
Imprisoned   *— for over 20 years*

                               — for 16 to 20 years

                               — for 11 to 15 years

                               — for 6 to 10 years

                               — for up to 5 years

Punished in some other way/s. In what way/s?...............................
....

12c. Why do you think this?...
....

13a. The judge has found one accused guilty of murder because he hit Jetta over the head and killed him.

Do you think this accused should be punished?
Yes   *No* [go to Question 13c]

13b. How do you think he should be punished?

Hanged
Imprisoned   *— for over 20 years*

                               — for 16 to 20 years

                               — for 11 to 15 years

                               — for 6 to 10 years

                               — for up to 5 years

Punished in some other way/s. In what way/s?...............................
....

13c. Why do you think this?...
....

14a. The judge has found all 25 accused guilty of murder and they can now be sentenced to death.

How will you feel if any of them are hanged?...............................

....

14b. Why would you feel this?...

....

15a. How will you feel if any of the 25 accused are not imprisoned and are allowed to return to Paballelo?...

....

15b. Why would you feel this?...
....

Questions (4a) to (15b) were posed in an open-ended manner, that is, respondents were *not* provided with a list of answers from which to choose their responses, but gave answers of *their choosing*.[11] In this way, the chance of interviewers biasing responses was reduced (Couper et al., 1987). To clarify responses further, respondents were asked to give reasons for their opinions. This also served to tap some of the covert assumptions that underlie attitudes, thus facilitating a more in-depth understanding of respondent's opinions.

The interviewers

Eighteen interviewers were trained in interviewing skills, with a focus on how to administer the interview schedule constructed for this particular survey. They were thoroughly briefed on research ethics and the prevention of bias at all stages of interviewing, from the introduction through to the recording of responses. Interviewers were selected on the basis of previous interviewing experience and proficiency in at least Xhosa or Afrikaans. Two of the interviewers were also fluent in Sotho. Interviewers worked in pairs of Xhosa and Afrikaans speakers.

The respondents

In an attempt to reflect *more stable, adult opinion*, only residents of eighteen years and over were interviewed. In each dwelling, the following occupants were interviewed when present: the householder; the householder's spouse; an elderly adult over the age of sixty years, who was neither the householder nor the spouse; and a young adult between the ages of eighteen and twenty-five years inclusive, who was neither the householder nor the spouse. This approach was adopted to include respondents of *both* sexes and of *varying* ages.[12] The focus on householders and spouses was a means of sampling *more balanced* opinion.[13] Dwellings were visited twice when potential respondents were not at home, or unavailable at the time. Before consenting to be interviewed, respondents were informed that the Institute had been instructed by the defence attorneys to conduct the survey, that the

---

11. The pre-recorded response alternatives that appear in italics on the interview schedule were used to assist the interviewers in the recording of responses only, and were *not* seen by the respondents.
12. Details of the characteristics of the respondents are presented in the text that follows.
13. The emphasis on sampling balanced, *adult opinion* was deemed important for the purposes of the court.

FIGURE 8.2: INTRODUCTION TO RESPONDENTS

We work for the Institute of Criminology at the University of Cape Town. We are working with the lawyers defending Pinkie Khumalo and the other 24 Paballelo residents who have been convicted of the murder of the municipal policeman called Jetta, in November 1985. This weekend, a group of us will be asking many Paballelo residents what *you* think about this case. The reason we are asking your opinion is that the court may want to know what the people of Paballelo feel. Unfortunately, we do not have time to ask everyone's opinion, so we have tried to be fair by choosing to ask people from one in every few houses. If you agree to answer our questions we will write down your answers, but we will not be taking down your name or address. There are *no right or wrong answers* to the questions we are going to ask you. It would help us a lot if you would answer our questions *openly and honestly*, because we need to know what you *really* think. Thank you for your time.

---

survey findings were to be used in the court case, and that respondents' identities would remain *confidential*.[14] All queries were answered as fully as possible. The aim of these measures was to improve the validity and reliability of responses and to reduce the number of respondents lost due to unavailability and refusals.

The sampling method

A *cluster, random* sampling method was used to achieve an *evenly distributed* survey sample. For this purpose, a map indicating the spatial distribution of dwellings was required. Despite numerous requests by the attorneys to the relevant government authorities, however, the only map provided was dated 1956 and thus could not be used to draw a *reliable* sample. This map had to be updated by adding those dwellings that had been built in the township since 1956. The updated map was used to select a random sample of dwellings and corresponding addresses. In Paballelo, the adult population of eighteen years and over has been estimated to be 5 689 (Rademeyer et al., 1987). According to the norms of social science, a five per cent sample of such a large background population is deemed to be representative (Hammond & McCullagh, 1977). The aim, therefore, was to interview at least 285 adult respondents. An initial sample of 400 addresses had to be selected, however, to allow for the inevitable loss of respondents that usually results from refusals and unavailability.

---

14. See Figure 8.2 for the Introduction to Respondents.

The survey procedure

The survey was conducted over a *weekend* in an attempt to include respondents who would otherwise have been away at work during the week. Interviewers were provided with a list of addresses and a map of the area in which the addresses were located. Sample dwellings that were visited twice, but remained unoccupied, respondents who were unavailable on a second visit and respondents who were too intoxicated to be interviewed were excluded from the sample. Respondents were interviewed in a language with which they were comfortable and, where feasible, they were interviewed in their home language. Two co-ordinators were based at a central point in the township, to assist interviewers with problems and queries. At regular intervals, interviewers returned completed interview schedules for checking by the co-ordinators. Errors, omissions, and ambiguities were clarified immediately.

The analysis of the findings

A list of the full range of responses to each question was constructed. Two researchers analysed the contents of the responses. From this analysis sub-categories emerged which were grouped into supra-categories according to common themes. For example, the response Many others have killed and have not been punished was placed in a sub-category titled Others are seen to go unpunished for killing. The response The police did not make a full investigation in this case was placed in a sub-category titled The pre-trial arrests/investigations are seen to have been unfair. Both of these responses were also placed in a supra-category titled The criminal justice process is seen to have been unfair. Each supra- and sub-category was allocated a different code. The two researchers conducted an independent content-analysis of all responses using the above-mentioned coding system. The two sets of independently-generated codes were compared and disagreements were discussed until agreement was reached between the two researchers. Two types of disagreements occurred, namely, contradictions, in which each researcher assigned a different code to the same aspect of a response, and additions, in which one researcher assigned more codes to a response than the other researcher. The resulting average inter-coder reliability level was high, at a 96 per cent level of agreement.

Characteristics of the respondents

Out of the original sample of 400 dwellings a total of 240 (60%[15]) had to be excluded for the following reasons: (1) in 29% of the cases the occupants of the dwellings were not at home or unavailable after two visits; (2) in 20% of the cases the respondents did not know about the offence; (3) in 7% of the cases the occupants refused to be interviewed; and (4) in 4% of the cases the respondents were too intoxicated to be interviewed. The remaining 160 (40%) dwellings yielded 330 interviews, or a 6% sample of the total estimated adult population.

The sample included 47% householders, 31% spouses, 21% young adults, and 1% elderly adults. This last percentage appears to be somewhat low, but this is due to the fact that the categories of householder and spouse subsumed many of the respondents over the age of sixty years. The home language of 60% of respondents was Xhosa, Afrikaans was spoken by 27%, Tswana by 5%, Sotho by 4%, while Afrikaans and Xhosa was spoken by 3%, Zulu by 0,2%, Venda by 0,2%, English by 0,2%, English and Xhosa by 0,2%, and Afrikaans and Sotho by 0,2% of the respondents. Of the interviews that were conducted, 57% were in Afrikaans, 39% were in Xhosa, 2% were in Sotho, and 2% were conducted in English.

At the time of interviewing, 24% of the respondents were between 18 and 25 years of age inclusive, 11% between 26 and 30 years, 12% between 31 and 35 years, 9% between 36 and 40 years, 9% between 41 and 45 years, 6% between 46 and 50 years, 7% between 51 and 55 years, 7% between 56 and 60 years, 6% between 61 and 65 years, 5% between 66 and 70 years, and 4% were 71 years and over. The average age of respondents was 41 years. Fifty two per cent of those who were interviewed were women and 48% were men. Respondents had been resident in Paballelo for an average of 19 years and 78% of those who were interviewed had been present in Paballelo on the day of the offence.

Overall, the 1988 survey sample appears to be *representative* of the sex and age distributions of the background population as described by Rademeyer et al. (1987). It is only in three of the eleven age categories that these two samples differ by more than three per cent. The 18- to 25-year and the 26- to 30-year categories are *under-represented* by 7% and 5% respectively, and the 31- to 35-year category is *over-represented* by 4%, in the 1988 sample. This may well be due to the fact that the majority of householders and spouses, who were the focus of the 1988 survey, seemed to fall into the 31- to 35-year age category.

---

15. All percentages have been rounded to the nearest whole number. Figures less than one have been converted to the nearest first decimal place.

The central findings[16]

Attitudes to the punishment of the accomplices

The majority of respondents (57%), stated that the accomplices should *not* be punished, whereas only 24% felt that the accomplices should be punished.[17] The most common reason given for *not punishing* these trialists (32%) was that respondents were not convinced of their guilt. The second most frequent reason given for not punishing (26%) was that these trialists had been affected by the way in which Jetta had behaved immediately prior to his death. The largest proportion of these responses focused on Jetta's shooting at people as the most influential aspect of his conduct on that day.

The reasons given by respondents who felt that these trialists *should be punished*, fell into three categories: (1) *punishment with leniency,* or those who felt that leniency should be shown in punishing these trialists (50%); (2) *punishment without leniency,* or those who did not mention leniency in punishing these trialists (37%); and (3) *punishment with other reasons,* or those whose responses fell into neither of these two categories (13%).[18]

The most frequently cited reason for *punishment with leniency* (25%) was that people felt empathy for these trialists and their families. The second most frequent reason cited for punishment with leniency (6%) was that these trialists had been affected by the way in which Jetta had behaved immediately prior to his death.

The most frequently cited reason for punishing these trialists *without leniency* (20%) was that they were guilty and must therefore be punished. The largest proportion of these responses showed that the accomplices should be punished because they had stoned, intended to stone, or contributed to a stoning (48%). The second most common reason for punishing without leniency (13%) was that people felt that punishment would serve a purpose. The central purpose mentioned was that of deterring these trialists from re-offending.

---

16. Only those findings directly related to attitudes to sentencing have been included in this chapter. Thus, the results for Questions (8a) to (10) have been excluded. See Hansson & Fine (1989) for these details. Copies of the booklet detailing the central findings were distributed to township residents.

17. The reader will notice that the percentages in this paragraph and in the four sections that follow do not always add up to 100%. The reason is that some of the respondents did not give definite answers. See Hansson & Fine (1989) for further details.

18. Including those who gave no reason or nonsensical responses.

Three *types of punishment* were most frequently selected as appropriate for these trialists, namely, imprisonment (12%), suspended sentences (3%) and corporal punishment (3%). The most common prison sentence suggested (67%) was up to five years inclusive. It is noteworthy that 80% of the responses in support of punishment indicated that people felt that prison sentences of *less* than 11 years were felt to be sufficient. Only 0,3% of the responses in support of punishment indicated that people felt that the death penalty would be appropriate for the accomplices.

Attitudes to the punishment of the co-perpetrators

The largest proportion of respondents (48%) stated that the co-perpetrators should *not* be punished, whereas 31% felt that they should be punished. The most common reason given for *not punishing* these trialists (27%) was that respondents were not convinced of their guilt. The second most common reason given (28%) was that people felt that these trialists had been affected by Jetta's behaviour immediately prior to his death, because he had shot at people.

Among the respondents who felt that these trialists *should be punished*, the most frequently cited reason for *punishment with leniency* (28%) was that people felt empathy for these trialists and their families. The second most common reason for punishment with leniency (5%) was that people felt that the criminal justice process had been unfair. The largest proportion of these responses indicated that this was because people felt that the state evidence had been unfair.

Among the respondents who felt that these trialists *should be punished*, the most frequently cited reason for *punishment without leniency* (27%) was that people felt that the co-perpetrators were guilty and must therefore be punished. The largest proportion of these responses (44%) showed that the co-perpetrators should be punished because they had assaulted, intended to assault, or contributed to an assault. The second most common explanation given for punishment without leniency (10%) was that people felt that punishing these trialists would serve a purpose. The central purpose outlined was that of deterring these trialists from re-offending.

Three *types of punishment* were most frequently selected as appropriate for these trialists, namely, imprisonment (16%), suspended sentences (4%), and corporal punishment (2%). The most common prison sentence suggested (79%) was up to five years inclusive. Only 1% of the responses in support of punishment indicated that people felt that the death penalty would be appropriate.

Attitudes to the punishment of the perpetrator

The largest proportion of respondents (43%) stated that the perpetrator should *not* be punished, whereas 36% felt that he should be punished. The most common reason given for *not punishing* this trialist (24%) was that respondents were not convinced of his guilt. The second most common reason given (22%) was that people felt that this trialist had been affected by Jetta's behaviour immediately prior to his death, because he had shot at people.

Among those who felt that this trialist *should be punished*, the most frequently cited reason for *punishment with leniency* (26%) was that respondents were not convinced of his guilt. The second most frequent reason cited for punishment with leniency (6%) was that people felt that this trialist had already been punished sufficiently.[19]

Among those respondents who felt that this trialist *should be punished*, the most frequently cited reason for *punishment without leniency* (29%) was that he was guilty and that he must therefore be punished. The largest proportion of these responses (82%) showed that people felt that the trialist should be punished because he was guilty of killing, intending to kill, or contributing to a killing. The second most common explanation given (10%) was that people felt that punishing this trialist would serve a purpose. The central purpose outlined was that of deterring this trialist from re-offending.

Three *types of punishment* were most frequently selected as appropriate for this trialist, namely, imprisonment (20%), a suspended sentence (5%), and the death penalty (4%). The most common prison sentence suggested (56%) was up to five years inclusive. It is noteworthy that 79% of the responses in support of punishment indicated that people felt that a prison sentence of less than eleven years would be sufficient for the perpetrator.

Attitudes to the death penalty in this case

By far the majority of the respondents (87%) were *against* hanging any of the trialists, with 41% of this group expressing *strong opposition* to the death penalty. Only 3% of respondents *supported* hanging any of the trialists, with a minimal 0,3% expressing *strong support* for the death penalty.

The most frequent reason given for *opposing* the death penalty (30%) was that respondents were uncertain about the guilt of the trialists. The

---

19. By this stage most of the trialists had already been in prison for almost three years.

second most common reason given for opposing the death penalty (20%) was that respondents felt that the trialists had been influenced by various situational factors, including the conduct of the deceased (8%) and the conduct of the police (5%).

The most common reason given for *supporting* the death penalty (88%) was retribution and the second most common reason given was that people felt that the death penalty would have a deterrent effect on others (8%).

Attitudes to release in this case

By far the majority of the respondents were *in favour* of releasing *any* of the trialists (69%), with 27% of these respondents *strongly in support* of release. Only 11% of the respondents *opposed* releasing any of the trialists, with 2% expressing *strong opposition* against release.

The most common reason given for *supporting* release (36%) was that there should be leniency because respondents felt empathy for the trialists and their families. The second most common reason given for supporting release (7%) was that people felt that the trialists had already been punished sufficiently.

The reason most frequently given for *opposing* release (36%) was that releasing any of the trialists would make the community fearful, due to the possibility of the trialists re-offending. The second most common reason given for opposing release (33%) was that people felt that the trialists were guilty and should therefore be punished.

The survey findings in summary

Although the judge had found twenty-five of the trialists guilty of murder and one guilty of attempted murder, the majority of the respondents in this study said that the twenty-six should *not* be punished *at all*. There were a small number of residents who *wanted* the trialists punished, but many of them said that the punishment should *not be severe*. There was very *strong opposition* to the death penalty as a punishment for the trialists, and a clear majority *supported* the immediate release of the trialists. Residents had similar feelings about punishment for all three categories of trialists. Those residents who did *not* want the trialists to be punished dropped from 56% for the accomplices, to 48% for the co-perpetrators, to 43% for the perpetrator. Those residents who *wanted* the trialists punished increased from 12% for the accomplices, to 16% for the co-perpetrators, to 20% for the perpetrator. These figures seem to suggest that some members of the community felt that the trialists should be punished according to their *degree of involvement* in the killing.

On the whole then, most people felt that the trialists should not be punished at all. Smaller numbers of people were not certain whether to punish them and some suggested punishment such as imprisonment. The main reasons they gave for *not* punishing the trialists were that they were uncertain of the guilt of the trialists and that they felt the trialists had been provoked by the way that Jetta had behaved just before he had been killed. People were especially upset that Jetta had shot a child.

Most of the residents who *wanted* the trialists punished felt that the punishment should *not* be severe because of the unusual circumstances in this case. Respondents felt that the guilt of the trialists was uncertain and said that they felt empathy for the trialists and their families. Furthermore, respondents believed that the way in which the trialists had been arrested, charged, and put on trial in this case had been unfair. Residents felt that the criminal justice process had been unfair in this case because the state evidence had not been proper. For example, some said that state witnesses had lied and that people wearing masks had identified the suspects. They added that the trialists had been provoked by the way in which Jetta had behaved as a municipal policeman prior to his death.

Those residents who *wanted* the trialists punished *severely* explained that the trialists were guilty and should therefore be punished for what they had done and that such punishment would serve to deter the trialists from re-offending. As regards capital punishment in particular, people rejected the death penalty as a form of punishment in principle and, in this case, because they felt empathy for the trialists and their families.

The main reasons respondents gave for *releasing* the trialists was that there should be leniency because people felt for the trialists and their families, who had already suffered a great deal. The main reason given for *opposing* the release of the trialists was that people felt that the community would react negatively. For example, people were afraid that the trialists would kill again and they felt that those who are guilty of offences must be punished.

The validity of these findings

One way in which social scientists have sought to validate empirical research has been to show that *different* studies of the *same* phenomena yield *consistent* findings[20] (Couper et al., 1987). Thus, the findings

---

20. This is known as reliability.

from the 1988 Paballelo opinion poll have been compared with those from a 1989 survey of township residents' attitudes to the death penalty that was conducted in Port Elizabeth (PE) in the Eastern Cape (Hendriks et al., 1989). It should be emphasized that these two surveys were conducted for *different purposes*, using *different samples*. The aim of the Paballelo study of township residents in the Northern Cape was to provide evidence on attitudes to sentencing, *including* the death penalty, for a *particular* court case. In contrast, the PE study of township residents in the Eastern Cape focused *only* on attitudes to the death penalty and was part of a wider investigation of South African life under a state of emergency.[21] Despite the differences, a comparison was made, as no other suitable studies were available at the time this chapter went to press.

Figure 8.3 is a summary of the pertinent results of both surveys in parallel. Overall, the Paballelo survey showed strong opposition to the death penalty, namely, 87% of the respondents. The PE survey demonstrated even greater opposition, namely, 93% of the respondents (Hendriks et al., 1989: 70). In actual fact, there is a greater similarity in the level of opposition than first appears. Since 10% of the Paballelo respondents did not know how they felt, that is, they neither supported nor opposed hanging, refused to answer the question, or gave nonsensical responses, only 3% *actively favoured* the death penalty, as compared to 7% of the PE respondents. The similar level of opposition to the death penalty on the part of these two samples of African township residents is *one* indicator of the reliability of these findings.

Although the majority in both samples of respondents opposed the death penalty, their reasons differed *markedly*. The two groups of respondents agreed on only two reasons and then to varying degrees, namely, religious reasons (1%:21%) and the possibility of judicial error (1%:17%). The differences in these percentages may be due to the fact that the Paballelo respondents gave a *wider range* of reasons for opposing the death penalty. This is probably because they were more directly involved, as they had been living in a township in which a capital offence had occurred. The majority of their objections were based on *particular* aspects of this incident, rather than on abstract principles. For example, they referred to the uncertainty of the trialists' guilt in this case and to the provocative behaviour of the deceased prior to his death. In contrast, the three most common objections raised by the PE respondents were more abstract in nature, namely, the cruel nature of the death penalty, religious reasons, and the possibility of

---

21. Conducted under the auspices of the Human Rights Trust.

FIGURE 8.3: PERTINENT FINDINGS FROM THE PABALLELO AND PORT ELIZABETH (PE) SURVEYS*

	Paballelo	PE
Reasons given for supporting the death penalty		
Retribution	88%	12%**
Deterrence	8%	88%**
The death penalty will serve a purpose (unspecified)	4%	0%
Reasons given for opposing the death penalty		
Uncertainty as to the trialists' guilt	30%	0%
Influence of situational factors on the trialists' behaviour***	20%	0%
Empathy is felt for the trialists & their families	15%	0%
Death penalty rejected in principle	12%	0%
The criminal justice process was unfair	9%	0%
The death penalty is too severe a punishment in this case	2%	0%
Execution will cause a negative community reaction	2%	0%
The killing was not premeditated	2%	0%
Religious reasons	1%	21%**
The trialists have already been punished sufficiently	1%	0%
The trialists are young	1%	0%
The trialists are of good character	1%	0%
The possibility of judicial error	1%	17%**
Some of the culprits have not been tried	1%	0%
The trialists will be missed	1%	0%
The death penalty has little deterrent effect	0%	2%
The death penalty is cruel	0%	27%
Moral reasons	0%	20%
The death penalty allows no chance for rehabilitation	0%	12%
There is no justice in retribution	0%	0,7%
The death penalty doesn't save on the cost of punishing	0%	0,3%
There is no reason for these trialists to hang	0,7%	0%
This was the first killing of a police officer in this area	0,3%	0%

---

* Data drawn from Hansson & Fine, 1989; and Hendriks et al., 1989.
** Reasons that were given by respondents in both surveys.

***	
Deceased's conduct	8%
Police conduct	5%
Crowd situation	2%
General conflict	2%
Provocation (source unspecified)	2%
Community support for the killing	1%

190

judicial error. Furthermore, in the PE sample, deterrence was the main reason given for supporting the death penalty (88%), whereas retribution was the central reason given by the Paballelo respondents (88%). This difference is probably due to the fact that the respondents in the Paballelo study included acquaintances, friends, and family of the deceased, who would have been more likely to have wanted retribution than the PE respondents, who were merely expressing opinions in the abstract. It is important for those conducting opinion polls, therefore, to note that the personal and situational context of respondents and the nature of the questions posed greatly influences the types of opinions expressed.[22]

The relevance of opinion polls

It is a penological truism that the attitude of the community to sentence is a factor that should be taken into account when deciding on the sentence to be imposed. This is of particular import when a court wishes to use forms of punishment other than imprisonment, for there may be strong opposition from the community to having offenders back in their midst. It is difficult for a court to assess the opinion of a community, particularly in South Africa where the apartheid system has produced communities that are geographically and ideologically isolated from one another. Surely then, a properly conducted survey that shows a community's attitudes to sentencing should be considered to be of relevance to a court? This did *not* prove to be the attitude of the court, however, in the case of the Upington 26.

A report on the Paballelo opinion poll was handed to the court as evidence in mitigation of sentence. Mr. Justice Basson ruled the evidence inadmissible on the grounds that it was *irrelevant*. He remarked during argument that it was the opinion of *a bunch of faceless and uninformed people*[23] (*S v Khumalo & 25 Others*, 1989).

Evidence based on findings from opinion polls is sometimes called into question, because it is said to be *hearsay*, that is, the actual persons who gave their opinions are not testifying before the court and thus the *reliability* of their opinions cannot be subjected to the scrutiny of the court.[24] In recent years, however, such evidence has been accepted by

---

22. For further discussion of these effects see, Williams et al. (1988).
23. Editors' translation of Afrikaans original.
24. Procedural devices that are employed to increase or test the reliability of evidence include the oath, cross examination, and the courts' observation of witnesses' demeanour (Paizes, 1983)

courts in a variety of cases (Paizes, 1983). In such cases, courts have had to decide on the *weight* that should be accorded such evidence, by considering carefully the *reliability* of survey findings and the qualifications of the experts who have drawn conclusions based on such data. In his comments to counsel and his judgment on this point, Mr. Justice Basson emphasized that he was *not even considering* the question of whether evidence based on the survey should be excluded because it contained *hearsay* evidence, or because it might be *unreliable*, but because he regarded evidence on the opinions of the community to be *inherently irrelevant*. In his view, the judge knew what the opinions of *right-thinking* members of the community were and, therefore, did *not* require further evidence on this matter.

Although courts have a wide discretion in deciding what evidence is relevant (Hoffmann & Zeffertt, 1981: 17), the breadth of this assumption on the part of this particular judge is, with respect, extraordinary. In a polarized society like South Africa, an all-white judiciary simply does not have access to the opinions of large sections of the black community. In *S v Khumalo & 25 Others* (1989), the judge certainly would *not* have had *direct* access to information about Paballelo, the particular community that was involved in this case. It should be remembered that neither of the assessors who sat with this judge to decide questions of fact were from Paballelo, or indeed the judge himself, were Africans. Nor can it be assumed that the opinions expressed by various witnesses, in the course of the trial on the factual issues involved, were sufficiently focused or informed to have portrayed the communities views on the question of sentencing reliably. There appears, therefore, to have been *no* factual basis from which the judge could have gauged, with any accuracy, the mood and temper of this community among whom the incident had taken place and into which at least some of the trialists would eventually have had to be released.

This last dimension is underlined by the survey finding that this community would have been prepared to have the accused back in their midst, to serve sentences of community service. Ironically, the judge was prepared to hear evidence from a social worker, who interviewed the individual accused and found that several of them could be recommended for community service. Surely, therefore, it is *inconsistent* to have excluded the survey evidence which would have been directly relevant to the question of whether community service orders would have been an effective form of punishment?

The complete sentencing outcome was as follows: Fourteen of the twenty-six trialists were sentenced to death. They included the perpetrator and two of the three co-perpetrators. Two were sentenced to eight years imprisonment. They included the co-perpetrator who was *not* sentenced to death because of his youth. Four were sentenced to six years imprisonment. Six were sentenced to six years imprisonment suspended for five years, on various strict conditions. One of the conditions was that the trialists would complete 1 200 hours of community service in an old age home and in a church, over a period of forty months, *without* payment.

This decision to exclude evidence based on an opinion poll also raises a more fundamental question: In a divided society like South Africa, how does a judge actually determine the interests and attitudes of a community, when that judge is not prepared to accept a scientifically valid survey of community opinion? In a future South Africa it will be necessary for judges to be far more sensitive to the needs and fears of *all* sectors of the community. In order to achieve this, imaginative legal techniques will have to be adopted and the very composition of the judiciary will require serious re-examination. Ultimately such questions need to be placed in the context of the debate about the *accountability* of the judiciary to a wider public.

Bibliography

Books and articles

Bernadt, Vukic & Potash (1988). Summary of the Facts. Unpublished Notes of the Attorneys. Cape Town: Bernadt, Vukic & Potash.

Couper, M. P., Mouton, J. & Stoker, D. J. (1987). *Introduction to Survey Methodology.* Pretoria: Human Sciences Research Council.

Fine, D. & Hansson, D. S. (1989). *Community Attitudes to Sentencing in the Case of the Upington 26.* (Booklet.) Cape Town: Institute of Criminology, University of Cape Town.

Hammond, R. & McCullagh, P. S. (1977). *Quantitative Techniques in Geography.* Oxford: Clarendon.

Hansson, D. S. & Fine, D. (1989). A Survey of Community Attitudes to Sentencing: The Case of the State vs Khumalo and Twenty-Five Others. Unpublished report prepared for the Court. Cape Town: Institute of Criminology, University of Cape Town.

Hendriks, N., France, F. & Riordan, R. (1989). Black Port Elizabeth's Attitudes to the Death Penalty. *The Journal of the Human Rights Trust Monitor* December: 70–3.

Hoffmann, L. H. & Zeffertt, D. T. (1981). *The South African Law of Evidence* 3rd edn. Durban: Butterworths.

Paizes, A. (1983). Public Opinion Polls and the Borders of Hearsay. *The South African Law Journal* 100: 71–91.

Rademeyer, Van Wyk, Muller & Company (1987). *Socio-Economic Survey Statistics*. Upington: Rademeyer, Van Wyk, Muller & Co.

West, M. & Ramphele, M. (1988). The Social Context of Paballelo. Unpublished report prepared for the Court. Cape Town: Department of Social Anthropology, University of Cape Town.

Williams, F. P., Longmire, D. R. & Gullick, D. B. (1988). The Public and the Death Penalty: Opinion as an Artifact of Question Type. *Criminal Justice Research Bulletin* 3: 1–5.

Newspaper articles

The Argus (2 February 1990).

Legal cases

S v Khumalo & 25 Others May 1989 unrep. (OPD).

Acts

The Criminal Procedure Act 51 of 1977.

CHAPTER NINE

Corporal punishment: Acceptable state violence?

Julia Sloth-Nielsen

Introduction

More than 40 000 people are whipped each year in South Africa, most of them juveniles (McQuoid-Mason, 1987).

It is noteworthy that while the state's use of violence has become the major focus for human rights organizations and anti-apartheid groups both within South Africa and externally, virtually *no* attention has been paid to the form of violence that is most frequently and pervasively inflicted by the state, namely, whippings imposed as a sentence by the courts. Judicial sentences of corporal punishment represent the most extreme example of the state's use of coercive power (Garland & Young, 1983). Legal provisions sanctioning corporal punishment imply that, in the final instance, the state will resort to bodily violence to impose its norms on those who offend. Whipping, even for juvenile offenders, clearly contravenes international conventions on human rights and has fallen into disrepute in most parts of the world. It was pointed out thirty years ago that flogging as a punishment had been abandoned in almost the whole of the *civilized* world and that South African legislation was exceptional (Kahn, 1960). Despite some amelioration in both the law and the practice of whipping, however, at present there would seem to be *no* possibility of its abolition. The central question addressed in this chapter, then, is why the South African state continues to rely upon flogging as a sanction. In this regard it is necessary to examine carefully the history of the use of corporal punishment as judicial sanction in South Africa. Aspects of the history of corporal punishment will be explored in order to suggest what function this sentence has served in

South Africa, and to gain a better understanding of the operation of this punishment today.

What will become clear, is that the imposition of whipping is not merely a relic of the past, an anachronism, abandoned elsewhere and overdue for reform here. This *progress or reform* perspective on the development of corporal punishment, although popular in current legal writing and a feature of recent judicial decisions on the topic of whipping, does not illuminate sufficiently the *particular* role played by whipping as a punishment in *our* society. Furthermore, the notion of *inevitable progress* also fails to explain the way in which the state has responded periodically to *crises*, by *increasing* the legal opportunities for the imposition of whipping. In essence, this approach does not take account of the wider *ideological* and *social implications* of the practice of judicially-imposed whipping.

It must be conceded that there is some evidence of public support for whipping as a form of punishment. Whipping was one of the sanctions imposed by the *Peoples' Courts*, alternative adjudicatory structures set up by black communities during 1985 and 1986. In addition, it has been alleged that there is considerable support among black people for the practice of whipping, since it is a customary form of punishment. The view that we are progressing belatedly from brutal to more civilized forms of punishment in South Africa does not take issue with the prospect that in a future South Africa, corporal punishment might indeed be retained and legitimized by reason of public support. The motivations for this analysis of the history of corporal punishment, therefore, are to expose the roots of this perception, to cast doubt upon its validity, and to discuss its implications for the future.

Three themes in the historical development of corporal punishment in South Africa

Corporal punishment: The seventeenth to the nineteenth century

The retention of whipping in South Africa, despite major shifts in penal practice in both Europe and in South Africa in the eighteenth and nineteenth centuries, is the starting point of this historical exposition. Prior to this period the focus of punishment was the body of the accused. Punishment was the public infliction of physical pain, a spectacle of suffering for all to see, a symbol of the might and power of rulers and kings. The development of custodial institutions, in particular prisons, is linked inextricably to the industrial revolution and the development of the factory. The prison was a symbol of a new form of power, designed to control individuals by disciplining the mind and the soul during incarceration, rather than through spectacular, but increasingly repulsive, public displays of suffering.

At the Cape in the seventeenth and eighteenth centuries, many different forms of bodily punishment short of death were available to the authorities, including floggings, brandings, and the severing of limbs (Venter, 1959). The authorities at the Cape were influenced, however, by developments in Europe relating to the rejection of torture and other *barbarous* punishments. Gradually they began to express their opposition to the infliction of physical punishment and the European notions of *moderate, measured* incarceration took root (Van Zyl Smit, 1984). In 1828, a Commission of Inquiry claimed that the prison system had expanded to fill the gap left by the abolition of the *vicious* punishments that had been used during the eighteenth century. Corporal punishment as a sanction, however, did not disappear with the reforms that occurred in the penal system throughout the nineteenth century. Flogging was retained in the colonies, despite the increasing distaste expressed by the colonial powers (Pete, 1984). In this respect there was an ever-widening divergence between penal developments in Europe and penal practice in the colonies.

A major causative factor for this divergence is to be found in the colonial experience of *slavery*. Although slave owners were forbidden to torture their slaves, there was widespread abuse of this rule. Slave owners repeatedly subjected their slaves to a variety of cruel and brutal practices under the guise of *moderate chastisement*. There was a clear link between corporal punishment administered by slave owners and whippings imposed by the courts (Ross, 1983). It would seem that slaves featured disproportionately as objects of legal physical punishment (Ross, 1983; and Venter, 1959).[1] During the process of the abolition of slavery[2], limits were placed upon the rights of slave owners to legally punish their slaves. The state also intervened in an unsuccessful attempt to monitor the imposition of whippings as chastisement (Rayner, 1986). Cape farmers were hostile to state attempts to curtail their rights to discipline slaves physically, and they continued to clamour for the re-introduction of the right to flog *servants* after the abolition of slavery (Rayner, 1986). In Natal, the Masters and Servants Ordinance 2 of 1850, which regulated conditions of employment between *masters and ser-*

---

1. For a contrary view, see Shell (1989).
2. Which commenced in 1807 and ended during the 1830s.

vants, retained corporal punishment as the sanction for violations of employment contracts, for neglect of duty, and for disobedience by *servants*. In the Cape, laws were enacted to protect the labour of erstwhile slaves to meet the increasing labour needs of the developing Cape Colony and to compel slaves to remain with their owners as servants and apprentices. The Masters and Servants Act 15 of 1856 provided for the harsh punishment of infringements by servants.[3] Ross (1983) points out that despite the *formal* abolition of slavery, old patterns of physically disciplining workers reasserted themselves and farm workers in particular were frequently subjected to whippings.

It is important to recognize the link between slavery, the growing labour demands of the colony, and flogging, for it is at this point that the South African penal experience diverges from the European progression toward the *civilization* of punishments. For the colonists, whipping was a *non-disruptive* form of labour control, one which was *demonstrably* punitive and, therefore, important for maintaining discipline among *unruly* workers in *outlying* areas. In addition, flogging was entirely consistent with the colonial ideology and imagery of the labouring classes.

It is to this second theme, the *ideological implications* of whipping, that the discussion is now turned. Pete's (1986) description of the development of the penal system in colonial Natal demonstrates that the practice of flogging was only partially shaped by the need to discipline black labourers. It was equally a reflection of the colonists' image of the black person (Pete, 1986). The white settlers viewed the large black population around them both as *children* and as *savages*. This served to justify the *guiding hand of the white person, leading black children in the paths of righteousness*. The black person's faculties of reason, like a child or an animal, were not sufficiently developed to allow the behaviour of that person to be altered in prison solely by ideological means. Physical coercion was thus seen as necessary to secure obedience, for this could be understood clearly by the black person. Imprisonment alone was seen as insufficient punishment for the *rebellious savages*: they had to be taught that the white man was superior. In a debate in 1876,[4] one member of the Natal Legislative Council argued that, *'[i]n many cases the Kaffir had such a thick skin that whipping had little effect'* (Pete, 1984: 136). In the same debate,

---

3. Ermacora (1976) describes similar South West African regulations promulgated in 1896 which permitted servants to be whipped for violation of duty.
4. Which centered on the proposed abolition of whipping for offences under the Masters and Servants Ordinance 2 of 1850.

another member maintained that, *'[t]he fact was, a Kaffir liked a master who was masterful'*, a view clearly indicative of the paternalistic ideology of the times (Pete, 1984: 136). The logic then, was that physical pain was the only way to impress upon *ignorant savages* their duties as servants to white people.

Contemporaneous accounts of floggings leave no doubt that these were indeed severe punishments. Corporal punishment for trivial offences against prison discipline formed an integral part of life for black prisoners in Natal. These punishments were unmerciful and frequently sadistically administered by white warders. In contradistinction to the treatment of black offenders, whites were whipped only infrequently. In addition, there was great concern about the degradation and humiliation that white offenders suffered in having to mix with blacks in prison and having to submit to the indignity of having to take orders from *Native* constables. The white person, it was believed, suffered severely from being deprived of liberty and this was sufficient. The *uncivilized* black person, on the other hand, could understand only physical pain (Pete, 1984).

It was not only in the British colonies that whipping was a racially differentiated form of sanction, one imbued with the image of the black person as an *uncivilized savage*. In the former South African Republic, now the Transvaal, corporal punishment was reserved *solely* for use on black offenders until 1880,[5] when legislation was passed permitting flogging as a punishment for white *escaped* prisoners (Law 14 of 1880). It is hardly surprising, therefore, that the vast majority of persons who have been subjected to whipping during this the twentieth century, have been blacks (Central Statistical Services, July 1977 to June 1988). The Lansdown Commission Report on penal policy in 1947 recommended that whipping be retained as a sentence, despite its abolition in most Western countries, chiefly because the Commission felt that this punishment was a deterrent of *'special efficacy'* for Africans who had not yet emerged from an *'uncivilised state'* (The Lansdown Commission, 1947: 484). In more recent decades, the paternalism in arguments supporting whipping has become more subtle, more underplayed. Now the logic of such arguments is that the state is serving the interests of the black population by retaining corporal punishment. After all, black witnesses testified before the Viljoen Commission in 1976 that corporal punishment was respected by the black community, that it was regarded as an effective deterrent, and that it should possibly be used more

---

5. Article 149 of the 'Grondwet of 1858' and Article 6 of Ordinance No 5 of 1864 (cited in The Viljoen Commission: para. 5.1.6.11.)

frequently. Nevertheless, the Commission did propose certain limitations on the use of corporal punishment. The Minister of Justice at the
time rejected some of these limitations because he felt that black South
Africans have *great faith* in whipping. One commentator asked whether
the Minister intended whipping to be reserved for black offenders only?
(Midgley, 1982). The paternalistic tone of the state's attitude to corporal
punishment in 1976 seems strangely reminiscent of the colonial concerns of the nineteenth century. The only change of emphasis seems to
be an appeal to the legitimacy of tribal custom, rather than to the
superior judgment of white rulers.

Corporal punishment: The twentieth century

This discussion of the colonial and racist notions that underlie the use
of corporal punishment does not reflect fully, however, the
development of corporal punishment in twentieth century South Africa.
In particular, the picture is incomplete without brief reference to judicial
responses to corporal punishment and to the restructuring of legislation
regarding whipping during the past century. The third focus, therefore,
is the role of the state in continuing to provide for a punishment that is
regarded elsewhere as being an *outmoded* and *barbaric* practice.

Throughout this century, both the law and practice related to whipping have been reformed significantly. Where floggings of 100 lashes
were not unknown at the end of the last century, the legal maximum
has been progressively decreased and now stands at seven strokes
(Section 292(2) of the Criminal Procedure Act 51 of 1977). In the forties,
the cat-o'-nine-tails was outlawed for use in flogging and the instrument
now used is a cane (Regulation 100(3) of the Prison Regulations promulgated in terms of the Prisons Act 8 of 1959). The age of a person
who may be whipped has been reduced repeatedly. At one time it was
sixty years, it has now been halved to thirty years (Section 295 (1) of the
Criminal Procedure Act 51 of 1977).[6] Women are now excluded from
the sentencing jurisdiction of the courts for whipping (Section 537 of
the Prisons Act of 1959 and Section 295 of the Criminal Procedure Act 51
of 1977). Except in the case of juveniles, no-one may be subjected to a
whipping more than twice and a second whipping may not be imposed
within a period of three years of the last sentence of whipping (Section 292(3) of the Criminal Procedure Act 51 of 1977). In addition, the

---

6. See, however, Section 54(2)(d) of the Prisons Act 8 of 1959 which permits
   the imposition of whippings for prison disciplinary offences on men up to
   the age of forty.

courts have increasingly expressed their dislike of the practice of corporal punishment. In the guidelines emerging from recent decisions it is clear that, at present, the tendency is to restrict the opportunities for the imposition of whipping. For example, it is now deemed undesirable to impose a sentence of whipping where the offence is not one aggravated by the use of violence (e.g. *S v Maisa*, 1968). It is also held that if previous whipping appears to have been ineffective, the repetition of such a sentence constitutes unnecessary brutality (*S v Nkoana*, 1985). Furthermore, it is maintained that to couple whipping with a long term of imprisonment is an unsound practice (*S v Sele*, 1985). This is merely a selection of some judicial limitations on the practice of whipping that have emerged from the courts.[7] Both the Lansdown Commission Report of 1947 and the Viljoen Commission Report of 1976 recommended considerable reform in the practice of whipping, although neither supported its abolition. Thus, the role of the judiciary in limiting the use of this sanction for adults should not be underestimated.

There are indications, however, that whipping remains an important mechanism in dealing with juvenile offenders (Midgley, 1975; and Hutchinson, 1983). Since juvenile whippings are not subject to compulsory review proceedings by Supreme Court judges, judicial disquiet has not significantly reduced the use of corporal punishment by magistrates (D'Oliviera, 1983). It would be premature indeed to assume that merely because the Supreme Court has criticized whipping as inhumane and brutal, that it is has become a *vestigial practice of little more than historical interest'* (Midgley, 1982: 402).

While the Supreme Court has been at pains to reduce the opportunities for the infliction of whippings, a consideration of the legislative structure of the punishment in this country provides a different perspective on the social context of corporal punishment. When the Nationalist government came to power in 1948, it ignored the thrust of the Lansdown Commission's recommendations that aimed to restrict corporal punishment. In 1952, the new government enacted legislation making whipping a *compulsory* sentence for certain offences (Criminal Sentences Amendment Act 33 of 1952). The courts were thus forced to sanction an orgy of whipping. At the time, compulsory whipping was deemed necessary for dealing with an alleged crime wave, but it is doubtful that any crime wave existed (Kahn, 1960). In 1955 additional offences were added to the list of those for which whipping was a mandatory sentence. These included the theft of goods from a motor vehicle and the receiving of stolen property. Of course, the majority of those who were whipped

---

7. For further detail, see Roberts & Sloth-Nielsen (1986)

were blacks. From mid-1957 to mid-1958, only 436 whites were sentenced to be whipped. In total, however, 18 542 offenders over the age of twenty-one years were sentenced to a whipping (Kahn, 1960). It should be emphasized that the fifties saw not only Nationalist accession to government, but also increasing political organization among blacks. Thus, despite protestations against mandatory whipping from the bench and the magistracy, it was only in 1965 when black political organization had been crushed and the rule of apartheid imposed upon the population that these compulsory sentencing provisions were relaxed.

There is further evidence to support the notion that the state resorts to physical violence, sanctioned by the legal system, in response to social turbulence. In 1986, during a period of severe political upheaval, the Criminal Procedure Act 51 of 1977 was amended to include the possibility of whippings as a sentence for offences such as public violence, sedition, arson, and malicious damage to property (Roberts & Sloth-Nielsen, 1986). This is a clear example of the state responding to a hegemonic crisis by emphasizing the physical force it will use to subdue its *unruly and uncivilized subjects*.

Setting standards: The future of corporal punishment in South Africa

In view of the legislature's periodic swing back to the punishment of the body and the latter-day paternalistic justification for continuing the practice of whipping, it may be supposed that possibilities for its abolition must lie with future governments of South Africa. There are compelling reasons why whipping should have *no* place in a legal system of the future in spite of indications of public support for the practice.[8] It is hoped that the following brief remarks will afford grounds for a reappraisal of this issue, especially the question of whether legally-imposed corporal punishment is acceptable, now or in the future.

This exploration of aspects of the history of whipping has shown that the notion of the unswerving reform of whipping, from a brutal form of punishment to one which is passably humane, does not accord with the reality of the development of corporal punishment. After all, there has been both reform and extension of the legislation pertaining to whipping. Despite reforms in the manner of infliction, corporal punishment

---

8. Shown perhaps in the use of corporal punishment by prefiguring institutions like Peoples' Courts.

remains a brutal and degrading punishment. Indeed, Mr. Justice Gubbay concluded in the recent Zimbabwean case of *S v Ncube* (1988) that whipping is a cruel and degrading sanction. He describes graphically the process it involves:

> Once the prisoner is certified fit to receive the whipping, he is stripped naked. He is blindfolded with a hood and placed face down upon a bench in a prone position. His hands and legs are strapped to the bench, which is then raised to an angle of 45 degrees. The ... calico square is tied over his buttocks and the kidney protector secured above his buttocks at waist level. The prisoner's body is then strapped to the bench. The cane is immersed in water to prevent splitting. The strokes are administered to one side across the whole of the buttocks. It is within the power of the officer administering the strokes to determine their strength, timing and, to some extent, their placement upon the buttocks. A second stroke upon the same part as an earlier stroke undoubtedly causes greater pain than were it to be placed elsewhere (*S v Ncube*, 1988: 714A–C).

Furthermore, the court rejected corporal punishment as contrary to the provisions of the Zimbabwean Constitution that outlaw inhuman or degrading punishment or treatment. Whipping, it was argued, is attended by acute pain and much physical suffering. Irrespective of the extent of regulatory safeguards, it is a procedure easily subject to abuse in the hands of a sadistic and unscrupulous prison officer, who might be called upon to administer such punishment (*S v Ncube*, 1988).

Despite reform, corporal punishment is no less brutal today than it was a century ago. The aura of official procedure that attends the imposition of corporal punishment, the certification of medical fitness to be flogged that precedes it, and the careful calculation of strokes and the measurement of rods does not detract from the fact that corporal punishment is, in essence, one human being inflicting violence upon another. As Mr. Justice Gubbay points out, whipping

> ... [b]y its very nature treats members of the human race as non-humans. Irrespective of the offense he has committed, the vilest criminal remains a human being possessed of common human dignity. Whipping does not accord him human status (*S v Ncube*, 1988: 772C).

Thus, one of the strongest arguments for the abolition of whipping in South Africa should be the desire to recognize the humanity of each member of this society. Treating people as objects, slaves, or savages does not embody the ideals of a South African legal system where each person is accorded equal worth.

To turn now to the broader ideological implications of whipping in the South African context, it is important to recognize that whipping imposed as a sentence, sanctioned by the courts, legitimates the state's use of violence in general. This point is made explicit by the European Court of Human Rights who, in 1978, were called upon to adjudicate in the case of *Tyrer v United Kingdom* (1978). Tyrer was a fifteen-year-old youth who had been sentenced to a caning by the juvenile court on the Isle of Man. He lodged an application at the European Commission of Human Rights, complaining that the infliction of a whipping violated Article 3 of the European Convention on Human Rights (1950), to which the United Kingdom is a signatory. Article 3 forbids *inter alia* the use of inhuman and degrading punishment. The court noted that whipping amounted to *'institutionalised violence, that is, violence permitted by the law, ordered by the judicial authorities of the State and carried out by the police authorities of the state'* (cited in *S v Ncube* (1988): para. 33). Whippings imposed by the courts and carried out by police officers and prison warders stamp an official seal of approval on what is essentially an assault on those who fail to act in accordance with society's norms. In a society such as ours, where legal and illegal violence has assumed truly horrific proportions, the starting point for reducing recourse to brutality must be a firm commitment by the state to outlaw violence in *any* form. Police officers should not be mandated to use the cane, whether privately below the courtroom with judicial approval, or publicly in the streets.[9] A system of punishment which includes whipping debases not only the individual who is punished, but the society as a whole. That state-sponsored violence perpetuates the prevalence of violence in society is difficult to prove empirically. However, there is evidence that between 1985 and 1986 the increase in the number of sentences of lashings handed down by the Peoples' Court in Nyanga corresponded with the increase in police brutality in the townships (Schärf & Burman, 1989). Those who participated in these courts claimed that the lashings they imposed were mild and fair in comparison with the treatment received by people at the hands of the state, in particular the security forces. The implication is that brutal punishments inflicted at the state's behest, create a climate in which recourse to personal violence against others becomes an authenticated mode of settling disputes. It is incumbent upon the state, therefore, to set the standard from which those who are governed can take their cue.

An issue that remains to be explored is the question of whether the peculiar South African context merits a different approach to the practice of whipping. As noted earlier, recent justifications for the practice of whipping hinge on the assertion that whipping enjoys the support of

---

9. A reference to the use of sjamboks and quirts by the SAP, particularly when dispersing crowds.

the black community and that whipping is consistent with customary notions of appropriate penal measures. Since anthropological evidence of corporal punishment as an indigenous tradition is not conclusive, the validity of this argument must be regarded as doubtful. Ndabandaba (1974) mentions that corporal punishment was not commonly imposed by traditional Zulu courts. Possibly the most illuminating example, however, comes from the Namibian courts. Some detainees who were members of the South West African Peoples' Organization (SWAPO) were freed from police custody only to be ferried, with the complicity of the police, to the Tribal Courts where they were flogged brutally. During an application to the Supreme Court for an interdict to prevent such thrashings, the victims

> ... proved the nature and development of criminal procedure under tribal law and custom. Corporal punishment was unknown until introduced by a Government official dubbed Shongola Hahn (Sjambok Hahn) (Soggett, 1986: 73).

This strongly suggests that at least in one part of southern Africa corporal punishment was *not* a traditional sanction, but became internalized only after conquering imperialists had imposed their forms of punishment upon the population.

It seems that the death sentence *was* a traditional tribal punishment. However, this does *not* mean that tribal tradition endorsed other forms of corporal punishment. Capital punishment was imposed for witchcraft to eradicate the sources of evil, not as a means of punishing offenders. The intention behind capital punishment can thus be distinguished from the purpose of corporal punishment.

Despite the tentative nature of this evidence, it may prove quite impossible now, in 1990, to determine the true content of indigenous law as it was *before* it became tainted by the experience of black communities at the hands of the colonists. The experience of the historical process described above undoubtedly continues to influence black communities' perceptions of the acceptability of whipping.

If the argument that the retention of corporal punishment is legitimized by indigenous traditional concepts does not hold water, then the assertion that there is informed community support for whipping should also be carefully re-examined. Does the community really wish to perpetuate the whipping practices of the past? For example, the sanctions advanced by Peoples' Courts were originally conceived to be *conciliatory* in nature. Violence, and hence corporal punishment, was discouraged for it was seen as an *'instrument of police brutality'* (Van Niekerk, 1988: 292). The fact that abuses and brutality did occur in practice does not detract from the fact that a *different concept* of adjudicative justice was *intended*. This new concept included practices such as dispute settlement and restitution rather than punishment, reintegration rather than the humiliation of offenders, and the re-education of delinquents, instead of the generation of hatred that results when the humanity of the recipients is destroyed through the imposition of physical punishment. These ideals should determine the response to corporal punishment as a sanction of the future. In rejecting violence, the state would be setting the precedent by which its commitment to the values of decency and human dignity could be measured. Corporal punishment has no place in the future of South Africa.

Bibliography

Books and articles

Central Statistical Services (July 1977 to June 1988). *Statistics of Offences*. Pretoria: Government Printer.

D'Oliviera, J. A. (1983). 'Corporal Punishment as an Alternative to, or in Part Commutation of a Sentence of Imprisonment'. *The Magistrate* 18: 191–203.

Ermacora, F. (1976). Flogging in Namibia. Unpublished Conference Paper. Dakar: International Conference on Namibia and Human Rights.

Garland, D. & Young, P. (1983). *The Power to Punish*. London: Heinemann.

Hutchinson, D. (1983). 'Juvenile Justice'. In *Criminal Justice in South Africa*. (Ed.) Olmesdahl, M. J. C. & Steytler, N. Juta: Cape Town

Kahn, E. (1960). 'Crime and Punishment 1910–1960'. *Acta Juridica*: 191–222.

McQuoid-Mason, D. (1987). Children in the Dock. Unpublished paper. Durban: University of Natal.

Midgley, J. (1975). *Children on Trial: A Study of Juvenile Justice*. Cape Town: National Institute for Crime Prevention and the Rehabilitation of Offenders (NICRO).

Midgley, J. (1982). 'Corporal Punishment and Penal Policy: Notes on the Continued use of Corporal Punishment with Reference to South Africa'. *Journal of Criminal Law and Criminology* 73: 388–403.

Ndabandaba, G. L. (1974). 'Crime and the African'.*Crime, Punishment and Correction* 3: 27–41.

Pete, S. (1984). The Penal System of Colonial Natal: From British Roots to Racially Defined Punishment. Unpublished LLM Dissertation. Cape Town: University of Cape Town.

Pete, S. (1986). 'Punishment and Race'. *Natal University: Law and Society Review* 1: 99–114.

Rayner, M. (1986). Wine and Slaves: The Failure of an Export Economy and the Ending of Slavery in the Cape 1806–1834. Unpublished Ph.D. Dissertation. USA: Duke University.

Roberts, A. & Sloth-Nielsen, J. (1986). 'Whippings: The Courts, the Legislature and the Unrest'. *South African Journal on Human Rights* 4: 224–9.

Ross, R. (1983). *Cape of Torments, Slavery and Resistance in South Africa.* London: Routledge & Kegan Paul.

Schärf, W. & Burman, S. (1989). Informal Justice and Peoples' Courts in a Changing South Africa. Unpublished paper. Cape Town: University of Cape Town.

Shell, R. (1989). 'The Family and Slavery at the Cape 1680–1808'. In *The Angry Divide.* (Eds.) Wilmot, J. & Simons, M. Cape Town: David Philip.

Soggett, D. (1986). *Namibia: The Violent Heritage.* London: Resi Collings.

The Lansdown Commission (1947). *The Lansdown Commission Report.* Pretoria: Government Printer.

The Viljoen Commission (1976). *The Viljoen Commission Report.* Pretoria: Government Printer.

Van Niekerk, G. M. (1988). 'People's Courts and People's Justice in South Africa'. *De Jure* 21: 292–305.

Van Zyl Smit, D. (1984). 'Public Policy and the Punishment of Crime in a Divided Society: A Historical Perspective on the South African Penal System'. *Crime and Social Justice* 21/22: 146–62.

Venter, H. J. (1959). *Die Geskiedenis van die Suid Afrikaanse Gevangenisstelsel 1652–1958.* Pretoria: HAUM.

Acts, ordinances, and conventions

Law 14 of 1880 of the Zuid Afrikaanse Republiek.

Ordinance 5 of 1864.

The Criminal Procedure Act 51 of 1977.

The Criminal Sentences Amendment Act 33 of 1952.

The European Convention on Human Rights of 1950.

The Masters and Servants Act 15 of 1856.

The Masters and Servants Ordinance 2 of 1850.

The Prisons Act 8 of 1959.

Legal cases

S v Maisa 1968 (1) SA 271 (T).

S v Ncube 1988 (2) SA 702 (ZSC).

S v Nkoana 1985 2 SA 395 (T).

S v Sele 1985 3 SA 1039 (0).

Tyrer v United Kingdom 1978 YB (European Court on Human Rights).

CHAPTER TEN

Community responses to police abuse of power: Coping with the kitskonstabels

Derrick Fine and Desirée Hansson[1]

Introduction

From late 1986 through 1987, a category of black police officers, officially termed *Special Constables*[2], were deployed in the majority of the urban and in certain of the rural African townships of South Africa. By February 1989, this *sub-force* was 5 000 strong (*Hansard* (House of Assembly Debates), 24 April 1989: col. 6383). Township residents have come to refer to these policemen as *instant constables* or *kitskonstabels*, due to their very limited, six-week training period. Kitskonstabels were part of the state's attempt to regain control in the African townships after the Black Local Authorities collapsed under popular resistance during 1984 and 1985. Chapter 2 has located the kitskonstabels, along with the municipal police and vigilantes, within the state's overall counter-revolutionary strategy.

> [S]erious abuses of power by kitskonstabels occurred in many areas from the first weeks of their deployment, ranging from fatal shootings, arbitrary assaults, and sexual abuse, to verbal abuse and harassment (Fine, 1989:58).

Between February 1987 and August 1989, the kitskonstabels killed forty-nine township residents and, by February 1988, they had been

---

1. The authors would like to thank the members of the Legal Education Action Project (LEAP) at the Institute of Criminology for their information, help, and support.
2. Appointed in terms of Section 34(1) of The Police Act 7 of 1958.

served with five Supreme Court interdicts restraining them from unlawful conduct (Fine, 1989).

The abuse of power by the kitskonstabels is not the primary concern here, for this topic has already been thoroughly discussed in Fine (1989).[3] Instead, this chapter focuses on the ways, both productive and counter-productive, in which African communities have coped with such abuses in the period between late-1986 and mid-1989. Community responses are critically assessed, problems are highlighted, and legal strategies are discussed. Particular attention is paid to the role that legal professionals and para-legals[4] have played in assisting communities to gain access to and redress through the criminal justice system.

A note on rural communities

Most of the illustrative examples used in this chapter are drawn from communities located in the Cape Province. This is due to the fact that the findings reported here are derived from fieldwork conducted by the Legal Education Action Project (LEAP)[5], which operates in the *Cape*. More importantly, many of the examples come from *rural* areas, for it is these communities which have faced high levels of repression and abuse by the security forces, in combination with a legal system which is often inaccessible and hostile. Our research has shown this to be particularly true of several communities in the Eastern Cape. This vulnerability seems to be produced by a number of factors, including a lack of awareness of basic legal rights and court procedures, insufficient legal representation, the lack of an independent criminal justice system[6], and repression which decreases cohesion, thus impeding a community's ability to deal with its legal problems effectively

3. For details of abuses on the part of the municipal police, see The Catholic Institute for International relations (CIIR) (1987), and for abuses committed by vigilantes, see Chapter 3 of this book.
4. People without formal legal qualifications, who are trained in practical legal skills like interviewing, the taking of statements, and the collection of evidence. At present, para-legals are working in legal firms, advice offices, and community organizations.
5. LEAP is part of the Institute of Criminology at the University of Cape Town, and is concerned *inter alia* with the monitoring of police abuses of power and the training of para-legals and advice workers, especially in rural areas.
6. For example, in a small town in the Klein Karoo, the magistrate is a reserve policeman. This means that he may arrest and pass judgment on the same person. Similarly, in Eluxolweni in Hofmeyr, the policeman directly responsible for kitskonstabels is also the public prosecutor.

(Dugmore, 1989). Furthermore, inaccessibility of rural communities and their underdeveloped infrastructure often places them beyond the reach of the mass media, both national and international, thus allowing the authorities ample opportunity for the abuse of power without having to face the negative consequences of public reaction.

Community responses to the kitskonstabels

General responses

Since their inception, the kitskonstabels have developed a reputation for misconduct, lawlessness, and violence. Despite the state's claims to the contrary, this conduct has meant that they have *no* legitimacy in African communities. How then have these communities come to deal with the kitskonstabels and the problems they have created?

Community responses have been varied, ranging from cowering submission to legal action and defiance. In areas where levels of political organization have been relatively low, kitskonstabel deployment has tended to result in unhappy submission and disillusionment on the part of residents. In areas characterized by higher levels of political organiz- ation, repression and the presence of kitskonstabels has produced frustration and disorganization. In general, however, progressive organ- izations in these areas have continued to address the problems facing their communities. Community Defence Committees have been intro- duced to develop ways of protecting the physical well-being of residents who are harassed by *inter alia*, the kitskonstabels, the municipal police, and vigilantes (The Catholic Institute for International Relations (CIIR), 1987). In a number of areas, advice offices or trained advice-givers have played important roles in dealing with problems related to kitskonsta- bels and policing in general.[7]

Pleas and letters to the authorities

Communities have resorted to measures such as pleas and letters to the authorities, unfortunately with minimal effect. The plight of the Thembalesizwe township in Aberdeen is a case in point. After the death of community leader, the Reverend Boy Jantjies, and futile attempts to lodge complaints at the Aberdeen police station, residents wrote to the regional headquarters of the police in Graaff Reinet in the following terms:

---

7. For example, in Botsabelo in the Orange Free State (OFS), and Victoria West, Mossel Bay, Oudtshoorn, and Aberdeen in the Cape.

Here in Aberdeen "special police" have recently been stationed ... The town was completely calm before these police arrived ... The special police are armed with a gun, bullets and a sjambok. If you get arrested by them, you are first handcuffed and then peppered with sjamboks and then still arrested and taken to the nearest police station to appear before the magistrate on some or other charge.

You are aware of the fact that a life has already been taken by the police here. On all the street corners the only topic of discussion is the actions of the police.

What is so strange for the community, is the fact that the police, while they are on duty, take strong drink with the community in public drinking places and then later pick on those who have not offered them drink. The public is fully aware of this and to crown it, there are many, in fact hundreds of witnesses to prove it.

We, the public ask in a friendly manner if this is the new policy of the law. All of us here are really on our nerves because what we know is right, is now suddenly not right ... A speedy and favourable reply would be appreciated before the community starts to work through other channels[8] (The Thembalesizwe Community, 1987).

Conditions, however, failed to improve and indeed degenerated to the extent that the community was forced to seek legal assistance with a view to obtaining a restraining interdict.

Counter-violence against the kitskonstabels

Two of the more prominent and distinct community responses have been counter-violence against the kitskonstabels and, by contrast, the institution of various forms of legal action. The extreme provocation and frustration experienced by communities that are subjected to unlawful conduct and brutalization at the hands of the kitskonstabels has inevitably given rise to counter-violence. Across the country kitskonstabels have been wounded, killed, and their homes and barracks have been fired upon and petrol-bombed.

Particularly in rural communities where residents and kitskonstabels often know one another on a first name or nickname basis, acrimony has been more personalized and has often manifested itself in brawls. Threats to their safety have led the kitskonstabels, in some areas, to live in separate barracks or in a particular part of a township. In Cape Town, for example, a great many kitskonstabels live in Crossroads, home of the *Witdoek* vigilantes and the base of the conservative township mayor, Johnson Ngxobongwana. In Bhongolethu, Oudtshoorn, all the kitskonstabels live in a block of fourteen houses on the edge of the

---

8. Editors' translation of Afrikaans original.

township's new extension and are protected by a special guard at night (*South*, 21 January 1987).

Obstacles to legal redress

Introductory comment

The pressing nature of the problems experienced by communities in relation to kitskonstabels has forced individuals and various communities to seek relief through *formal legal intervention.* Obtaining legal assistance, however, is by no means automatic, particularly for rural communities which are also usually those that are most severely affected by repression and poverty. There are numerous obstacles that impede individuals and communities in their efforts to obtain effective legal redress in matters relating to police action.

Lack of knowledge about legal rights

Many residents, particularly in rural areas, are simply unaware of their legal rights in relation to police procedures such as the use of force, entry, search and seizure, arrest and detention, questioning, interrogation, and the making of statements. As a result, their rights are more likely to be violated by kitskonstabels who are themselves neither particularly well-acquainted with the law, nor law-abiding. Furthermore, residents usually have little knowledge of available legal channels and procedures like criminal charges, civil claims, and interdicts. It is for this reason that projects such as LEAP have focused attention on the legal education of communities in basic legal rights and procedures.[9]

Lack of legal and other resources

Lawyers who are prepared to take on matters such as those involving the kitskonstabels are in short supply and are almost non-existent in rural areas. For many rural lawyers, it is deemed prudent to avoid *political* matters that could jeopardize their commercial work and existing relationships with magistrates, prosecutors, and the police. Lawyers who do take on such cases, therefore, are usually based in the larger cities and so face the constraints of money, time, and distance involved in travelling to rural areas. Service organizations such as the

---

9. LEAP uses educational workshops and accessibly-written booklets.

Black Sash, Advice Office Forum[10], LEAP, and the Legal Resources Centre (LRC) have tried to reduce the dependence of rural communities on city-based lawyers by training local residents as advice-givers or para-legals. These people are trained in the practical skills of interviewing, advising, the taking of statements, and the collecting of evidence.

When evidence of the injuries suffered by residents is material to the legal relief being sought, professional medical attention and a medical certificate are important. In rural areas, district surgeons are often the only doctors available and in general they are, unfortunately, not well-disposed toward victims of police action. Some district surgeons have been reluctant, and some have even refused, to assist in respect of civil claims and interdicts. On occasion, they have actually charged a fee for their services, which most township residents cannot afford (Hofmeyr Interdict, 1987).

The high rate of unemployment and poverty endemic in African townships means that the victims of kitskonstabel abuse are not usually in a position to afford legal services. Certainly in rural areas, state legal aid is not generally made available for matters that are deemed to be *political*. Thus, victims must depend on sources such as the Dependents' Conference of the South African Council of Churches for assistance. Financial constraints also impede residents' ability to meet the additional expenses of transport to lawyers and doctors and even the cost of medical treatment itself.

Difficulties with the criminal justice system

There has been effective institutional *support* for kitskonstabel abuses in the form of direct encouragement as well as non-intervention on the part of the regular South African Police (SAP). For example, in Oudtshoorn, members of the SAP joined a kitskonstabel in an assault on a Bhongolethu resident (Oudtshoorn Interdict, 1987), and in KwaNdebele, they maintained a passive presence whilst kitskonstabels attacked Vlaklaagte residents with pick-handles and pangas (CIIR, 1987). Furthermore, the Minister of Law and Order himself praised the kitskonstabels as follows:

> They have done excellent work but radicals do not like them [because] these constables do not put up with any nonsense from them (*Hansard*, 4 September 1987: col. 2839).

---

10. A structure which assists in the training and co-ordination of advice work in the Cape Province.

Township residents have experienced various difficulties in attempting to lay charges against kitskonstabels. The police have used a range of tactics to discourage legal action of this type. On occasion statements have been taken, but no docket has been opened. It has been commonplace for the police simply to refuse to take a statement. Complainants and witnesses have been harassed and intimidated frequently, by being assaulted or by having their families threatened. In many instances complainants' themselves have been charged with an offence, after trying to lay a charge against the kitskonstabels. There has been a tendency for thorough investigations to be conducted in only a small number of cases, usually those in which there is strong evidence or those which have already produced adverse publicity.

A problem experienced by rural communities is that of the local police acting as prosecutors. Communities see this as a problem, because the particular policeman who prosecutes has often been involved in, or is at least associated with, the kitskonstabel abuse that has given rise to the case in question. The situation in Hofmeyr is a case in point. Here a certain Warrant Officer Pretorius functioned as a policeman working closely with the kitskonstabels on patrol and in the charge-office, and at the same time also acted as court prosecutor. Eluxolweni resident Mabhuti Bhunta was beaten by three kitskonstabels and then locked in a cell at the police station, allegedly because he was drunk. He described Pretorius' dual role as follows:

> I asked Warrant Officer Pretorius for a doctor but did not receive any assistance at all. My body was sore all over and my right forearm was bleeding from where I had been struck by the gun handles. My mouth was also bleeding.
> On the Monday I was taken to court and charged with being drunk. Warrant Officer Pretorius was now playing his role as the prosecutor. I was not given any chance to talk in the court. I was not even asked to plead guilty or not guilty. I was found guilty and fined R30 (Bhunta, cited in Hofmeyr Interdict, 1987).

Warrant Officer Pretorius asserted, however, that there is nothing untoward about police officers acting as prosecutors in small towns where there are no permanent state prosecutors. He commented further:

> I can only presume that the fact that the majority of people who are charged, are found guilty, creates this feeling against my conduct as the state prosecutor (Pretorius, cited in Hofmeyr Interdict, 1987).

Another example of dual roles occurs when magistrates serve as police reservists in rural areas. For example, it is alleged that a magistrate in the town of Ladysmith, in the Little Karoo, is a police reservist, who after being involved in the arrest of suspects, is openly hostile when they appear before him in court (LEAP, 1988–9).

Problems related to repression

An assortment of problems related to repression by the police in general, and by other agents of state control, also inhibit legal redress, either directly or indirectly. The threat to those involved in legal action of ongoing harassment, surveillance, and even detention or prosecution inevitably deters complainants, potential litigants, or witnesses. For example, several deponents and assistants faced detention, harassment, and prosecution after involvement in the Hofmeyr Interdict (LEAP, 1988–9). Lawyers and their assistants have not escaped such harassment. For instance, while working on an interdict restraining kitskonstabels from assaulting township residents in Oudtshoorn, a Port Elizabeth attorney, Kobus Pienaar, was visited by two security policemen who accused him of inciting people not to give information to the police (*South*, 21 January 1987). Harassment has taken many other forms, from death threats and assaults to the slashing, deflating, or inflating of car tyres and the searching or ransacking of offices and homes (*The Argus*, 1 December 1987; and *New Nation*, 5 April 1989).

A problem which has begun to affect lawyers and para-legal assistants increasingly is denial of access to areas affected by *inter alia* kitskonstabel abuse. In terms of Regulation 2(3) of the Security Emergency Regulations, all police, including kitskonstabels, can summarily order people not normally resident in an area to leave the area,

> ... if they are of the opinion that it is necessary for the safety of the public, the maintenance of public order or the termination of the State of Emergency (The Security Emergency Regulations, 9 June 1989).

Such action has also inhibited fieldworkers from entering rural areas to monitor repression and to provide various welfare and educational services. In Beaufort West, for example, the security police interrupted a workshop on child care and expelled certain participants from the area. The legal challenge against this action was, however, successful (*Christian Women's League & Others v Minister of Law and Order*, 1989). In addition, political repression in the form of the restriction of organizations and the detention and restriction of members impedes the attempts of community organizations and advice services to assist communities with legal and other problems. A most alarming trend has been the high incidence of arrests and attacks on the membership and vandalism of the offices of advice and service organizations, particularly in the Eastern Cape and Border regions (*New Nation*, 27 October 1988).

A battery of media censorship provisions, including the Media Emergency Regulations (1989), and Section 27 of the Police Act 7 of 1958, have hindered the publication and exposure of abuses by kitskonstabels and others. Another more indirect method that has been employed by the state to minimize legal redress is the attempt to prevent money entering the country to cover the legal costs of political cases against kitskonstabels (The Fundraising Act 107 of 1978; and The Foreign Funding Act 26 of 1989).

In court cases lawyers may have to overcome the hurdle of the indemnity provisions under Regulation 15 of The Security Emergency Regulations (9 June 1989). This indemnity has already been invoked, albeit unsuccessfully, in a murder trial involving a kitskonstabel in Cape Town (*S v Mkohle*, 1987). Lawyers may also be hindered by being denied access to necessary documents. It is the state's privilege to withhold subordinate legislation like the Police Standing Orders and documents like the Minutes of Joint Management Centres and those containing orders given to SAP members (Section 66 of the Internal Security Act 74 of 1982).

The following quote illustrates residents' general disillusionment with seeking redress for police abuse through the criminal justice system:

> … [w]e have given up hope to see culprits in the police force suspended from their service or even being convicted of violence against us (LEAP, 1988–9).

Standard methods of legal intervention

Lawyers' letters

Standard methods of legal intervention, such as lawyers' letters, criminal cases, and civil claims, have all been attempted on different occasions in matters involving kitskonstabels. Lawyers' letters have usually been the first response in attempts to secure relief without having to resort to costly interdict proceedings. The purpose of such letters is to request cessation of unlawful behaviour by kitskonstabels, failing which further action would be contemplated. For example, in Zakhele township in the Eastern Cape, such a lawyer's letter was sent to the SAP Divisional Commissioner regarding the alleged unlawful behaviour of seven kitskonstabels, deployed in June 1987 (Lawyers for the Zakhele Community, 15 December 1987). The response to this letter merely acknowledged receipt and said that the matter was receiving attention (The Divisional Commissioner of the SAP, 15 January 1988). Little improvement in the situation resulted and several subsequent incidents of serious assaults on residents necessitated the institution of civil claims. In practice, such letters seem to have had very little positive effect, for their success rests on the often faulty assumption that the officers ultimately responsible for kitskonstabels will be inclined to convey the contents of these letters to their subordinates, and that the kitskonstabels will accept and act in accordance with such admonitions.

Criminal charges

The difficulties encountered by residents who attempt to lay criminal charges have already been mentioned above. The extent to which lawyers can improve the chances of matters being investigated and prosecuted is debatable. On occasion the presence of lawyers has ensured the recording of a complaint by the police on duty in a charge-office. In rural towns, where lawyers are frequently not available, the presence of a respected adult member of the community, such as a priest, a teacher, or a social worker, has reduced the likelihood of complainants actually being physically harassed or assaulted *at* the charge-office. An alternate strategy for complainants who fear recriminations is to request that complaints simply be noted in the Charge-Office Occurrence Book. In this way the complaint is placed on record *without* a criminal charge being made.

The tactic of getting *many* complainants to lay criminal charges in a *co-ordinated* manner has had a positive impact. In East London, the Black Sash assisted large numbers of Duncan Village residents to lay sixty-three charges against the municipal police. This, it has been reported, has largely deterred the municipal police from further unlawful conduct (Black Sash, 1988). Lawyers enlisted in more serious criminal cases and in inquest proceedings have played an important follow-up role by ensuring that charges are indeed properly investigated, and in pre-empting or countering any attempts to harass clients, or to force them to amend or to make new statements to the police.

Complainants' difficulty in identifying perpetrators has been a serious obstacle to the institution of criminal charges. Ironically, this has been less of a problem in the rural areas where residents tend to know the kitskonstabels by sight and usually also by name. Given the fact that kitskonstabels are not known for their propensity to identify themselves when complainants do not know them, residents often have the difficulty of identifying their assailants at identity parades. When perpetrators deliberately try to disguise themselves by wearing plain clothes and/or balaclavas, the prospects of there being sufficient identity for the purposes of criminal charges are decreased further.

Civil claims

Since the inception of kitskonstabels, a large number of civil claims have been brought against them. Given the many obstacles to legal redress already discussed, these claims probably only represent the tip of the iceberg. Additional problems specific to civil claims have also had a detrimental effect.

Section 32 of the Police Act 7 of 1958 stipulates that notice be given to the Commissioner of the SAP within five months that a civil claim is to be brought. As a result, a number of civil claims have prescribed because of delays on the part of clients and, sadly, because of lawyers failing to appreciate the urgency of these matters. The extremely long periods between actual events, the institution of legal action, and hearings or attempts at settlement often sap residents' motivation for bringing civil claims and, of course, also tend to dim their memory of events.

As with criminal charges, residents have had difficulties identifying the perpetrators of unlawful action for civil claims. People have tended to confuse the different police uniforms, primarily those of the kitskonstabels with those of the municipal police or private security guards. Furthermore, the fact that kitskonstabels often perpetrate offences whilst out of uniform or when disguised by balaclavas has made it extremely difficult to distinguish them from members of vigilante groups.

Civil claims have been dogged by a lack of material evidence to substantiate verbal allegations. The problems relating to medical evidence have already been mentioned above. In addition, the shortage of cameras in townships results in a paucity of photographic evidence. Particularly in rural areas, some time usually elapses before lawyers arrive on the scene. Greater awareness among residents of the importance of collecting these and other types of supporting evidence, such as bullets and torn clothing, would greatly enhance the prospect of winning civil claims.

Unfortunately, the Minister of Law and Order has not seen fit to release the specific figures of compensation pay-outs to victims of kitskonstabel abuse. It is significant, however, that pay-outs for civil claims by the police in general, increased by a dramatic 85 per cent during the period in which kitskonstabels were deployed. Between July 1986 and July 1987, R1 856 499 was paid out, as compared with R3 440 733 for the period July 1987 to June 1988 (*The Argus*, 14 February 1989). The case of *Nyuka & Two Others v Minister of Law and Order* (1988) is an interesting example of an out-of-court settlement by the police. In this matter Oudtshoorn-based journalist Nkosinati Nyuka and two other Bhongolethu residents were paid R31 500 (*The Weekly Mail,* 31 March 1989). It was alleged that Nyuka had been assaulted with rifle-butts and then shot in the back and side by three apparently drunk kitskonstabels while he was returning from covering a community event for the local newspaper, *Saamstaan.* It was alleged that one of the kitskonstabels also shot into the crowd that gathered. Members of the crowd, Gladys Ngalo and Lindiwe Phillips, were shot and as a result the latter was partially crippled. In keeping with similar tendencies in other matters involving kitskonstabels, the three victims were arrested and charged with public violence, after they had received medical treatment. None of the kitskonstabels have been charged with any offence arising out of this incident, in spite of the fact that the Control Prosecutor in Oudtshoorn wrote to the Attorney General's office, stating that in his opinion they had acted unlawfully (The Control Prosecutor, 23 October, 1987).

For litigants, the decision of whether or not to accept an offer of an out-of-court settlement is difficult, but too often the delay in waiting for the completion of extended litigation becomes the deciding factor. Although the Minister of Law and Order usually makes such out-of-court payments without any admission of liability, this is tantamount to an admission in everything but name. For the police, however, it has the benefit of limiting the adverse publicity generated by press coverage of a lengthy trial.

Brief comments on legal interventions

The standard methods of legal intervention outlined above, while useful in appropriate circumstances, are of limited effect in preventing the repeated, arbitrary, brutal, and unlawful conduct that is characteristic of kitskonstabels. Lawyers' letters are an *interim* measure and are seldom expected to have any *major* deterrent effect. Criminal charges and inquests are limited to individual perpetrators and have been shown to have a poor record of success. Private prosecutions are extremely rare. Civil claims are limited to the prospect of monetary compensation and take considerable time. Accordingly, when pleas and letters by the community and lawyers and attempts at laying criminal charges have been unsuccessful, communities have been obliged to apply for urgent interdicts to restrain kitskonstabels from systematic, unlawful conduct. In such situations, when all other legal means have been exhausted, residents have a real fear that the pattern of abuse will continue.

The use of individual and community interdicts

The first type of interdict that was attempted was the *individual* interdict. This is brought by an *individual* and is limited to restraining *individual* kitskonstabels from unlawful conduct in situations where they have been responsible for misdemeanours, or where there is insufficient evidence to show a pattern of abuse involving other kitskonstabels. In July 1987 in KwaNdebele, a resident of Gemsbokspruit successfully brought such an interdict against two kitskonstabels (*Ngwenya v Sibanyoni & Three Others*, 1987). Another form of individual interdict is that in which an individual applicant seeks a restraining order against an *entire force*. This may be done when a *pattern of abuse* has emerged in a particular area. In April and May 1987, two such interdicts were successfully brought against the municipal police in Duncan Village township in East London (*Makibeni v Gompo Town Committee*, 1987a; and *Makibeni v Gompo Town Committee*, 1987b). It soon became apparent, however, that individual interdicts were of little use in restraining the kitskonstabels as a force involved in a systematic pattern of abuse that affected a whole community. As a result, residents sought legal protection for sections of a community or for an entire community. In these cases a *community* interdict restraining kitskonstabels as a force from unlawful conduct has been used.

The first type of community interdict is where an organization, or group of organizations, bring an urgent application to protect their members from unlawful actions. In June 1987 the KTC branch of the Cape Youth Congress (CAYCO) brought an application for an interdict to restrain the SAP and by implication the kitskonstabels, from unlawfully interfering with lawful meetings held or organized by CAYCO in the KTC area, and from unlawfully assaulting or threatening to assault people attending, or wishing to attend, such meetings (KTC Interdict, 1987).[11] The Divisional Commissioner of the SAP in the Western Cape attempted to settle the matter out of court by offering an undertaking, but the applicants refused and continued to request the protection of a court order. An interim order was granted and the matter was postponed indefinitely (KTC Court Order, 5 June 1987). At present the return date has still not been set. This interim interdict appeared to have *some* effect for a *limited* period, but its actual and continued effect has been difficult to assess, given the volatile and dynamic political climate in KTC. The

---

11. CAYCO was subsequently declared a restricted organization in terms of The Security Emergency Regulations (24 February 1988).

interdict was certainly *politically significant* in asserting the right of a then-unrestricted organization to hold meetings during a state of emergency. Similar interdicts have been used in other areas.[12]

The second type of community interdict is where representative organizations, institutions, or community leaders, armed with a mandate from affected residents, bring an urgent application to protect an entire community from unlawful abuse. This is illustrated in the three examples that follow.

In July 1987 in Oudtshoorn, the Bhongolethu Civic Association (BHOCA), on behalf of the residents of the Bhongolethu township, sought a community interdict to restrain all members of the SAP, including the entire kitskonstabel force of sixteen in their personal capacities, from unlawful conduct against any resident of the township (Oudtshoorn Interdict, 1987). Sixteen affidavits were placed before the court to substantiate the community's case. Once again the state attempted to settle the matter out of court, by undertaking to instruct all SAP members to refrain from unlawful conduct and to obtain personal undertakings to this effect from individual kitskonstabels. The state went to great lengths to avoid the granting of an interim order, as is reflected in this perplexing extract from the State Attorney's letter to the applicants' attorneys:

> We wish to advise further that great prejudice attaches to a court order [as opposed to an undertaking] such as the one sought by your clients, as this invariably leads to misquotations in the press and undermines the authority of First and Second Respondents [the Minister of Law and Order and the Divisional Commissioner of Police] and therefore their ability to maintain law and order (The State Attorney, 23 July 1987).

Counsel for the applicants accepted the state's undertaking which, although included in the court record, was unfortunately *not* made an order of court. Nevertheless, the details of the application could be published as they formed part of the proceedings held in open court.

The major disadvantage of an interim order *not* being sought and granted is that applicants have to return to court to obtain an interim order in the event of an undertaking not being honoured. This is exactly what took place subsequently. The abuses perpetrated by kitskonstabels in Bhongolethu continued unabated, in spite of an undertaking from the highest authority to put an end to this misconduct. Between September 1987 and January 1988, the kitskonstabels shot, wounded, and killed a number of Bhongolethu residents (Oudtshoorn Interdict,

---

12. The situation in Pietermaritzburg is described in detail in Chapter 3 of this book.

1987). As a result, a further urgent application was brought for a community interdict to restrain the SAP as a force, as well as fifteen kitskonstabels in their personal capacities (Oudtshoorn Interdict, 1987). In response, the SAP made its standard undertaking. An interim interdict was granted and was made an order of court, which meant that kitskonstabels violating this court order could be committed for contempt of court (*City Press*, 24 January 1988). In February 1988 the matter was settled. A final interdict was granted with respect to both the first and second applications, *without* admission of liability by the state and with each side having to pay their own costs (Oudtshoorn Court Order, 18 February 1988; and *The Argus*, 18 February 1988). The potential sanction for breaking either of these final orders was, similarly, committal for contempt.

While Bhongolethu residents did express serious doubts about the long-term deterrent effects of this interdict, they felt that although sporadic incidents of assault and harassment continued, the interdict had *reduced* the *overall* level of arbitrary violence by kitskonstabels (LEAP, 1988–9; and *New Nation*, 25 February 1988). In December 1988 residents did take further legal action. Five Bhongolethu residents brought an application to have the particularly notorious kitskonstabel, Basie Mdewu, tried for contempt of court, as he had repeatedly broken the court orders. Although this matter was referred for oral evidence, to date it remains to be heard.

Events in the Thembalesizwe Township in Aberdeen provide a second example of the use of interdicts in dealing with police abuse. In January 1988 a community leader, James Nonnies, sought a community interdict on behalf of the residents, to restrain all members of the SAP as a force, all twelve of the kitskonstabels in their personal capacities, and two regular SAP members in their personal capacities from unlawful conduct against any resident of the township (Aberdeen Interdict, 1988). Considerable evidence was placed before the court in the form of thirty-six affidavits.

In response, the state gave an undertaking to ensure that all the respondents would not act unlawfully against residents. The twelve kitskonstabels and the two regular SAP members gave a similar undertaking. The state again attempted, unsuccessfully, to resolve the matter out of court. It was decided by agreement that the state would not contest the matter and that no order would be made regarding costs. The state's undertaking was made an order of court and a final interdict was granted in January 1988 on these terms (Aberdeen Court Order, 14 January 1988; and *The Argus*, 15 January 1988). Although the state did not admit liability, residents felt that the final interdict was a significant victory for the community (*New Nation*, 21 January 1988). Three days after the court order was granted, one of the most notorious of the kitskonstabels, Pokori Dunjana, flagrantly violated the order and an application for contempt of court was brought (*Jacobs & Two Others v Dunjana & One Other*, 1988). The state, however, defended Dunjana by claiming that the order had not been brought to his attention at the time of the violation (*The Weekly Mail*, 5 February 1988). Finally, the application was withdrawn for technical reasons and each side agreed to pay its own costs (*City Press*, 13 March 1988). The lesson to be learnt from this experience is the importance of incorporating *personal service with immediate effect* in the terms of such court orders.

It was not long before residents reported further violations of the court order and within a month two residents brought another application. This was against a different kitskonstabel, Phindile Gomo, for a brutal assault committed off-duty with his service shotgun (*Claasen & One Other v Gomo*, 1988). The state decided *not* to defend Gomo and at the hearing in March 1988, he failed to appear. Mr. Justice Alexander described Gomo as 'a foul-mouthed bully [and] a danger to the community' (*The Argus*, 2 April 1988). Gomo was sentenced to two months imprisonment for contempt of court, of which he eventually served six weeks. On his release he was *not* admitted back into the kitskonstabel force (LEAP, 1988–9) It is significant that the state left Gomo to his own devices, probably because his case was weak and it was felt that one kitskonstabel was an expendable *bad egg*. Thembalesizwe residents reported that while Gomo's imprisonment did not stop all kitskonstabel abuse, it did have a *noticeable* deterrent effect (LEAP, 1988–9).

In November 1987 a similar application was brought to protect eight residents of Eluxolweni, a township in Hofmeyr in the Northern Cape (*Fuba & Seven Others v Minister of Law and Order & Seventeen Others*, 1987). An interim order was granted, protecting these particular residents from unlawful abuse (Hofmeyr Court Order, 6 November 1987). When kitskonstabels continued to engage in violence on a wide scale, the application was amended and brought by the Midlands Division of the South African Council of Churches, on behalf of all the residents of Eluxolweni (Hofmeyr Interdict, 1987). This application sought to restrain all of the members of the SAP, including the entire force of thirteen kitskonstabels and a particular SAP sergeant, from unlawful conduct against any resident of the township. In the first application fourteen affidavits had been placed before the court. In the broader amended application, these were supplemented by thirty-seven additional affidavits. Characteristically, the state was only prepared to give an out-of-court undertaking. In February 1988, after stringent opposition on the part of the state, an interim interdict was eventually granted protecting the entire community from unlawful abuse (Hofmeyr Court Order, 12 February 1988). This effectively expanded the limited interdict which had been granted in November 1987 and which had protected particular residents only. The matter was postponed *indefinitely* for the hearing of oral evidence. To date this has not taken place and, accordingly, the interim interdict has remained in force.

This interdict, while reducing the *frequency* of unlawful assaults on residents, was *not* successful in tempering kitskonstabel conduct *in general*. In February 1988 one of the applicants, Mondile Duna, was blinded after being shot by a kitskonstabel. In June 1988 Fusile Daniso, another applicant, was brutally assaulted by eight kitskonstabels, disguised in women's clothing and headed by Zola Winter. As a result, Daniso brought an application for contempt of court against all eight kitskonstabels (*Daniso v Winter & Seven Others*, 1988). In contrast to the state's treatment of Gomo in Aberdeen, these kitskonstabels were defended, presumably because the state could not afford to sacrifice more than half of the kitskonstabel force in this area. The essence of the state's defence was a *complete denial*.[13] It is cause for concern that these kitskonstabels continue to walk the streets of Eluxolweni fully armed, and that a court date has still not been set. Residents have reported, however, that the mere bringing of the contempt application has resulted in a *slight improvement* in the conduct of the kitskonstabels (LEAP, 1988–9).

In interdict and contempt proceedings in which the state has chosen to file *opposing* affidavits, the following central themes have been raised in defence: The state has claimed that most of the allegations against kitskonstabels are fabricated and are part of a concerted campaign to discredit the kitskonstabels. Furthermore, this type of interdict and the attendant publicity are said to be tactics in the strategy of total onslaught against the state (e.g. Oudtshoorn Interdict, 1987). Action such as that taken by the kitskonstabels is said to be justified against *radicals intent on overthrowing the existing order* (e.g. Hofmeyr Interdict, 1987). It is claimed that kitskonstabels are subject to strict supervision and control and are disciplined for any misconduct (e.g. Hofmeyr Interdict, 1987). It has also been common for the state simply to deny allegations against kitskonstabels (e.g. KTC Interdict, 1987). Furthermore, the state has launched political and personal attacks to discredit the good faith of applicant organizations or individuals. In the case of the Bhongolethu

---

13. See Chapter 5 for further details of the range of police responses to allegations of misconduct.

Civic Association (BHOCA), this strategy backfired on the state (Oudt-shoorn Interdict, 1987). A survey of the community strongly refuted the state's allegations that the applicant, BHOCA, was *not representative* of the township residents (LEAP, 1987). Attempts have also been made to discredit individual residents, usually by reference to their being *comrades*[14] or to their having criminal records (Aberdeen Interdict, 1988).

On occasion, the state has resorted to more technical grounds of defence in their attempts to defeat or deviate applications. For instance, the argument of lack of personal service was used in the contempt of court application in Aberdeen (*Jacobs & Two Others v Dunjana and One Other*, 1988). In the Hofmeyr Interdict (1987), the state sought to prevent the Midlands Council of Churches from intervening as the First Applicant. It was argued that the Midlands Council of Churches did not have legal standing, because it had no local interest in the matter. This attempt failed. Mr. Justice Rein ruled that in law, the Midlands Council of Churches *did have* sufficient interest in the matter (Hofmeyr Interdict, 1987).

The use of community interdicts as a legal means of defending communities from abuse by kitskonstabels has certainly set a precedent which can be, and indeed has been, used to deal with similar forms of repression by other forces, such as the municipal police (e.g. *Gubula & 10 Others v Paballelo Town Council & 23 Others*, 1989; and *Masomothane & Six Others v Kayamandi Town Committee & 13 Others*, 1988).

While the successful use of the legal process to prevent the infringement of human rights is to be welcomed, a word of caution is necessary. The fact that the court acts *after the event*, in the sense that a serious pattern of abuse must be established to persuade the court to grant an interdict, limits its capacity to prevent abuse. Conditions in rural areas differ materially and, as a result, the success of interdicts in stopping abuse has varied considerably. At best, community interdicts have had a deterrent effect on arbitrary abuse, although to varying degrees in different areas. In our experience, this strategy has proved most successful in Aberdeen, moderately successful in Oudtshoorn, and relatively unsuccessful in Hofmeyr.

It is also important to recognize that high levels of repression and the obstacles to redress that have been outlined above sometimes make it *impossible* for a community to take the organizational steps that are necessary to apply for a community interdict. Beaufort West is just such a community, for despite widespread abuse by the police, *no* community legal action has been taken (LEAP, 1988–9).[15] In 1987 and 1988

---

14. Members of the anti-apartheid movement.

in particular, vigilante violence created a climate of fear and lawlessness, to the extent that it was only possible to bring *individual* interdicts in an attempt to restrain vigilantes (e.g. *Dlamini & Another v Jwara*, 1987; *Hadebe & Two Others v Zuma*, 1987; *Mkhize & Eight Others v Zuma*, 1987; *Mkhize & Another v Ntombela & Seven Others*, 1987; and *Zulu & Another v Zondi & Three Others*, 1987). A further, even more serious implication is the fact that various applicants and witnesses have been subjected to severe harassment and have even been assassinated (CIIR, 1987). Such consequences of taking legal action have led residents and human rights lawyers to seriously question the wisdom of bringing applications against vigilantes, who seem to be allowed and even encouraged to operate *outside* of the law (CIIR, 1987). Events in June 1986 in the Cape Town squatter communities in KTC are perhaps the best illustration of the difficulty of enforcing interdicts in situations of alleged police collusion with vigilantes. Here, an interdict was obtained restraining the SAP, the South African Defence Force (SADF), and vigilante leaders from unlawful attacks on the residents of KTC (*Mbewana & Five Others v Minister of Law and Order & Nine Others*, 1986). Nevertheless, two weeks after the court order was granted, vigilantes attacked and destroyed a large part of the KTC area. Furthermore, it is alleged that the SAP did *not* intervene and, at some points, even *assisted* the vigilantes (CIIR, 1987).

One crucial lesson has been learnt from the experience of bringing community interdicts against kitskonstabels: It is essential in situations where the state offers an undertaking, to *insist* that this is made an *order of court*. Failing this, a most important weapon in enforcing interdicts is lost, namely, being able to have perpetrators of continued abuse committed for contempt of court. The threat of a committal for contempt seems to have been the *only* factor which has had a *marked* deterrent effect on the conduct of kitskonstabels.

It must be noted that interdicts restraining kitskonstabels by no means prevent the state from employing *alternate means* of quashing township resistance. In Hofmeyr, for instance, surveillance by the security police was continued and criminal charges were used to tie up large numbers of activists in protracted trials. In April 1988, sixty-eight people were on trial in six cases, ranging from murder to public violence (LEAP, 1988–9).

---

15. The situation in the Pietermaritzburg area, described in Chapter 3 of this book, is even more critical.

Conclusion

To conclude on a more positive note: The actual involvement of residents themselves in the organizing and bringing of community interdicts has proved to be an extremely valuable experience in itself. It has restored some faith in the value of collective legal action and has enabled communities to regain some space in which to pursue legitimate social and political activities with less arbitrary interference. In addition, it has helped to train residents in advice-giving and para-legal skills which, it is hoped, will assist their communities in the longer term. Finally, the exposure of violations of human rights and socio-economic problems has, to some extent, lessened the isolation of rural communities.

Bibliography

Books and articles

Dugmore, C. (1989). Access to Justice in Rural Areas. Unpublished paper. Cape Town: Institute of Criminology, University of Cape Town.

Fine, D. (1989). 'Kitskonstabels: A Case Study in Black on Black Policing'. *Acta Juridica*: 44–85.

Hansard (House of Assembly Debates.) April 1989. Pretoria: Government Printer

Hansard (House of Assembly Debates) September 1987. Pretoria: Government Printer

Legal Education Action Project (LEAP) (1987). Unpublished Survey Results. Cape Town: Institute of Criminology, University of Cape Town.

Legal Education Action Project (LEAP) (1988–9). Unpublished Files. Cape Town: Institute of Criminology, University of Cape Town.

The Black Sash (1988). *Greenflies: Municipal Police in the Eastern Cape*. Cape Town: Esquire Press.

The Catholic Institute for International Relations (CIIR) (1987). *Now Everyone is Afraid: The Changing Face of Policing in South Africa*. Cape Town: CIIR.

Newspaper articles

City Press (24 January 1988).

City Press (13 March 1988).

New Nation (21 January 1988).

New Nation (25 February 1988).

New Nation (27 October 1988).

New Nation (5 April 1989).

South (21 January 1987).

The Argus (1 December 1987).

The Argus (15 January 1988).

The Argus (18 February 1988).

The Argus (2 April 1988).

The Argus (14 February 1989).

The Weekly Mail (5 February 1988).

The Weekly Mail (31 March 1989).

Letters

Lawyers for the Zakhele Community. Letter to The Divisional Commissioner of the SAP (15 December 1987).

The Control Prosecutor (Oudtshoorn). Letter to the Attorney-General (23 October, 1987).

The Divisional Commissioner of the SAP. Letter to Lawyers for the Zakhele Community (15 January 1988).

The State Attorney. Letter to the Attorneys for the Bhongolethu Community (23 July 1987).

The Thembalesizwe Community. Letter to The Divisional Commissioner of the SAP (1987).

Acts and regulations

The Foreign Funding Act 26 of 1989.

The Fundraising Act 107 of 1978.

The Internal Security Act 74 of 1982.

The Media Emergency Regulations of 9 June 1989.

The Police Act 7 of 1958.

The Security Emergency Regulations of 24 February 1988.

The Security Emergency Regulations of 9 June 1989.

Legal cases, court orders, and interdicts

Aberdeen Court Order (14 January 1988) (ECD).

Aberdeen Interdict 1988 (ECD).

Christian Women's League & Five Others v Minister of Law and Order 1989 unrep. (CPD).

Claasen & One Other v Gomo 1988 unrep. (ECD).

Daniso v Winter & Seven Others 1988 unrep. (ECD).

Dlamini & Another v Jwara 1987 unrep. (NPD).

Fuba & Seven Others v Minister of Law and Order & Seventeen Others 1987 unrep. (ECD).

Gubula & 10 Others v Paballelo Town Council & 23 Others 1989 unrep. (NCD).

Hadebe & Two Others v Zuma 1987 unrep. (NPD).

Hofmeyr Court Order (6 November 1987) (ECD).

Hofmeyr Court Order (12 February 1988) (ECD).

Hofmeyr Interdict 1987 (ECD).

Jacobs & Two Others v Dunjana & One Other 1988 unrep. (ECD).

KTC Court Order (5 June 1987) (CPD).

KTC Interdict 1987 (CPD).

Makibeni v Gompo Town Committee 1987a unrep. (ECD).

Makibeni v Gompo Town Committee 1987b unrep. (ECD).

Masomothane & Six Others v Kayamandi Town Committee & 13 Others 1988 unrep. (CPD).

Mbewana & Five Others v Minister of Law and Order & Nine Others 1986 unrep. (CPD).

Mkhize & Another v Ntombela & Seven Others 1987 unrep. (NPD).

Mkhize & Eight Others v Zuma 1987 unrep. (NPD).

Ngwenya v Sibanyoni & Three Others 1987 unrep. (KwaNdebele).

Nyuka & Two Others v Minister of Law and Order 1988 unrep. (CPD).

Oudtshoorn Court Order (18 February 1988) (CPD).

Oudtshoorn Interdict 1987 (CPD).

S v Mkohle 1987 unrep. (CPD).

Zulu & Another v Zondi & Three Others 1987 unrep. (NPD).

CHAPTER ELEVEN

The resurgence of urban street gangs and community responses in Cape Town during the late eighties

Wilfried Schärf [1]

Introduction

The proliferation of extra-parliamentary political organizations and the associated increase in political turbulence in South Africa from 1983 onward changed the balance of forces within oppressed communities. The changes were numerous and complex. The change that forms the focus of this chapter is the large-scale marginalization of male youths that occurred during and after widespread political mobilization within African and coloured townships. For many marginalized youths, urban street gangs became the most important social support network. On the whole the township communities in which such gangs resided and operated perceived them to be negative in effect.

In this chapter the central forces that gave rise to the resurgence of urban street gangs at this particular point in the history of Cape Town are sketched. Secondly, some of the efforts that have been made by

1. I wish to thank Nompumelelo Mbebe, Lindiwe Kota, and Baba Ngcokoto for conducting some of the interviews on which this paper is based. I would also like to thank Potifa Nkhoma, Lungile Daba, and Dinga Sikwebu for their valuable information on street gangs in African townships. I would like to acknowledge Lauren Nott of the National Institute for Crime Prevention and the Rehabilitation of Offenders (NICRO) Cape Town for her brave and pioneering work on gang engagement in coloured townships.

groups in the most affected communities, to curb gangs without police intervention, are discussed. Finally, these community initiatives are assessed and theoretical questions are posed about the limits of community intervention in situations that are shaped by structures that are beyond their control.

The marginalization of township youths

Background: Gangsterism before 1986

The resurgence of urban street gangs in coloured townships and the first appearance of such gangs in African townships in Cape Town need to be understood not only in the light of the overt political challenge to the state and the fluidity of personal roles that resulted from social turmoil, but also against the background of an exceedingly criminogenic society. Verwoerdian apartheid sought to keep the black population of South Africa disorganized and economically dependent. Further, all attempts made by blacks to burst out of this structural straight-jacket were criminalized. However, this policy was not applied to the coloured population with equal vigour. The intention seemed to be to co-opt coloured people to form a buffer against the African population and some attempts were made to this end following the Sharpeville disturbances in 1960 (Schärf, 1984a).

Economic dependency was ensured by preventing the accumulation of capital by blacks. Influx control was designed to confine the surplus African population to the economically impoverished homelands. Housing policies denied Africans freehold rights and any other relatively stable form of land tenure and thus robbed them of the opportunity of using their homes as collateral for loans. Licensing provisions in the townships were extremely restrictive, thus limiting opportunities for the growth of a black middle class (Kane-Berman, 1978). All forms of street trading without licences, otherwise known as the informal sector, were made illegal. Even the commodification of domestic services such as beer brewing was criminalized. This ensured that the state's sorghum beer breweries and retail bottle stores retained their monopoly of the townships, thus making each *racial group* pay for its own reproduction (Kane-Berman, 1978; and Schärf, 1984a). In addition, the education system for blacks was designed to perpetuate the *status quo* by keeping blacks under-skilled (Kane-Berman, 1978). Until the late seventies job reservation protected whites from competition in the job market (Hinds, 1985). There were thus pitifully few legal avenues to *financial success* open to Africans. To become an Urban Bantu Councillor[2] on a Black Local Authority was to enter into a political alliance with the apartheid state and such submission to the political patronage of the state led inevitably to confrontation with local township populations (Bloch & Wilkinson, 1982; and Swilling, 1988). Two predictable developments followed such a choice: Councillors attempted to enrich themselves and their supporters by means of their own form of patronage and large-scale corruption characterized their incumbencies (The Van der Walt Commission, 1985). Secondly, it was often politically too costly for councillors to use South African Police (SAP) assistance in ruling the townships. Therefore, with the blessing, and sometimes even the con-nivance, of the police they recruited right-wing vigilante forces to fulfil this function (Haysom, 1986; Haysom, Chapter 3, this volume; Schärf et al., 1987; and *The Weekly Mail*, 21 December 1989). What happened in the townships outside cities had its parallels in the homelands[3] where corrupt leaders, chosen and groomed by the apartheid state, ruled by means of patronage and state sponsored or condoned terror (Haysom, 1983; Hinds, 1985; *Hansard* (House of Assembly Debates), 24 April 1989; *The Weekly Mail*, 21 December 1989; and South African Pressclips, 1977–82).

Many Africans who chose not to take this path sought opportunities for survival in the *illegal* informal sector. They supplied or ran she-beens[4], produced or sold illegal intoxicants like marijuana and mand-rax[5], engaged in illicit moneylending, hawking, confidence trickery, and gambling, and ran illicit goods agencies or forged documents, especially drivers' licences.

In South Africa, unemployment among African males, particularly those under the age of twenty-five years, has always been exceedingly high. However, the official figures have continued to underplay the seriousness of the unemployment problem in South Afica (Moll, 1986). When Verwoerdian apartheid proved unworkable following the Soweto uprisings, political strategy occasioned the state to seek out a group of fledgeling entrepreneurs who could form the backbone of the newly nurtured, black middle class. The only sizable group that possessed entrepreneurial skills were the shebeen owners, and the state, with encouragement from liquor capital, thus focused on these shebeen owners and commenced a process of legalizing the distribution of liquor

---

2. Later renamed Community Councillors.
3. See Chapter 3.
4. Illegal bars in the townships.
5. Otherwise known as Methaqualone.

by Africans in townships. Ironically, the state seemed to be rewarding shebeeners' success as law breakers, whereas previously they had been vilified in political rhetoric (Schärf, 1984a) and persecuted by the police.

There was thus considerable structural inducement to Africans to seek survival opportunities on the *wrong side* of the law. The position of Africans in the Western Cape was worse than that described above. The coloured labour preference area policy meant that Africans were only legally entitled to be in the region if they had a job which no coloured person was willing or able to perform (Eiselen, 1955). This policy, which operated until 1984, also justified the state providing minimal housing and recreational and educational facilities for Africans in this region.[6]

Poverty was thus virtually guaranteed for the majority of Africans living in the Western Cape (Wilson & Ramphele, 1989). Youths were particularly vulnerable to poverty. Their lack of work experience and their reputation for being politically active made them less desirable employees than older men, who, having families to support, were less likely to risk losing their jobs by challenging the *status quo.*

Under these circumstances a high incidence of gang-formation among African youths in the townships could have been expected. This, however, only occurred in 1986, after the first two States of Emergency had produced turmoil in the townships. Prior to 1986, informal methods of control exercised over the youth by the older generation, parents, teachers, and community leaders appears to have prevented gang formation in African townships. When these forms of social control were swept away by the escalation of violence and the changing role of the youth in the liberation struggle, gang formation proceeded apace.

In the coloured townships, where the youth was structurally less deprived, street gangs had been a feature of the poorer sectors of townships from the forties onwards (Pinnock, 1982). The massive dislocation caused by removals under the legislation which defined and enforced separate *group areas* for officially defined ethnic groups during the seventies had an accelerating effect on gang formation. The fragmentation of extended families, the collapse of the informal economy, and the effect of new surroundings and growing alienation within communities increased the pace and scope of gang formation (Pinnock, 1982).

These gangs were parasites in the townships. They ran shebeens

---

6. For example, teachers training and technical colleges, theological seminaries and universities were not provided until after the repeal of influx control laws in 1986 (Schoombee & Davis, 1986).

which sold liquor and illicit drugs, they operated as moneylenders and extortioners, and they ran protection rackets and agencies for goods stolen within the townships and in white suburbs.[7] They also robbed and raped members of their own communities and indulged in gang fights over territory, markets, and women. They severely curtailed residents' freedom of movement, particularly at night and on weekends, and inhibited religious worship and political mobilization. Yet, to their members, gangs were a source of survival, for they provided a sense of manhood and dignity denied to them by society. They were also a form of social security: a brotherhood, where standing up for each other and helping a gang-brother were part of the ethos, if not always the practice. The close relationship between street gangs and prison gangs ensured that a member was always supported by a community of brothers in and outside of prison (Lötter & Schurink, 1986; and Haysom, 1981). This constituted a form of social security which the apartheid state did not offer the *underclasses*. Gang sub-culture had a profound effect on the values of the rest of the underclass. Gang notions of manhood, their images of women, their language, *ourokertaal*[8], their ability to sometimes *beat the system* and their skill at dealing with the police in order to win space for their survival strategies were particularly influential (Schärf, 1986b). The gangs became the source of *action* in the form of music, highs, women, kicks, excitement, and power. Above all, gangs constructed their own notion of dignity and pride in a society where the formal value system accorded them neither.

Gang membership and media coverage of gangs seems to have peaked in 1981 (Schärf, 1983) and diminished between 1982 and 1985. The police have claimed credit for this apparent reduction in gangsterism, maintaining that it is due to considerable numbers of senior gangsters having been imprisoned for lengthy periods (Schärf, 1984b). Some members of gangs, however, say that the publicity engendered by research into gangs robbed them of their mystique, so diminishing their attraction (Schärf, 1984c). Sociologists commissioned by the Prisons Service to study prison gangs have suggested that improved conditions and policies in prisons have reduced inmates' need to rely on prison gangs for protection and goods (Lötter & Schurink, 1986). However, Pinnock's (1982) argument that gang formation resulted from the fragmentation of community structures in the context of a declining economy suggests that the relative quiescence of gang activity and

---

7. Several gangs actually specialized in particular commodites like clothing, cars, electrical appliances, bicycles, guns, etc.
8. Translated as the language of old marijuana smokers.

reduced membership between 1981 and 1985 may have been due to increasing cohesion as social networks were reconstructed in communities.

African gangsterism after 1986

Introductory comment

Whatever the factors were that produced this period of quiescence, 1986 saw a striking resurgence of gangsterism in coloured townships in Cape Town and the emergence of gangs in African townships for the first time. More systematic research than that which has been completed is required for a thorough understanding of the social forces that enabled this resurgence of gangsterism. The discussion that follows is, therefore, somewhat tentative.

Until 1985, inter-generational relationships in African townships, unlike those in coloured townships, were generally characterized by adults holding the authority to lead, discipline, and chastise youth. Cultural tenets of respect for seniority and the tradition of extended family guardianship over youths seemed to prevent youths from seeking alternate support structures like gangs. This is not to imply that deviance among youth was absent. *Hooliganism*, as it was called, was fairly rife in the African townships during 1985. In fact it reached such proportions, that from mid-1985[9] communities set up People's Courts to deal with the problem (Burman & Schärf 1988; Schärf, 1986a & 1988a; and Schärf & Ngcokoto, in print). This *hooliganism*, however, was not perpetrated by gangs, but by loose groups that had no structure or continuity.

The formation of gangs in African townships seems to have developed out of three converging sets of factors: first, there was the education crisis in the schools, the lack of alternative education, and thorough political conscientization in a context where youth had little hope of employment; secondly, there was the call that was made to the youth to become impromptu soldiers or *Young Lions*, i.e., militaristic populism; and thirdly, there was the politicization of sport.

The education crisis in the schools

From 1976 schools in African townships in the Cape Town area were in a state of perennial ferment, with large-scale disruptions occurring in

---

9. Recent interviews with a founder member of the first People's Court, however, suggest that it was started in early 1985 (Schärf, 1989b).

1980, 1984, and for the greatest part of 1985 (Abrahams, 1988; Hall, 1986; and Hyslop, 1988). Essentially the education crisis was a battle for power between the state, which had long imposed its form of education, and scholars, sometimes supported by pockets of teachers and parents, who began challenging the state education system. The challenge was aimed at many of the anomalies of the apartheid system, such as the vast disparities in *per capita* expenditure on black and white pupils, the fact that black pupils, unlike whites, had to buy their own textbooks and stationery, the refusal of the state to allow students' representative councils to organize and mobilize, the detention of students and teachers, and the dismissal or transfer of teachers who were considered to be politically radical. Student challenges took the form of school and class boycotts, marches, rallies, attacks on school property, and, sometimes, attacks on teachers and their vehicles. During boycotts, students fostered the myth that they were involving themselves in *People's Education*, an alternative form of education that was to challenge the racially discriminatory *'gutter education'* provided by the state. In reality, however, there were only a few *alternative* programmes and after this limited range of programmes had been exhausted during a boycott, slogans, songs, and chants were introduced. This did not keep all scholars entertained and a considerable drift away from schools occurred. Those that remained politically involved claimed the moral high ground and excluded those who sought something more entertaining and exciting than shouting slogans. This may appear overly cynical, but the political mobilization of pupils was relatively haphazard and uneven. In defence of the student leadership, one must concede that they were under severe pressure, often having to meet secretly, being hunted, harassed, and detained by the police (Syren, 1989). Nevertheless, the outcome was that in the desire to mobilize support for protest against the apartheid state, very little in-depth political conscientization and building of organization took place. As the boycotts dragged on, more and more scholars dropped out of political organizations and sought other forms of entertainment. One form of entertainment that was not affected by ideological tensions was that of competitions for dance-groups known as *mapantsula*. Many youngsters imitating the wave of break-dancing styles that began in the United States joined mapantsula dance groups.

Not only did the student leadership exercise a tenuous authority over scholars, but the relationship between teachers and pupils underwent very serious changes. The state attempted to shift the unpleasant task of controlling pupils onto black principals and teachers. In trying to perform this task principals in particular, with some noteworthy exceptions, came to be seen as reactionary. Whatever respect they had enjoyed from students was gradually undermined during 1984 and 1985. Teachers too, found it increasingly difficult to exert authority over scholars. Thus, in this highly important sphere of socialization, both peer leadership and structural authority were weakened. This left a great many youths without role models or structures for containment.

A compounding factor was the apparent futility of completing school only to be left jobless on the streets. African males who do not have a tertiary level of education have severely limited chances of being employed. They must compete with older, more experienced, and politically docile men for jobs as manual labourers in which a school leaving certificate would certainly be of little assistance. This awareness of the uselessness of school qualifications became manifest at the same time that the turmoil in schools was causing disaffection with the education system itself (Schärf, 1989c).

The Young Lions and their relationship to adults

Disaffection and loss of respect for the institutions of the older generation seemed also to manifest itself in the domestic sphere, with the rise of the *Young Lions*. Compared to other regions, there were relatively few mass street protests in the Western Cape during the first few months of 1985 (Hall, 1986). Street protest escalated rapidly however, after the shootings at Langa near Uitenhage in the Cape (The Kannemeyer Commission 1985) and the death of Goniwe and others in the Eastern Cape. Throughout the country youth were exhorted to join the liberation struggle, to become Young Lions and to *shake off* the oppressors (Bundy, 1987; Johnson, 1988; and Seekings, 1988). Youths perceived this call to become soldiers as a mandate from the entire oppressed stratum of society to take up the fight in the streets on their behalf. The increasingly violent clashes between protesters and the armed forces encouraged a militaristic style of thinking on both sides. Extreme stereotypes became the norm. It was a case of *us versus them,* with very few intermediate categories. The *us* included township youths and everyone who supported the liberation struggle against the demonstrably brutal apartheid state. This group appropriated the status and the label of *comrade*, which became a passport to legitimacy, to power, and to the moral high ground. The label was all too often appropriated by marginalized youths without much justification, for it served their opportunistic goals well (Schärf, 1989a; and Schärf & Ngcokoto, in print).

In this very heady time, the youth seemed to take the authority they had been accorded further than was initially intended by adults. Their control of the streets and their sense of representing adults made them feel as if they were in command of the townships. The youth developed a noticeable arrogance toward the older generation, amplified by developments in squatter politics in Cape Town. Here, the state had nurtured warlords whose interests became increasingly threatened by the movement for democratization. Squatter leaders thus mobilized adult vigilante forces which constituted a real threat to the youth. Squatter leaders and their sizable following were severely discredited among the youth as reactionary traditionalists who were being manipulated by the enemy, the state. This rift between the generations was allegedly encouraged by certain police and broke out in open skirmishes between the *fathers* and comrades (Cole, 1986, and Haysom, 1986). As thinking became increasingly polarized, adults in general became associated with the more conservative attitudes rejected by the majority of youths.

The outcome of these processes was that youths were wrenched away from the moral authority of the older generation and cast adrift, guided only by the ambivalent and unsystematic political conscientization offered at school. This made it far more difficult for parents who were already experiencing problems controlling their children to prevent them from being drawn into or from drifting toward street gangs. For those with no discernible support structure, street gangs became a strong temptation.

The politicization of sport

It is difficult for outsiders to envisage the degree to which youths virtually politicized every aspect of township life. One's social circle, the organizations to which one belonged or did not belong, and one's leisure activities had to be chosen on the basis of whether they were for or against the liberation struggle.

Sport was no exception and during the early eighties the non-racial sports body, the South African Council of Sport (SACOS), became increasingly influential in the townships. It adopted a strategy of encouraging sports clubs to refuse to play against clubs that did not subscribe to a policy of non-racial sport. Soccer was one of the most popular forms of sport among African male youths and many clubs attracted sizable followings. The SACOS policy resulted in the formation of a relatively insular league, because many clubs were not considered to be politically acceptable. Since sponsorship from multi-nationals and big local companies was also taboo, the SACOS leagues limited their resources and attracted little coverage in the mainstream mass media. The National Soccer League (NSL) was labelled as politically unacceptable and SACOS even sought to penalize members who watched NSL games on television. Whole teams were punished by being barred from playing a number of future fixtures, because some of their members had been seen watching NSL games on television in shebeens. Frequently disaffected players left clubs and stopped playing sport altogether. Eventually, SACOS league soccer in Cape Town all but collapsed (Schärf, 1989c).

As was mentioned above, the only leisure activity that seemed relatively unaffected by these ideological prescriptions were the mapantsula dance competitions. Groups created, rehearsed, and performed certain dances and held competitions. Rivalry developed into animosity when groups who thought they should have won, did not. Winning groups were then accused of bribing the judges. Since dance groups were usually composed of youths who resided in a particular geographic area, skirmishes became a matter of protecting territory. As the cycle of attacks and counter-attacks developed, the dance groups came to be seen as street gangs. In fact, it became increasingly difficult for any youth between the ages of twelve and nineteen years who lived in a particular locality to avoid being labelled as a gangster. Members of one of the African street gangs, the *Ntsaras*, who were interviewed, stated that they had joined this gang because they had been accosted by members of opposing gangs who insisted that they must be Ntsaras since they lived in Ntsara territory (Schärf, 1988c). Once these gang skirmishes resulted in fatalities, wars broke out between rival gangs, and the cycle of revenge killings accelerated (*The Cape Times*, 17 August 1986). Groups developed into fully fledged gangs that focused on fighting their rivals and on exerting their power over females, particularly teenage girls in their territory. Their sense of power also spread to the economic terrain and gangs began to rob the vulnerable.

The route through dance groups was not the only passage into gangs in the African townships. Another route was provided by the prison system itself. The South African prison system is not famous for its success at reforming or *rehabilitating* prisoners. Although no official recidivism rates are published, research has shown that a substantial proportion of ex-inmates seek out, or end up in, survival activities on the wrong side of the law (e.g. Pinnock, 1982; and Schärf, 1984a). Ex-inmates carry the mystique of the prison gangs with their particular languages, hierarchical roles, rituals, tattoos, and value systems, all of which accord them high status among township youths who are themselves at risk of imprisonment. Ex-inmates who joined African street gangs were usually older than the youths in the dance troupes. They were also more concerned with economic activity which required that they protect sources of income on their turf, from opposition groups. They were thus not averse to the territorial battles being fought by youths. Precisely what influence these ex-inmates exerted on youths is not yet clear. In Langa, for example, the differences between the senior and junior members of the Ntsara gang were so marked, that the juniors became known by another name, the Young Deserters. What is certain, however, is that African gangs were not as tightly structured as coloured gangs. Over many years the latter had developed a particular style, language, hierarchy, and illegal economic infrastructure. By contrast, the gangs emerging in African townships had hardly any noticeable rights of passage, no discernible hierarchy or leadership, and relatively loose and fluid internal rules (Schärf, 1988c; d; e; and 1989f; i). Another feature that distinguished African from coloured gangs was the degree to which the former resorted to spells and tokens from spiritualists, diviners, *witchdoctors*, alternative healers, or *inyangas*. In coloured gangs the use of *doekoms* for anti-police vials and good luck charms for court appearances is still practiced, but their use is not widespread. The use of *magic* and *lucky tokens* to ensure invincibility is common in African gangs. Many youths believe that the charms or spells they buy at stiff prices from the inyangas will protect them from injury or death.

The threat posed by street gangs severely curtailed the mobility of township residents. By mid-1989 township residents nation-wide identified gangs as one of their most serious problems (Schärf, 1988b; 1989b; d; e; h; i; *South*, 14 December 1989; *The Weekly Mail*, 18 August 1989; and *The Argus* 17 August 1989). Gangs had become an issue of such deep-seated concern that extra-parliamentary political organizations stated gangsterism as one of their priorities for action. When the United Democratic Front (UDF) *unbanned itself* in the Western Cape in early August 1989, it was announced that one of the key campaigns would be to address the problem of crime and gangsterism (Carolus, 4 August 1989).

Thus far, some of the social processes which may have created pre-conditions for gang formation have been highlighted. Broad social and structural factors, however, form only part of any explanation of gang formation. Not all youths who are subject to such social processes join gangs. Those who do, reach gangs via different trajectories and each of these paths is shaped, at least to some extent, by circumstances specific to the individual concerned. It should thus be emphasized that, 'structure, culture and biography blend in a complex way to produce particular social forms' (Hall et al., 1976: 57).

Gang engagement: Romantic myth or realistic possibility?

Theoretical context

The question of central importance here is whether social forces exist which have the potential to counteract gang formation and activity. Particularly in South Africa, practice without a clear theoretical basis runs the risk of merely perpetuating the existing oppressive status quo. It is thus important to examine critically theoretical approaches which could inform intervention that is aimed at reducing or removing gangsterism in the townships.

Structural functionalist approaches to criminology and idealist versions of Marxist theory have maintained that since crime is caused by forces inherent in the social and economic structure, it can be prevented or controlled only by changing these structures radically (e.g. Taylor et al., 1973; and Young, 1979). Gang formation and activity are therefore regarded as the products of structural strain, remediable only through drastic surgery. Some Neo-Marxists have taken this argument even further, by claiming that the crimes of the marginalized are a form of resistance against the dominant classes (e.g. Hall et al., 1978). A school of criminology known as Left Realism has criticized these approaches to crime as somewhat Utopian (e.g. Matthews & Young, 1986). History has shown that revolutions do not automatically eradicate crime. Furthermore, the economic crimes of the marginalized, whether perpetrated for political or non-political reasons, are less frequently aimed at the dominant classes than at the oppressed. Interventions that do not alter the fundamental structure of society are thus necessary, if only to ameliorate the suffering of those who fall victim to crime. It is this latter approach which informs the modes of intervention discussed in this chapter.

Negotiating with gangs

It is true that many of the marginalized coloured and African youths of Cape Town are aware of and angry about their oppression and have participated in political protest of some sort. For a significant number, however, the purpose of such participation has been to have fun or, more importantly, to use the confusion of conflict situations to steal. Only in rare cases have negotiations between political organizations and gangs succeeded in reducing the extent to which gangs have misused political events.[10] However, whether the success of such an approach hinges on gang members understanding and being willing to abide by a strategy of targeted and disciplined political protest, that is, the raising of political consciousness, or whether it is merely a product of the greater power of the politically active group is difficult to assess. It has been noted that by late 1985, coloured gang members were older, more educated, and more politically aware (Schärf, 1986b). Whereas previously gangs had tended to attract marginalized youth between twelve and fifteen years of age who had little formal education (Pinnock, 1982), the political crisis in the schools in 1985 combined with poor employment prospects seems to have resulted in older ex-scholars with more formal education joining gangs (Schärf, 1986b). Although it is likely that the more politically aware communicated their political views to other gang members, maturity, education, and political awareness have had minimal effects on relations between gangs and political organizations. There have been a few instances in which gangs have co-operated with political initiatives taken by communities, but they have also assisted the police, one example being to coerce residents participating in a stayaway to vote in the tricameral parliamentary elections.

The police and gangs

From late 1984 in the coloured townships and from 1986 in the African townships[11], residents began perceiving street gangs as being more than a mere nuisance and by mid-1989 they were seen to be a serious social problem (Schärf, 1986b; and 1989b; d; e; h; i). In response, various sectors of coloured and African communities in Cape Town have taken a range of initiatives.

The successive States of Emergency have contributed indirectly to the marginalization of youth and thus to the increase in gang membership, by preventing or impeding informal mechanisms of social control that had previously retarded gang-formation and gang activity in the townships. It is thus important to understand how community initiatives, informal mechanisms of social control, have interacted with state-initiated, formal means of social control. The interaction between formal and informal agents of social control is always complex. In South Africa this relationship is further complicated by the fact that the police lack legitimacy, for the majority of the population perceive them to be

---

10. Prior to June 1987, political organizations in Bonteheuwel were successful in applying this strategy.
11. To date, there are no known white street gangs in Cape Town.

instruments of the oppressive apartheid state. Shapland and Vagg (1988) have argued that the co-operation of informal structures of ordering is a pre-condition for successful, formal policing. Police forces are thus encouraged to establish and maintain a *partnership in policing.* In South Africa the police have established such partnerships with white communities and with a few sectors in oppressed communities, namely, those who have chosen to form expedient alliances with the apartheid state. Some of the homeland élites (Africa Contemporary Record, 1974; Carter et al., 1967; and Rogers, 1976) and sectors of squatter communities not only co-operate with the police, but supply extra-legal informal armies or police forces, in the form of vigilantes to do the *dirty work* of the police[12] (*Hansard*, 24 April 1989; Haysom, 1986 and *The Weekly Mail*, 21 December 1989).

The way in which the police have used street gangs presents a dilemma for community workers and leaders. They have begun to question on what basis the police define certain people as criminals, gangsters, or comrades (Schärf, 1988e; 1989g; 1989h). A number of Ntsara gang members named as their friend a policeman who had consistently exploited differences and precipitated open conflict between sectors of the African community in Cape Town (Hollands, 1988; and Schärf, 1988c; e). Furthermore, it has been alleged that this policeman encouraged the conflagrations in Crossroads and KTC, in which about 70 000 squatters lost their homes and most of their belongings (*The Methodist Church in Africa and 21 Others v Minister of Law and Order & Others*, 1986). It has also been alleged that the police pit opposing gangs against one another and use gangs to provide information about illegal or politically-motivated activity in townships (Schärf, 1984c; and Schärf, 1989g; i).

It is perhaps telling that although gangsterism has been experienced as a major problem in the townships of Cape Town, especially since 1988, special police units to counteract gangs were only set up in the coloured townships as late as May 1989 (*The Cape Times*, 10 May 1989) and in the African townships, in August 1989 (*The Cape Times*, 24 August 1989). Only fifty policemen were assigned to these units in comparison with the hundreds who have been trained and made available for dealing with political protest in the Cape Town area (The Commissioner of the South African Police, 1988). Political protest is thus clearly the most important *crime problem* for the police. It is hardly surprising that sectors of communities suffering from gang predation lost faith in the formal agents of social control. As a result, various community

---

12. See Chapter 3 for details of the methods employed by vigilante forces.

groups have begun initiating their own interventions for dealing with the gang problem. Generally these attempts have taken two forms: hard tactics involving physical confrontation and intimidation; and soft tactics such as persuasion and investigation. Since coloured and African street gangs differ, and because the configuration of social movements and the cultural images of the role of youths differ, the efficacy of interventions in African and coloured townships vary. Therefore, the efforts made by these communities to deal with gangs are discussed separately.

Gang engagement in coloured townships

In the coloured townships there is a relatively long history of sporadic attempts, by a range of groupings, to lessen the negative impact of gang activity on residents. The account that follows is not exhaustive, but highlights the most important forms that such efforts have taken.

Even before the mass removal of people from District Six in terms of the Group Areas legislation there were community initiated attempts to curb street gang activity. Pinnock (1982) describes how sons of shopkeepers in District Six formed a group that watched for pilfering and robberies close to their fathers' shops or stalls. This group, however, eventually became the legendary Globe gang of District Six. In the late seventies, after the Group Areas removals to the Cape Flats, gang membership and activity escalated dramatically. In response, groups of adults formed street patrols at night and on weekends. These Peacekeepers or Peacemakers, as many of them were called, attempted to establish an intimidating presence in their particular sectors of townships. When they came across youths whom they suspected of being gangsters, a form of confrontation, either physical or verbal, usually took place. Less frequently, the youth was taken home and his parents were informed of his gangster activities. The problematic relationship between oppressed communities and the police produced ambivalence on the issue of whether gangsters should be handed over to the police, but usually the Peacemakers preferred to administer punishment themselves. Increased confrontation between youths and adults for control of particular areas resulted. After an initial period of violent confrontation between the Peacemakers and street gangs, the Peacemakers attempted to draw gang members into their social and recreational networks, particularly soccer clubs. This approach met with limited success, for many *converted gangsters* soon *defected*. Defectors constituted a danger to the Peacemakers, since they were able to inform the gangs of the Peacemakers' tactics, signals, strengths, and weaknesses. The police complicated matters by publicly discouraging Peacemakers from operating, unless they did so under the command of the police, and Peacemakers were encouraged to become reserve policemen. This illustrated a lack of understanding by the police of community values, which made it unacceptable for Peacemakers to become formally linked to their oppressors. The image of the Peacemakers suffered a heavy blow when groups wearing Peacemakers' jackets and identifying themselves as Peacemakers raided and smashed houses and flats. Allegations were made that the Peacemakers had been infiltrated by the gangs and that they had become more self-serving than was acceptable. The fact that the Peacemakers gradually acquired a negative image in communities led to their eventual demise around 1982. Thereafter gang activity continued unimpeded (Pinnock, 1982; Video Lab, undated; and Williams, 1985).

By late 1985 gang activity had again reached such proportions that attempts to address the problem were renewed. To illustrate, the work of a church in Lavender Hill was severely hampered, because it was situated on the boundary of three gang territories. Gang wars were thus fought around and on the church premises which impeded the use of church facilities and attendance at services and functions. The church sought advice from those who had researched street gangs on non-violent solutions to this problem and several strategies were prioritized. It was astonishing that most of the teachers in this area had little or no understanding of the structure, background, and dynamics of gang life. Although they were able to recall many anecdotes about isolated incidents, they had no conception of their possible role in preventing or deterring the formation of gangs and gang activity. The first step then was to inform teachers at the seven schools in the area about gangs. With the co-operation of school principals who made attendance compulsory, two introductory meetings were held at which some 150 teachers were addressed. Thereafter attendance was no longer compulsory and only three teachers participated in the series of workshops that followed. The aim of these workshops was to train teachers to identify children between the ages of nine and fourteen years who were possibly at risk of dropping out of school and joining gangs. Once teachers had identified such children, they were to inform the school social worker who would investigate their domestic circumstances and intervene where possible to deter children from joining gangs. Poor attendance, however, caused the failure of this part of the initiative.

The second strategy was aimed at persuading the three gangs to make the church and its surrounding area neutral territory. A number of religious workers who had established rapport with certain gangsters and who enjoyed immunity from attacks in gang territory, undertook this task. They also set up an evening coffee shop at the church community centre and invited all youths in the area to attend as individuals and not as members of any organization or gang. On the whole, attendance at the coffee shop was limited and gangsters did not attend regularly. Those gangsters who did attend were relatively peripheral within their gangs and some did eventually leave the gangs. This was seen as a success, but the real success lay in the fact that the status of neutral territory had been achieved for the church.

A third tactic was to conduct a community survey of people's knowledge about, attitude toward, and ideas for dealing with the gang problem. A questionnaire was constructed so as to encourage township residents to believe that they could do something about gangs, rather than merely continuing to accept gang rule out of fear. Although several months were spent on designing this questionnaire it was never completed or administered, because community efforts were deflected to the more pressing political events of early 1986.

The fourth and last strategy was an attempt to enlist the assistance of a *six-star general* in a prison gang, who had recently been released from prison and who had begun a one-man crusade to keep children out of prison and out of street gangs. By the time the church initiative began, this man had already gathered a significant following, for he enjoyed instant respect among the young gang members who had not yet experienced prison. It soon become apparent, however, that his crusade was not only strongly evangelical, but contained an element of *fund-raising* for his own cause. He also began to attract suspicion and open hostility from older gang members whose potential labour force and livelihood he was undermining. For these reasons and because he proved to be something of a maverick, most of the volunteers working on the church initiative chose not to work with him.

In 1988 another initiative emerged in the high schools in Mitchell's Plain. An initial attempt simply to encourage gangster scholars to become members of political organizations failed. Scholars who were part of political movements then ran a series of workshops on gangs through their Student Representative Councils (SRCs). Their aim was to investigate ways of reducing fighting and victimization in and around schools.

They were assisted by a graduate student who was researching gang engagement. The project included the technikon and all thirteen high schools in Mitchell's Plain. Since the relationship between pupils and principals in Mitchell's Plain was more cordial than was the case in many of the African townships, school principals were supportive of efforts to raise awareness about gangs (Soal, 1988).

The impact of gangs on the schools of Mitchell's Plain varied greatly and so different strategies for drawing gangsters into discussions and meetings had to be developed. In some schools gangs actually broke up SRC meetings, in some they supported SRC meetings, while in others the gangs had little impact at all (Soal, 1988). Overall relations were sufficient to allow the SRCs to envisage a joint committee of scholars and gangsters for the planning of gang awareness programmes (Soal, 1988). The Mitchell's Plain Schools Congress (MIPSCO) held many meetings to plan ways of involving gangsters in a joint committee without this initiative being seen as a moral crusade or as a confrontation. This task proved more difficult than had been anticipated and the joint committee had not convened by the time the assisting graduate student completed her research in this area. Unfortunately then, the outcome of this programme is not known.

During the long build-up to constituting the joint committee, a questionnaire was administered that yielded some interesting findings. The aim of this questionnaire was to involve scholars in the process of finding out what they and others thought and, more specifically, to highlight similarities and differences between those scholars who join political organizations and those who join street gangs. In preliminary discussions with scholars it became quite clear that contrary to previous research findings, academic performance was not a reliable predictor of the type of group a scholar is likely to join (e.g. Pinnock, 1982). A number of gang members were model students whose entry into the gangs had been precipitated by factors other than poor school performance (Soal, 1988). The most noteworthy difference between gangsters and members of political organizations was found in their *terrains of interest*. SRC members were interested in the narrowly-defined area of mobilizing support for and involvement in protest around political problems. Since their interests did not lie in the terrain of leisure, their ideas for mobilizing people were limited to more serious pursuits. This *style* drew those who were interested in serious matters and the expression of anger and did not attract those interested in leisure or simply in having fun. The latter scholars were thus drawn into gangs. This finding showed an important limitation of these SRCs and a potential avenue for gang engagement, namely, the use of leisure activities to mobilize political support and, at the same time, to discourage gang activity.

Initiatives to engage gangs using the terrain of leisure emerged in Lotus River and Parkwood Estate, two sub-economic townships that had suffered greatly from gang wars and gang predation. From the middle of 1988 onward, the members of a soccer club in Lotus River became increasingly exasperated by the inadequacy of police efforts to intervene in gang wars. Finally, several gruesome murders resulted in an angry reaction on the part of residents. Preliminary meetings were held with a view to forming a peacemaker-type vigilante force to defeat the gangs. During this planning phase the National Institute for Crime Prevention and the Rehabilitation of Offenders (NICRO) was called upon for assistance. After assessing the area, NICRO concluded that none of the existing groups were capable of defeating the gangs. Political organizations, churches, service organizations, welfare agencies, school SRCs, teachers, taxi-owners, and sports clubs were not strong enough to counter the gangs, nor was a combined effort feasible, given the different agendas, power structures, and resources of these groups. Attempts were thus made to dissuade the soccer club from pursuing its intended goal of confronting the gangs. Unfortunately this advice was only heeded after at least two soccer club members had been killed in conflict with the gangs. The situation came precipitously close to an escalating retributive cycle when the soccer club members desisted and instead put their energies into a gang awareness campaign which included raising awareness among women about the helping agencies available to survivors of rape and other sexual assaults. Whether there was any sustained follow-up to this approach is not known.

The initiative in Parkwood Estate involved ex-offenders who had committed themselves to dissuading youth from following in their footsteps. They joined the youth and cultural organizations operating under the auspices of a church and attempted to alert the youth to the negative aspects of imprisonment. They organized a range of cultural events that were aimed at uniting residents and several of these events succeeded in this regard, as social networks developed that fostered mutual assistance in times of danger. This, however, had little effect on the level of gang activity and from the information available, it is not possible to assess its success in preventing youths from joining gangs.

Finally, in early 1988 civic associations affiliated to the UDF announced their intention to raise awareness about gangs as a strategy for countering gang activity and formation. The Advice Office Forum, a network of advice offices operating in the Cape, also became part of this programme. The programme does not seem to have progressed beyond this statement of intent, however, probably because of the limited number of available activists. Furthermore, at this time it was difficult to hold public meetings because of the State of Emergency and a number of meetings convened to deal with the gang issue were broken up by the police (Schärf, 1989d; e).

In sum then, prior to the unbanning of political organizations in February 1990, all the attempts to deal with gangs in coloured townships seem to have met with a common fate. None have developed far beyond the planning phase, as existing social and political networks have not been strong enough to sustain any challenge to gangs, which remain by far the most powerful organized social force in coloured townships.

Gang engagement in African townships

Informal civic management structures have been in operation since the birth of African townships and squatter settlements.[13] In both instances they developed because African township residents did not feel that formal state structures served their interests. Historically, existing formal structures served to enforce laws that sought to exclude the African population from the Western Cape both physically and economically.[14] Little was done by local authorities that benefited or promoted the interests of Africans (Burman & Schärf, 1988).

From the thirties onward in formal African townships (those built and owned by the state) civic associations took the form of street and ward committees comprising residents who were elected by peers living in the same street. These committees settled disputes among neighbours and acted as spokespeople for residents when requests were made to administration boards. They were also concerned with residents' safety and to this end, they mobilized informal neighbourhood police forces to patrol at times when the streets were dangerous (Burman & Schärf, 1988). Although these committees performed what, until the late seventies, was essentially a political function, they were not affiliated to any particular political movement (Burman & Schärf, 1988).

Street committees effectively retarded gang-formation in African townships. This punitive influence dwindled after the Soweto riots, when the state attempted to replace the merely consultative Urban Bantu Councils with a system of African local government or Community Councils (Kane-Berman, 1978). Community Councils were politically controversial. The extra-parliamentary opposition saw them as a ploy to deny full political equality to Africans (Humphries, 1988). Many members of street committees became Community Councillors, but street committees that worked closely with Community Councils were seen to be politically *tainted*. By 1985 their activities had been severely curtailed by the open hostility experienced against them by politicized Africans, particularly youths. During this period of heightened political conflict, the roles of policing and disciplining that had been fulfilled by

---

13. This was not the case in coloured townships.
14. For example, the coloured labour preference policy, influx control, job reservation, business licencing laws, and health regulations.

adults were *taken over* by youths. Previously adult street patrols had been mobilized by street committees to perform informal policing functions. In Nyanga East and in the KTC squatter camp this became the role of the youth working through their People's Courts (Burman & Schärf, 1988; and Schärf & Ngcokoto, in print). These structures were not affiliated to particular political organizations, even though some of their members were political activists.

It should be emphasized that in 1985 People's Courts did not have to deal with gangs, because gangs had not yet emerged in African townships. People's Courts are mentioned here to contrast the high levels of civic awareness and responsibility that characterized African communities with the almost complete absence of such commitment typical of coloured communities in Cape Town. Civic structures strengthened by a pervasive civic consciousness in African townships constitute social groupings that are in a position to intervene should socially damaging groups arise.

It is thus noteworthy that gangs began forming in African townships only when the street committees had been weakened and when the People's Courts had been smashed by the police. In fact, by mid-1986, no significant informal structures remained to fulfil the disciplinary role in African townships. Street gangs were thus free to grow in number and in power. By 1988 street gangs had become such a problem that community initiatives emerged to counteract them. By this stage political conflict on the streets had been dampened and extra-parliamentary political organizations had been severely restricted by the Security Emergency Regulations (24 February 1988). Conditions were therefore favourable for street committees to engage in activities more openly than during the *time of the comrades*. The street committees, none of which were directly linked to any political movement, commenced a three-pronged initiative to address the problem of gangsterism in many sectors of African townships (Schärf, 1988b).

The first aspect of this initiative was the re-introduction of street patrols at nights and on weekends. *Fathers* volunteered to patrol and they accosted and chastised youths whom they suspected of being gangsters. If the parents of a suspected gangster lived in the area over which a street patrol had authority, then the boy was taken to his parents and they were informed of his activities or his status as a gangster (Schärf, 1988b). Parents were then expected to discipline the boy or in the case of a single female parent, to give the patrol or the street committee the authority to do so.

The second aspect involved a similar process, but was implemented by street committees. They surveyed their areas to identify gangsters and informed parents. Besides expecting some form of disciplinary intervention on the part of parents, the street committees also attempted to identify and intervene in family or other problems that could have precipitated a youth's entry into a gang. For example, if the problem was identified as being the absence of a father figure in the home, then a male neighbour or other suitable member in the area was assigned to *keep an eye* on the youth concerned (Mbebe, 1989).

The third aspect of the initiative was to call meetings of residents and gangsters, where the aim was to try and understand the reasons for gang formation and for gang wars of retribution and counter-retribution. Although no satisfactory explanation of gang wars emerged, these meetings did serve to put pressure on the gangs.

This initiative spanned the best part of fourteen months and its success varied across areas. Not all street committees were equally active or equally well organized, so the quality and frequency of effort was not uniform. Gangsters who lived in areas where street committees were active simply moved their activities to areas where street committees were not as effective, or joined branches of their gangs in other areas. Neighbour supervision also varied in its efficacy. One of the central problems was that adults who worked could not supervise youths during the day. It was the police, however, who were probably the most significant damper on this community initiative. After a home was set alight and a number of gangsters were killed during street patrols, the police felt obliged to intervene as it was important for their public image to be seen to be dealing with the gang problem (Mbebe, 1989; and *South*, 18 May 1989). They began firing teargas at street patrols, detained some of their members (*The Weekend Argus*, 4 March 1989), and also attempted to bring about truces between rival gangs by encouraging gangsters and their girlfriends to play soccer and netball together (*The Cape Times*, 23 January 1989; and *The Cape Times*, 15 April 1989). Given the fact that the police had previously fueled the animosity between gangsters and comrades, members of the street committees and community workers viewed these police interventions with scepticism and bemusement (Mbebe, 1989; and Schärf, 1988b; 1989g). More importantly, however, some street committee members felt that police interventions undermined their moral authority to discipline their children (Schärf, 1988b; 1989). It is hardly surprising, therefore, that a community with such perceptions came to view police interventions that were given much media attention as mere publicity stunts that could have little lasting effect (Schärf, 1989g; i). In late 1989 the police launched a twenty-man, *gang busting unit* in African townships. Thus far none of the people interviewed had any information about the activities of this unit. Most of our interviewees who were involved in gang engagement initiatives derided these *gang busters*. Despite discouragement from the police, street committees have maintained their concern about gangster-ism and remain one of the most important mechanisms of informal ordering and policing in African townships.

Another rather different form of community initiative emerged during the first half of 1989. This took the form of a play about gangs which was developed and presented by the New Africa Theatre Group, an organization based in the townships. The drama was presented in the townships and comprised a social commentary on the various groups that have an interest or a role in gang phenomenon, including the gangsters themselves, the civic organizations, the street committees, the police, the inyangas, and the youth affiliates of the UDF. It parodied the roles of many of the parties involved in gang engagement initiatives, not least the double dealing of the police. This approach proved to be highly effective in stimulating renewed efforts to curb gangs in the African townships.

Two other gang engagement initiatives emerged in African townships during 1989. The first was the product of a group of concerned profes-sionals and the second was initiated by political organizations working through civic associations and youth groups. The group of concerned professionals consisted of teachers, community workers, social work-ers, and guidance advisers. They began by discussing gangs in general and more specifically, the reason why gangs had emerged in African townships at this time. The group agreed that gangsterism is a complex phenomenon for which there are several contributory causes, including the crisis in the schools, the demoralization suffered by youth who are faced with bleak prospects of employment, the collapse of community structures as a result of the State of Emergency and state repression, the loss of parental control, police brutality, and the lack of recreational resources in the townships (Schärf, 1989i). It was decided that this group would attempt to spread their understanding of gangs among fellow professionals and that they would try to set up meetings with gangsters. They encountered a major difficulty in this regard, as there were no discernible gang leaders with whom these proposals could be dis-cussed, or who were in a position to call the desired meetings. Further-more, when gangsters did attend meetings, the structure, ethos, and aims of gangs could not be ascertained, because none of the gangsters saw themselves as spokespeople for their gangs. Nevertheless, this did assist the group of professionals in establishing a more appropriate intervention. They began participating in large community meetings concerning gangsterism, where they shared their understanding of the history, structure, and aims of gangs, and they started directing their work with youths whom they encountered in their professional capacities toward preventing youngsters from joining gangs (Schärf, 1989i).

The initiative undertaken by the political organizations complemented the work of the street committees, the theatre group, and the group of concerned professionals. Political organizations had additional motives for treating the gang issue as an important problem. Gang activity had seriously impeded the work of political organizations. The police had encouraged hostility between the gangs and the comrades which had made people less willing to attend political meetings. The police had used the gangs as a source of information about political organizations and gangsters had become potential police recruits, either as *kitskonstabels* in uniform or as paid informers. The most important concern of youth organizations was the negative effect on their image of large numbers of youths who appeared not to be susceptible to political recruitment (Schärf, 1988d; and 1989d; h). The most prominent youth organization in the African townships, the Cape Youth Congress (CAYCO) claimed that gangs were able to emerge and flourish because CAYCO had been severely restricted in February 1988. This argument implied that the lifting of restrictions on CAYCO and on the UDF would enable successful gang engagement. In the light of a previous unsuccessful attempt, however, this claim did not seem credible. Previously CAYCO had attempted to recruit and *re-educate* marginalized and undisciplined youth through the Nyanga East Youth Brigade Court structure. In fact these youth actually *overran* the court and deflected it from its intended aims (Schärf & Ngcokoto, in print).

The approach of the UDF affiliates to the gang problem involved some remarkable alliances between the Amasolomzi and UDF aligned youths who tried to deter gangsters by sweeping through the townships, flushing out and beating gang members. This punitive action was coupled with a recruitment drive which aimed at drawing individual gangsters in to the youth affiliates of the UDF. Large public meetings with gangsters proved unsuccessful, however, because of poor attendance by gang members, their unwillingness to speak publicly about their activities, and their disposition toward CAYCO. Smaller groupings were more successful and did dampen gang activity, at least to some extent. For example, CAYCO set up an interim committee comprising CAYCO and gang members in Section Two of Guguletu (Mbebe, 1989). The UDF's Defiance Campaign also attracted many of the younger gangsters who were drawn to activities like the invasion of white beaches. The adult civic structures also began addressing the gang issue and sent a delegation to the inyangas to try and dissuade them from providing gangsters with *black magic*, as this seemed to be fueling gang wars (Schärf, 1989i). By November 1989 the gang issue was perceived to be less of a problem than it had been and one interviewee even said that the township streets had returned to normal, meaning that activities such as pickpocketing and robbery still occurred but were perpetrated by individuals rather than by groups (Schärf, 1989h).

Conclusion

It is quite clear from these descriptions that the composition and dynamics of street gangs and informal social control groups differ considerably in coloured and African townships. Contrary to theoretical predictions, the economically and politically more oppressed African communities have not engendered as much gangsterism, nor have their informal social networks, with the potential to curb gangsterism, suffered as much fragmentation as has been the case in coloured communities. One must conclude, therefore, that the structural functionalist conceptions in mertonian and neo-marxist approaches must be augmented if they are to be applied to the Cape Town context. Midgley (1975) has suggested that the African population of Cape Town has not internalized Western material aspirations to the same extent as the coloured population and so has not experienced as much structural strain. As tempting as this explanation may be, it fails to explain why the Moslem population of Cape Town, which is structurally in the same position as other coloured people and which most definitely subscribes to Western material goals, has not spawned a larger number of street gangs.

It is submitted that the answer to this question lies in differences between the elements of respective cultures that hold sway in particular contexts. The religious, social, economic, and familial networks in Moslem culture are more closely knit than those which operate within the non-Moslem coloured population. These networks function both as a mechanism of social control and as a source of social and economic support. In the Moslem community, therefore, structural strain may be counteracted by cultural forces which serve to reduce the likelihood of youth being marginalized. Historically-rooted, ethnographic research may thus hold promise as a means of correcting overgeneralizations in criminological theory. That theoretical excursus, however, although long overdue, must await a time in which more relaxed contemplation will be possible. Suffice it to say that the examination of community initiatives aimed at counteracting the marginalization of youth has served to highlight some of the shortcomings of existing theory. It has also exposed the limitations of community initiatives in counteracting structural imbalances. None of the initiatives discussed in this chapter addressed the two central issues of unemployment and preventive education at the primary school level. Nor was sufficient attention paid to the prospects of individual as opposed to group interventions. *Big Brother* or *Buddy System* programmes that involve the adoption of children who are at risk of becoming gangsters by peers should be explored, along with the development of systematic educational programmes about gangsterism for primary school children. Recreational programmes and after-school care could be initiated on a wide scale in high-risk areas. Preventive efforts aimed at youths who are at risk of becoming gangsters are likely to be much more cost-effective in the long-term, than having to resort to police assistance that has proven unreliable and ineffective. A police force which has no legitimacy within a community cannot hope to establish a partnership with that community and is thus prone to become corrupt, brutal, and self-serving.

As South Africa moves towards a more democratic social order, policing strategies are being scrutinized increasingly. The existing practice of policing gangs is highly unsatisfactory, as are the political policing practices of the apartheid state. This chapter has demonstrated that apart from preventive programmes and structural changes, the most successful method of policing gangs involves the combined effort of informal and formal social control groups. This approach should form the foundation of future gang engagement initiatives.

Bibliography

Books and articles

Abrahams, S. (1988). *Education in the Eighties.* Cape Town: Department of Adult Education and Extra-Mural Studies, University of Cape Town.

Africa Contemporary Record (1974). *Afrikaner Politics in Trouble: South Africa 1973.* London: Rex Collings.

Bloch, R. & Wilkinson, P. (1982). 'Urban Control and Popular Struggle: A Survey of State Urban Policy 1920–1970'. *Africa Perspective* 20: 2–40.

Bundy, C. (1987). 'Street Sociology and Pavement Politics: Aspects of Student Resistance in Cape Town, 1985'. *Journal of Southern African Studies* 13: 303–30.

Burman, S. & Schärf, W. (1988). Informal Justice and People's Courts in a Changing South Africa. Unpublished paper. Bologna: International Sociological Association.

Carter, G., Karis, T. & Stultz, N. M. (1967). *South Africa's Transkei: The Politics of Domestic Colonialism.* London: Heinemann.

Cole, J. (1986). *Crossroads: The Politics of Reform and Repression 1976–1986.* Johannesburg: Ravan Press.

Eiselen, W. W. W. (1955). *Die Naturel in Wes Kaapland.* Pretoria: Suid-Afrikaanse Buro vir Rasse-aangeleenthede.

Hall, M. (1986). Resistance and Revolt in Greater Cape Town. Unpublished paper. Cape Town: Centre for African Studies, University of Cape Town.

Hall, S., Critcher, C., Jefferson, T., Clarke, J. & Roberts, B. (1978). *Policing the Crisis: Mugging, the State and Law and Order.* London: MacMillan.

Hansard (House of Assembly Debates). April 1989. Pretoria: Government Printer.

Haysom, N. (1981). *Towards an Understanding of Prison Gangs.* Cape Town: Institute of Criminology, University of Cape Town.

Haysom, N. (1983). 'Ruling with the Whip: A Report on the Violation of Human Rights in the Ciskei'. *Occasional Paper* (5). Johannesburg: Centre for Applied Legal Studies, University of the Witwatersrand.

Haysom, N. (1986). 'Mabangalala: The Rise of Right-Wing Vigilantes in South Africa'. *Occasional Paper* (10). Johannesburg: Centre for Applied Legal Studies, University of the Witwatersrand.

Hinds, L. S. (1985). 'Apartheid in South Africa and the Universal Declaration of Human Rights'. *Crime and Social Justice* 24: 5–43.

Hollands, G. (1988). 'Death of a Tough Cop'. *Frontline* 8: 12.

Humphries, R. (1988). 'Intermediate State Responses to the Black Local Authority Legitimacy Crisis'. In *Government by the People.* (Eds.) Heymans, C. & Tötemeyer, G. Cape Town: Jutas.

Hyslop, J. (1988). 'School Student Movements and State Education Policy: 1972–87'. In *Popular Struggles in South Africa.* (Eds.) Cobbett, W. & Cohen, R. London: James Currey.

Johnson, S. (1988). '"The Soldiers of Luthuli": Youth in the Politics of Resistance in South Africa'. In *South Africa: No Turning Back.* (Ed.)

Johnson, S. London: David Davies Memorial Institute of International Studies.

Kane-Berman, J. (1978). *Black Revolt— White Reaction.* Johannesburg: Ravan.

Lötter, J.M. & Schurink, W. J. (1986). *Gevangenisbendes: 'n Ondersoek met Spesiale Verwysing na Nommerbendes onder Kleurlinggevangenes* 2nd edn. Pretoria: Human Sciences Research Council (HSRC).

Matthews, R. & Young, J. (Eds.) (1986). *Confronting Crime.* London: Sage Publications.

Mbebe, N. V. (1989). A Contextual Study Exploring the Gang Phenomenon in the African Townships of the Cape Peninsula and Community Attempts at Curbing and Redirecting Gang Activity. Unpublished Honours Dissertation. Cape Town: Institute of Criminology, University of Cape Town.

Midgley, J. (1975). 'Crime and Normlessness: Anomie in an Urban South African Community'. In *Crime and Punishment in South Africa.* (Eds.) Midgley, J., Steyn, J. H., & Graser, R. Johannesburg: McGraw-Hill.

Moll, T. C. (1986). *An Overview of the Sources of Labour and Employment Statistics for Regional Planning.* Pretoria: HSRC.

Pinnock, D. (1982). Towards an Understanding of the Structure, Function and Cause of Gang Formation in Cape Town. Unpublished Masters Dissertation. Cape Town: University of Cape Town.

Rogers, B. (1976). *Divide and Rule — South Africa's Bantustans.* London: International Defence Aid Foundation (IDAF).

Schärf, W. (1983). *An Introduction to Gangs.* Cape Town: Institute of Criminology, University of Cape Town.

Schärf, W. (1984a). The Impact of Liquor on the Working Class with Particular Focus on the Western Cape: The Implications of the Structure of the Liquor Industry and the Role of the State in this Regard. Unpublished Masters Dissertation. Cape Town: University of Cape Town.

Schärf, W. (1986a). People's Courts and Informal Justice. Unpublished paper. Stellenbosch: Law, State and Society Working Group.

Schärf, W. (1986b). Street Gangs, Survival and Political Consciousness in the Eighties. Unpublished paper. Cape Town: Centre for African Studies, University of Cape Town.

Schärf, W. (1988a). 'People's Justice'. *Sash* 30 March: 19–23.

Schärf, W. (1989a). 'The Role of People's Courts in Transitions'. In *Democracy and the Judiciary.* (Ed.) Corder, H. Cape Town: Institute for A Democratic Alternative for South Africa (IDASA).

Schärf, W., Hofmeyr, B., Tom, M., Van Zyl, M., Walton, M. & Watson, R. (1987). 'Policing Apartheid's Crisis: Western Cape'. *South African Outlook* 117 January: 5–7.

Schärf, W. & Ngcokoto, B. (in print). 'Images of Punishment in the People's Courts of Cape Town 1985–7: From Pre-figurative Justice to Populist Violence'. In *Political Violence and the Struggle in South Africa.* (Eds.) Manganyi, C. & Du Toit, A. Cape Town: Southern Books.

Schoombee, J. & Davis, D. (1986). 'Abolishing Influx Control: Fundamental or Cosmetic Change?' *South African Journal on Human Rights* 2: 8–19.

Seekings, J. (1988). 'Political Mobilisation in the Black Townships of the Transvaal'. In *State, Resistance and Change in South Africa.* (Eds.) Frankel, P., Pines, N. & Swilling, M. Johannesburg: Southern Books.

Shapland, J. & Vagg, J. (1988). *Policing by the Public.* London: Routledge.

Soal, S. (1988). Engaging Street Gangs: A Contextual Study Exploring Student and Teacher Perceptions of Gang Activity and the Relationship Between Gang and Political Organisations in the High Schools of Mitchell's Plain, Directed at Generating Guidelines for Engaging with Gangs. Unpublished Honours Dissertation. Cape Town: Institute of Criminology, University of Cape Town.

South African Press Clips (1977–82). *The South African Security Services.* Cape Town: Barry Streek.

Swilling, M. (1988). 'Taking Power from Below: Local Government Restructuring and the Search for Community Participation'. In *Government by the People.* (Eds.) Heymans, C. & Tötemeyer, G. Cape Town: Jutas.

Syren, C. J. (1989). Living in Fear: The Experiences of Parents of Political Activists in Coloured Cape Flats Townships 1985–88. A Socio-Psychological Study. Unpublished Masters Dissertation. Cape Town: University of Cape Town.

Taylor, I., Walton, P. & Young, J. (1973). *The New Criminology: For a*

Social Theory of Deviance. London: Routledge & Kegan Paul.

The Commissioner of the South African Police (1988) *Annual Report of the Commissioner of Police.* Pretoria: Government Printer.

The Kannemeyer Commission (1985). *Report of the Commission Appointed to Inquire into the Incident which Occurred on 21st March 1985 at Uitenhage.* Pretoria: Government Printer.

The Van der Walt Commission (1985). *Report on the Investigation into Education for Blacks in the Vaal Triangle following upon the Occurrences of 3 September 1984 and thereafter.* Pretoria: Government Printer.

Williams, J. J. (1985). The Geography of Urban Movements in Metropolitan Cape Town. Unpublished paper. Durban: University of Natal.

Wilson, F. & Ramphele, M. (1989). *Uprooting Poverty: The South African Challenge.* Cape Town: David Philip.

Young, J. (1979). 'Left Idealism, Reformism and Beyond: From New Criminology to Marxism'. In *Capitalism and the Rule of Law.* (Eds.) Fine, B., Kinsey, R., Lea, J., Picciotto, S. & Young, J. London: Hutchinson.

Newspaper articles, television programmes, videos, and public speeches

Carolus, C. (4 August 1989). Speech. Cape Town: University of Cape Town.

South (18 May 1989).

South (14 December 1989).

The Argus (4 March 1989).

The Argus (17 August 1989).

The Cape Times (17 August 1986).

The Cape Times (27 August 1988).

The Cape Times (23 January 1989).

The Cape Times (15 April 1989).

The Cape Times (10 May 1989).

The Cape Times (24 August 1989).

The Weekend Argus (4 March 1989).

The Weekly Mail (17 August 1989).

The Weekly Mail (21 December 1989).

Video Lab (undated). *The Peacemakers of Manenberg*. Documentary. Cape Town: Video Lab.

Interviews

Schärf, W. (1984b). Unpublished Interview with Captain Van der Westhuizen. Cape Town: Institute of Criminology, University of Cape Town (UCT).

Schärf, W. (1984c). Unpublished Interview with Four Ex-Reformatory Inmates. Cape Town: Institute of Criminology, UCT.

Schärf, W. (1988b). Unpublished Interview with the Chairperson of the Street Committee in Section 1, Guguletu. Cape Town: Institute of Criminology, UCT.

Schärf, W. (1988c). Unpublished Interviews with Members of the Ntsara Gang. Cape Town: Institute of Criminology, UCT.

Schärf, W. (1988d). Unpublished Interview with a Student on Gangster Activity. Cape Town: Institute of Criminology, UCT.

Schärf, W. (1988e). Unpublished Interview with a Member of the Ntsara Gang. Cape Town: Institute of Criminology, UCT.

Schärf, W. (1989b). Unpublished Interview with One of the Founder Members of the Nyanga East People's Court. Cape Town: Institute of Criminology, UCT.

Schärf, W. (1989c). Unpublished Interview with Former Executive Member of the Western Cape South African Council of Sport (SACOS). Cape Town: Institute of Criminology, UCT.

Schärf, W. (1989d). Unpublished Interview with the Convenor of the Advice Office Forum and a Member of the Heideveld Civic Association. Cape Town: Institute of Criminology, UCT.

Schärf, W. (1989e). Unpublished Interview with a Community Worker at the Foundation for Social Development. Cape Town: Institute of Criminology, UCT.

Schärf, W. (1989f). Unpublished Interview with a Para-legal Worker. Cape Town: Institute of Criminology, UCT.

Schärf, W. (1989g). Unpublished Interview with a Member of the New Africa Theatre Group. Cape Town: Institute of Criminology, UCT.

Schärf, W. (1989h). Unpublished Interview with a Member of the Cape Youth Congress (CAYCO). Cape Town: Institute of Criminology, UCT.

Schärf, W. (1989i). Unpublished Interviews with Members of a Group of Community Workers, Social Workers and Teachers involved in Gang-issues. Cape Town: Institute of Criminology, UCT.

Schärf, W. (1990a). Unpublished Interview with Don Pinnock on Gang Engagement in Grahamstown. Cape Town: Institute of Criminology, UCT.

Legal cases

The Methodist Church in Africa & 21 Others v The Minister of Law and Order and Others (1986). 13082/3 unrep. (CPD).

Acts and regulations

The Security Emergency Regulations of 24 February 1988.

The Group Areas Act 41 of 1950.

Index